I0896525

American Indian Intellectuals of the Nineteenth and Early Twentieth Centuries

Dedicated with affection to the memory of the "Horse and Buggy Ethnographers" and to their spiritual descendants of a later day.

This edition dedicated to the memory of
Katharine Douglas Pringle Massel, 1907–2002.

American Indian Intellectuals of the Nineteenth and Early Twentieth Centuries

Edited by
MARGOT LIBERTY

RedRiver books

UNIVERSITY OF OKLAHOMA PRESS
Norman

Library of Congress Cataloging-in-Publication Data

American Indian intellectuals.
American Indian intellectuals of the nineteenth and early twentieth centuries / edited by Margot Liberty.—Red River books ed.
p. cm.
Originally published: American Indian intellectuals. St. Paul : West Pub. Co., c1978, in series: Proceedings of the American Ethnological Society ; 1976.
ISBN 0-8061-3372-4 (pbk. : alk. paper)
1. Indians of North America—Biography. 2. Anthropologists—United States—Biography. 3. Intellectuals—United States—Biography. I. Liberty, Margot. II. Title.

E89 .A47 2002
970.004'97'00922—dc21
[B]

2001055606

1976 Proceedings of the American Ethnological Society
Robert F. Spencer, General Editor

"Jesse Cornplanter, Seneca, 1889–1957" © 1978 by William N. Fenton. Reprinted by permission.

Copyright © 1978 by West Publishing Co. Red River Books edition published 2002 by the University of Oklahoma Press, Norman, Publishing Division of the University, by arrangement with West Group. Preface by Margot Liberty © 2002 by the University of Oklahoma Press. All rights reserved. Manufactured in the U.S.A.

1 2 3 4 5 6 7 8 9 10

The paper in this book meets the guidelines for permanence and durability of the Committee on Production Guidelines for Book Longevity of the Council on Library Resources, Inc. ∞

Contents

Preface to the Red River Books Edition

The 1974 survey by William Sturtevant that led to this book brought in more than one hundred suggestions of names of American Indian scholars and intellectuals from respondents all over the country. Many others have been suggested who are very deserving of biographical treatment. The "limiting factor" in choosing which to include here was not the value of the scholar's work, but the availability of a person who could write it up. This usually meant someone who had worked intensively in the Indian scholar's field, and often with that person as a researcher or co-author. The shortage of such knowledgeable "informants" on the work of Indian scholars continues.

The first use of the term "American Indian intellectuals" appears to have been by Margaret Mead and Ruth Bunzel in *The Golden Age of American Anthropology* (1960), a volume recalling the Boasian years in which so much foundational American Indian ethnography was collected.

American Indian Intellectuals of the Nineteenth and Early Twentieth Centuries began as a symposium at the American Anthropological Association in 1976. The AAA component organization that sponsored the symposium was the American Ethnological Society. It was published as the 1976 proceedings volume of that organization by West Publishing Company of St. Paul, Minnesota, which at that time held the contract with AES for its publications series. *American Indian Intellectuals* (as it was originally titled) sold out within a year and has been out of print now for years, despite continuing demand from a large number of people who have wanted to use it in classes or for their own research.

The question of reissuing this book was linked to the question of its possible revision for a second edition. Scholars were found for a series of new studies that were presented as papers at the AAA meetings of 1992 in San Francisco. Many new subjects, most centered upon work in linguistics, were presented and discussed. A revision and/or second volume was considered, but the papers from contributors were not completed.

The decision to reissue the first collection was based also upon continuing requests, especially from college teachers in Native American studies and American Indian history. One feature uniformly appreciated was the comparison obtained here, in one volume, concerning geographical areas as well as relative traditionalism versus acculturation toward mainstream cultural models.

There is good geographical diversity here—numerous tribes and a majority of North American culture areas are represented. The tribes represented include Blackfoot, Catawba-Cherokee, Cayuga-Oneida, Cherokee, Northern Arapaho, Northern Paiute, Omaha, Osage, Pawnee, Santee Sioux, Seneca, Teton Sioux, Tsimshian, and Zuni.

Culture areas represented here include the Southwest (Flora Zuni), the Northwest Coast (William Beynon), the Basin (Sarah Winnemucca), and with particular strength the Iroquois Northeast (Ely Parker, Arthur Parker, Alexander General ["Deskahe"], and Jesse Cornplanter), and the Plains (Charles Eastman, James Murie, Francis La Flesche, John Joseph Mathews, George Bushotter, and William Shakespeare).

The Iroquois, especially the Senecas, are the most represented tribe here (four out of sixteen chapters). They range from Eli Parker, General Ulysses Grant's assistant in the Union army during the Civil War, to Arthur Parker, who was tormented by the conflicts he experienced in museum work. Alexander General, Deskahe, was Cayuga-Oneida, a major longhouse ritualist. And William Fenton's beautiful biographical tribute to Jesse Cornplanter (also a Seneca) is a classic example of the best collaboration possible between Indian and white scholars. A major dilemma exists here. Should a tribal member become "educated," imperiling traditional roles and responsibilities, or remain "a Blanket Indian," less able to cope with the mainstream world? This dilemma remains today. Similar contrasts appear among the Plains representatives here—from the highly sophisticated La Flesche (who appeared in a most uncharacteristic buffalo robe in his obituary) to George Eastman, the Santee Sioux writer and physician; William Shakespeare, the sad Arapaho educator; and Buffalo Child Long Lance, the fraudulent actor whose escapades delight tribal college students because of his skill at hoodwinking gullible whites.

From the fifteen studies here of individuals poised between old and new ways of life, students can develop comparisons between individuals who were highly sophisticated and well educated in mainstream schools (Ely Parker, John Joseph Mathews, and Emmet Star) to the very traditional (Richard Sanderville, Jesse Cornplanter, William Beynon, and Alexander General) with little if any such alien indoctrination. They can also assess the ideology that led them to record traditional culture for posterity. Thus the sketches here, presented in one volume, balance and complement full-length biographies that are appearing elsewhere.

Native American students in present-day colleges and universities have very few Indian role models for their own studies and careers. This work provides a useful selection of models. It will also be useful to students in developing countries elsewhere around the world, where the issue of native scholarship concerning native tradition is only beginning to be addressed.

In conclusion, Garrick Bailey, an Osage tribal member, writing of the Osage tribal historian John Joseph Mathews, says that old men who avoided Mathews when he was a boy changed when they became elders. The younger Osages didn't care about their traditions, "and the old men sat by themselves seeing the cultural disintegration of their people." As Mathews said, "They were afraid that their moccasin prints would be washed by the sheet waters of oblivion. Then they started talking—they wanted to live on in word symbols. That's the only chance they had; they thought that they would be gone. . . . They could go to Spirit Land but . . . they might lose their culture. They might be absorbed by the I'n-Shta-He, the white man. So they started talking."

MARGOT LIBERTY

October 2001

ACKNOWLEDGMENTS

Numerous people and institutions have assisted in the preparation of this book.

Initial inspiration and formulation derived from discussions between John V. Murra, William C. Sturtevant, and others at the 1974 meeting of the American Ethnological Society at Worcester, Massachusetts. Many scholars responded with helpful suggestions to a prospectus mailed from the Smithsonian Institution in July (see Appendix to this volume). In addition to the authors published herein these included David Aberle, Lowell Bean, Robert Bieder, Edmund Carpenter, Helen Codere, Frederica de Laguna, Vine Deloria, Jr., Fred Eggan, Christian Feest, David French, William Hodge, Dell Hymes, Alvin Josephy, Nancy Lurie, D'Arcy McNickle, Alfonso Ortiz, Arnold Pilling, Ronald Rohner, Wayne Suttles, George W. Stocking, Jr., and W. Raymond Wood. John B. Cornell, the American Ethnological Society's 1975 president, gave assistance in selecting the topic presented here for the 1976 Symposium, held in Atlanta March 31–April 3, and in exploring support possibilities which culminated in welcome assistance from the Wenner-Gren Foundation for Anthropological Research. The sessions themselves benefitted substantially from the co-chairmanship of Bill Sturtevant. Tape recording and transcription were made possible through assistance from the Oral History Program of the University of Pittsburgh. Stephen Zupcic and Margie Gillcrese were particularly helpful. Financial assistance was also received from the Faculty Grants Committee of the Faculty of Arts and Sciences, and from the Provost's Research Development Fund, at the University of Pittsburgh.

I am indebted to my colleagues at the University of Pittsburgh for clarifying discussion on a number of points: I would like to thank in particular Alan McPherron and Richard Scaglion. I am also indebted to Arthur Tuden and to Eileen Kane. Hazel M. Johnson of Hillman Library was exceptionally helpful on many occasions. Alexander Spoehr gave very generously of his time in discussing concepts to be included in the Introduction, and in reading a preliminary draft. Capable research and editorial assistance was provided by Jamie McIntyre, Mary Lou Vanzin, Amy

Masters, and Joni Harlan; and patient and efficient typing by Donna Rawe. Betty Arens of the Handbook of American Indians Office, Smithsonian Institution, kindly assisted in checking on the identities of a number of individuals listed in the Appendix.

My children Paula and Henry Liberty endured disruption of the dining room for a period of four-odd months, and I am grateful for their patience. I also thank Esther Marine and Herbert C. Schulberg.

The contributors themselves have been most understanding through the trials of delayed correspondence, lost pictures, and other annoyances. It has been most stimulating to work with them, and I feel very privileged to have made their acquaintance.

Finally, I am deeply indebted to the memory of John Stands In Timber of the Northern Cheyenne tribe: teacher, co-author, and friend; to the memory of my father, Henry F. Pringle; to continuing inspiration from my mother, Helena Huntington Smith; and to Katharine and Mark Massel.

CHAPTER ONE

AMERICAN INDIANS AND AMERICAN ANTHROPOLOGY

MARGOT LIBERTY

The present volume represents an effort to bring together biographical sketches of some of the most outstanding North American Indian intellectuals of the nineteenth and early twentieth centuries—individuals who for the most part made lasting contributions to the enterprise of anthropology, although a few were more involved politically, or as writers, than they were as scientific scholars. They represent a wide range of kinds of human beings—from different historical periods, different educational and tribal backgrounds, and very different views of the world surrounding them, as well as personal roles played within it. Their contributions have varied as greatly as their personalities. But a unifying theme appears in the following pages—a theme of awareness of lifeways precious because they were unique, each in its own way, and more precious because they were vanishing. Linked to this awareness was dedication to the task of preserving at least something for the future—born in part from sadness and in part from the new perspective gained through contact with the non-Indian world. It was also born from the ability, in Shakespeare's terms, "to love that well which thou must leave ere long."

Other notes recur here—of anger at exploitation and crusading for reform; of showmanship at times and making financial or political gain from widespread loss and tragedy; of "reverse exploitation" of anthropologists reported somewhat wryly by several authors (see Fenton in particular); and of conflict and sometimes heartbreak amid the relentless currents of change which engulfed each in his or her own way. There is in fact no more poignant record of the pressures of acculturation than some of the personal vignettes presented here.

The discussion which follows seeks to place the individuals portrayed in the context of their times. It ranges across 150 years of American history, from 1825, three years before Ely Parker was born, through the 1960's: when a different Shakespeare was seeking validation as an Arapaho tribal historian and Flora Zuni was at peak influence and activity. It deals with Indian history linked to broader political and economic events in mainstream American life, and it deals with some key aspects of American anthropology: a milieu to which most of the men and women portrayed here had important ties.

Finally, it addresses the issue of exploitation of Indians by anthropological scholars: an issue broached in recent years by anthropologists and Indians alike.

I

The Indian subjects of this volume were nearly all born in the nineteenth century, continuing to live into the twentieth. Their period witnessed the final fulfillment of American "Manifest Destiny" with all its concurrent shocks upon the Indian world. The quarter century 1825–1850 saw the essential closing of the beaver trade as the Bureau of Indian Affairs, established in the War Department in 1824, began its operations; the removal of almost all Indians from the eastern United States in connection with the 1830 Removal Act; George Catlin's observation of the first recorded Plains Sun Dance in 1833; the thrust of settler caravans westward along the Oregon Trail in 1843 (a year after the American Ethnological Society was established in New York); research among the Chippewa by Henry Schoolcraft, begun in the 1820's; the annexation of Texas and subsequent Mexican War and the 1849 Gold Rush (which all but wiped out the Indians of California); the 1849 shift of the Bureau of Indian Affairs to the Department of the Interior; and disastrous disease epidemics in the Great Plains. The religion of Handsome Lake, the Seneca prophet, became established among the Iroquois. Along with Ely Parker (1828), Sara Winnemucca (1844) was born during this period.

Between 1850 and 1875 Lewis Henry Morgan, in collaboration with Parker, published the first scientific account of an Indian tribe (1851) and conducted far-ranging research among the tribes of the Missouri and beyond. Despite the Fort Laramie Treaty of 1851, war broke out in the Plains and raged for some thirty years, as the Reservation Policy replaced Removal as the keynote in national Indian affairs. Gold and silver strikes in the mountain West were followed by trail herds of cattle moving east from Oregon and north from Texas. The Homestead Act was passed in 1862. The Civil War interlude was followed by Grant's so-called Peace Policy in which Indians on reservations were supervised by missionaries while those off them were chased by the Army. The science of anthropology began in earnest, with the publication of major theoretical works here and abroad (Hallowell 1960; Hoebel 1972) partly in association with American museums founded in the 1860's (Darnell 1974; Mead and Bunzel 1960). Francis La Flesche (1857), Charles Eastman (1858), James Murie (1862), George Bushotter (1864), Emmet Starr (1870), and Richard Sanderville (1873) were born during this period.

The last quarter century of the 1800's began with the celebration of the American Centennial in Philadelphia in 1876, and the spectacular event that summer which befell George Armstrong Custer on the Little Big Horn River in Montana. Plains Indian resistance ended a year later, despite final spasms which culminated in 1890 at Wounded Knee. The southern buffalo herd was destroyed by 1878 and the northern herd by 1883, in conjunction with the completion of the transcontinental railroad. Indian children by the hundreds were sent to off-reservation boarding schools beginning with Carlisle in Pennsylvania, established in 1879. The Plains Sun Dance was outlawed in 1883, vanishing or going underground (as it did in a number of locations) for the next fifty years. In 1887 the Dawes Allotment Act spearheaded national Indian policy in a drive for assimilation through the assignment of small farms to individuals, which was to reduce the remaining Indian land base from 132 to 32 million acres by 1928. The winter of 1886–87 ended the era of the open-range cattle industry, and Wounded Knee ended any Indian hope of turning back to buffalo days, even in dreams, after 1890.

Meanwhile anthropologists had engaged surviving Indian cultures on several fronts in what was to become a fifty year obsession. The Bureau of American Ethnology was founded in 1879; area research in the Southwest proliferated in the 1880's; Plains salvage ethnography began with J. O. Dorsey, Alice Fletcher, and Francis La Flesche; James Mooney recorded the throes of the Ghost Dance in 1890; in 1891 John Wesley Powell's linguistic classification of North America was published; in 1893 the World's Fair Congress of Anthropology was held in Chicago; in 1897 the Jesup Expedition began investigating the origins of American Indians and the cultures of the Northwest Coast; and university departments emerged as major theatres of anthropological activity, though the museums continued to be critically important for some years. Over this period Franz Boas rose to dominance as the key figure in what has been termed the "golden age" of American Anthropology (Mead and Bunzel 1960), to continue for another twenty years. The period outlined is of particular importance here, as many of our subjects were born within it: Arthur Parker (1881), William Beynon (1888), Jesse Cornplanter and Alexander General (1889), Buffalo Child Long Lance (1891), John Joseph Mathews (1894), and Flora Zuni (1897). Only Will Shakespeare (1901) awaited the turn of the century.

The period between 1900 and 1925 witnessed the peak of land allotment activity and the giving of fee patents to individuals by 1924, the year when Indians also became U.S. citizens. The national Indian population began to recover from its lowest level (about 250,000 in 1850: Wax 1971:32–35) despite widespread belief that Native Americans had indeed reached "The End of the Trail" (the name of a famous equestrian statue unveiled at the San Francisco Exposition of 1915) and were about to vanish permanently. Salvage ethnography directed from museums, especially the American Museum of Natural History, was at its peak, as in Sun Dance studies sent out for nine years (1907–1916) among sixteen tribes of the Plains. The Native American Church became firmly established as a major force in Plains religion. The American Anthropological Association was established in 1902. Boas and his students, bent upon historical reconstruction of Indian cultures, dominated the period through World War I and into the Depression. By the end of the period it was believed that Indian culture was essentially gone, although much had been preserved for posterity—owing in part to the work of the subjects of this volume who were then most active in collaboration with anthropologists (Tax 1955; Laguna 1960; Hayes 1960; McNickle 1973; Darnell 1974; Stocking 1976).

The second quarter of the twentieth century brought momentous events to Indians and to anthropology. Investigation of reservation conditions led to widespread demands for Indian policy reform which were initiated under the Indian Reorganization Act of 1934, born of the Depression. Known as the "Indian New Deal," the Act reversed the push toward assimilation which had characterized almost fifty Allotment-oriented years. It lifted the ban on native religion and other aspects of tribal culture, encouraged tribes to organize politically, and initiated other liberal policies whose effects tended to be mitigated by World War II. Thousands of Indians served in the armed forces during the war, and were encouraged to "relocate" from their reservations to urban areas afterwards, in a return to assimilationist goals which were to reassert themselves in the Termination policy of the 1950's. New interests appeared among American anthropologists, including acculturation and culture and personality studies, while new theoretical approaches sparked by British and French scholarship rose to primary importance throughout the world. A massive shift away from North American studies to other topics and world areas took place as anthropology entered its boom period of expansion, and global rather than internal interests prevailed. Never again did Native American subject matter regain its old importance: by the late 1950's, in fact, academic specialists in North America were becoming rare (Murphy 1976:6). Many of the Indian scholars in this volume were nonetheless publishing their work, or seeing it published, during this period (Officer 1971; Wax 1971; McNickle 1973).

Since 1950 the trend of anthropology away from primary concern with Indian subject matter has accelerated. In a note of mutual disenchantment, Indian communities at the same time have become critical of anthropologists per se: a reaction shared by other members of the so-called Third World (Deloria 1969:83–104; Medicine 1971; Hymes 1974:5; Fontana 1973; Maynard 1974). The percentages of articles in three anthologies published by the American Anthropological Association are instructive: between 1888 and 1920, 63 percent were clearly devoted to North American Indian topics (de Laguna 1960); between 1921 and 1945, 46 percent and between 1946 and 1970, 18 percent (Stocking 1976 and Murphy 1976). Urban Indian migration has continued: an estimated 50 percent of the national Indian population was in urban areas by 1970 (Wax 1971: 157–193; Bahr, Chadwick, and Day 1972; Liberty 1974). Pan-Indian culture, distinguished from continuing tribal identity, has been defined (Howard 1955; Wax 1971:135–156). Political activism associated with the Vietnam War and its aftermath, and linked to Black Power in association with the rise of the American Indian Movement, has reached national headlines on a number of occasions, especially in 1972 and 1973 (Deloria 1969:169–195; Steiner 1968; Josephy 1971; Burnette and Koster 1974; Washburn 1975). Nonetheless, interest in Indian subjects in the seventies continued (Liberty 1976) and a major updating of the state of knowledge of Indian cultures is underway at the Smithsonian, to appear as a twenty-volume revision of the old two-volume *Handbook of American Indians* (Hodge 1907, 1910) beginning publication in 1978. To a considerable degree this effort has led to revitalization of interest and enthusiasm among specialists in North American Indian culture, each of whom was beginning to think of himself as the last of the Mohicans. The AES symposium of 1976 upon which this volume is based assisted in the process of mutual recognition: many of the authors represented here are *Handbook* contributors, and most of their subjects were responsible in one way or another for material which will appear in *Handbook* pages.

To date, twelve volumes of the twenty-volume *Handbook* have been published:

Volume 4 *History of Indian-White Relations* (1988)
Volume 5 *Arctic* (1984)
Volume 6 *Subarctic* (1981)
Volume 7 *Northwest Coast* (1990)
Volume 8 *California* (1978)
Volumes 9 and 10 *Southwest* (1979, 1983)
Volume 11 *Great Basin* (1986)
Volume 12 *Plateau* (1998)
Volume 13 *The Plains* (2001)
Volume 15 *Northeast* (1978)
Volume 17 *Languages* (1996)

Continuing in preparation are eight more volumes. These include:

Volume 1 *Introduction*
Volume 2 *Indians in Contemporary Society*
Volume 3 *Environment, Origins, and Population*
Volume 14 *Southeast*
Volume 16 *Technology and Visual Arts*
Volumes 18 and 19 *Biographical Dictionary*
Volume 20 *Index*

II

Because of the work of and the data base provided by American Indians, anthropology in the United States has assumed a different character from that which developed in other parts of the world. The 18th century, and particularly the 19th century, brought ceaseless confrontation with "savages" within or beyond national borders as the drive to understand them or at least to cope with their vexatious and challenging presence continued. It has been suggested recently that American national character itself has been shaped in major ways by this general fact of life (Fiedler 1968:6–7). Specific themes in U.S. anthropology have included, among others; (1) the four-field focus still dominant organizationally at least in most academic settings; (2) the focus upon salvage ethnography, associated with strong historical or diachronic interests; (3) the geographical or ecological focus initiated by the wide range of North American environmental settings; (4) the concern with material culture and with "cultural anthropology" as opposed to "social anthropology" distinguished elsewhere by 1945; and (5) the concern for culture change which was closely linked to events on reservations in the nineteenth and twentieth centuries. Each of these themes will be touched upon briefly below.

The traditional four-field American focus, which combines ethnology with physical anthropology, archaeology, and linguistics, has inevitably given way to some extent to centrifugal forces of specialization within recent years (Hymes 1974:5; Stocking 1976:23–28; Murphy 1976:2). It seems generally accepted that this approach was strongly associated with the problems, practical and otherwise, associated with the North American Indian presence:

> American anthropology has been built upon detailed studies of the living behavior, the buried remnants of earlier periods, the vanishing complicated languages, and the remembered customs of the American Indians . . . Had there been no American Indians, Anthropology would have been taught and perhaps elaborated in the United States on the basis of German, British and French models that were developed as Europeans struggled to produce order from the accounts brought back by those few travellers who sought colonial enterprise in faraway lands. But American anthropology would not have been the same. (Mead and Bunzel 1960:2–3)

It has also been observed that European work began with analysis of folklore and folklife which minimized the need for study of variation in race and language, so that ethnology remained the dominant force or focus abroad (Darnell 1974; Voget 1975:676–696). Despite present day specialization, a number of American scholars still find value in the four-field approach (Murra 1976:5–6; Murphy 1976:19); and the need for appreciation and awareness of "the fundamentals of mankind . . . including each and every expression of human nature" has been underlined by a major scholar of quite different origin (Levi-Strauss 1966:124).

A second theme of U.S. anthropology has been its strong historical interest coupled to the early push to record Native American cultures while they remained in living memory. Memory ethnography thus became a major activity for as many years as informants linked to traditional times survived, and it is in this area of salvage work that most of the Indian subjects included here were most active. In this context anthropology is seen by some today as having functioned as an intellectual aftermath to warfare, a "child of Western imperialism"—the U.S. cavalry galloping off one end of the set as the "horse and buggy ethnographers" (Robert Lowie's phrase) entered at the other (de Laguna 1960:95; Clemmer 1974:215; Stocking 1976:21). Their American Indian preoccupation lasted until about 1920 (Stocking 1976:2) among a generation of scholars "steeped in fieldwork" who "settled down under the leadership of Franz Boas to detailed empirical research," "patiently taking down word by word the broken memories of old men" (Mead and Bunzel 1960:7). Nonetheless, an extraordinary record was preserved, one which increases geometrically in value as the years go by (Levi-Strauss 1966:124).

A third theme of U.S. anthropology has been its focus upon cultural variation through space as well as time. The range of environmental settings in North America led directly to questions concerning the effect of geographical factors upon human life; to Wissler's food areas, later culture areas; to Kroeber's 1939 refinements in North American classification; and eventually to modern approaches under the rubric of cultural ecology (Harris 1968:339–341, 374–376; 663–664; Voget 1975:676–696). This progression was closely tied to the needs of the museums which dominated anthropological research for decades: the Smithsonian, the Peabody Museum, the American Museum of Natural History, and the Field Museum in Chicago. The placement of American Indian materials in conjunction with natural history collections, which has infuriated Indian observers, derived from museum perspectives and requirements, as did the American stress upon collections of material culture needed for museum display, also a subject of recent controversy (Henry 1970).

Fourth, the museums have reinforced the association between the four fields, seeking to present "the complete human texture of historical man with a given physique in a given environment" (Mead and Bunzel 1960:9–11). Thus "cultural anthropology" was an American perspective sharply challenged by the rise of British functionalism and synchronically oriented "social anthropology" in the 1930's (Stocking 1976:14–15, 23; Murphy 1976;11). Though most contemporary American scholars have incorporated the newer emphasis (e.g., Eggan 1954, 1964) "cultural anthropology" or the older "ethnology" remain the dominant terms in American academic departments (Stocking 1976:18, 23).

Finally, the American Indian situation in the late nineteenth and early twentieth centuries was one generally of such rapid and drastic change as to focus anthropological attention upon the nature of cultural change itself. Other regions of the world in which contact between Western and native life existed were in general less overwhelmed, their indigenous cultures—often linked to larger populations—less quickly and totally destroyed. Studies of change were of course linked to the historical interest of the Boasian school, but in the reservation setting they took on a particular note of urgency. The stresses upon individuals which derived from acculturation are clearly reflected in the essays which follow; see for example the chapters on Arthur Parker and Richard Sanderville, and Warbonnet's statement in Loretta Fowler's essay.

Thus, to some at least, "It would be impossible to over-estimate the importance of the American Indian in the development of anthropology in the United States" (de Laguna 1960:453). Aside from the five themes or emphases sketched above (and others could be added) certain theoretical approaches have derived from this particular body of data. I will hazard a few statements concerning cultural anthropology alone (much more could be said from the perspectives of archaeology and linguistics).

Scientific kinship studies, for one, began with Lewis Henry Morgan, deriving from initial insights gained among the Iroquois which he carried far afield. Thus of six classic types of kinship systems eventually described for the whole world, four (Eskimo, Iroquois, Crow, and Omaha) bear native North American names. As suggested above, the concept of the culture area was also developed here, as was awareness of close adaptational strategies to a wide spectrum of natural resources. The concept of the archaic in particular, paralleling the Old World Mesolithic, derived important new insights from ethnographic analogy with contemporary peoples living very close to nature (as in the Basin and California, particularly) in very ancient ways. Of high-level political organization North American cultures have taught us little, despite such developments as the Iroquois League—native populations were generally sparse and small, scarcely able to compete with advances made by non-literate groups elsewhere (Lowie 1948). But we have been able to trace the rise of legal authority in tribes of the Plains, other studies of law reaching back through Yurok to Eskimo in a valuable range of low- to middle-level complexity (Hoebel 1954). In life cycle studies, the simple food collecting cultures have provided important data on female puberty beliefs and ritual, especially from the Northern Subarctic—while the region as a whole is strikingly lacking in severe initiation ritual for boys and men. In the area of marriage, sparse settlement on the band level of sociopolitical organization has provided insight into marital alliance as a "social bonding" mechanism, important in recent theoretical work in several countries—the institution of cross-cousin marriage being of key importance (Steward 1936; Eggan 1966). But the range of hunting and gathering societies available for study has extended from the simplest to the most complex types recorded anywhere (from the Great Basin and

Subarctic to the Northwest Coast)—providing invaluable information on the ranges of cultural development possible in groups in which domesticated food production does not exist.

In the particularly American area of culture and personality studies, again there is important regional data which has led to new insights and theoretical approaches. Such data include among other things material on the Arctic Hysterias and the Windigo Psychosis reported from the far north; Kwakiutl and Zuni materials utilized in Ruth Benedict's controversial Dionysian-Appollonian dichotomy; and Iroquois ethnohistorical materials utilized in Anthony F. C. Wallace's psychoanalytical assessment of the Seneca (Benedict 1934; Barnouw 1963:366–374; Wallace 1969). In studies of culture change, we have for comparison some of the most conservative as well as some of the most rapidly changing preliterate societies (e.g., the Pueblos and the equestrian Plains) ever reported anywhere. And as a final note we can look to the field of material culture and technology with its associated aesthetic themes and values—in which the art of the Northwest Coast is joined by Pomo basketry, Navajo weaving and silverwork, and many kinds of pottery (as well as Arctic technological genius) in an area of unbounded diversification just beginning to be analyzed. The further use to which all of this material will be put cannot yet be predicted. It will, however, in all likelihood be utilized increasingly by Indians themselves (Levi-Strauss 1966; Murra 1976) as time goes by.

III

There exists considerable rhetoric today on the part of Indians and anthropologists alike, concerning the putative exploitation of the former by the latter. Vine Deloria Jr.'s 1969 chapter "Anthropologists and Other Friends" is well known, and his position in it is strongly stated. Anthropologists do research which has no useful application; they deplore modern reservation life as a comedown from the aboriginal past; they create blocks in the road toward Indian personal development because they provide excuses for failure, alcoholism, and so forth; they abandon their Indian subjects of research in times of trouble; they reinforce stereotypes of all kinds; and they are overfunded via research grants which would better be donated outright to the treasuries of the tribes concerned (Deloria 1969:83–104). Nancy Lurie in a perceptive review traced some of this recent dissatisfaction to its proper sources (1969:39–41 ff.), and there was a stormy session of the American Anthropological Association in San Diego in 1970 devoted to assessment of some of Deloria's charges—in a kind of self-scourging ritual which has continued in one form or another at most meetings of the Association since (cf. Henry 1971; Ortiz 1971). Nonetheless, research interest among anthropologists today is, as stated above, largely directed elsewhere—no longer is the old saw true (if it ever was) that come summer, every Indian family consists of assorted kinsmen and animals plus an anthropologist. But the question of exploitation persists, and the subjects of this volume may provide insight into some of its dimensions.

The individuals described herein differ in so many ways that it is difficult to make valid general statements concerning them, on exploitation or anything else. Did Morgan, for example, exploit Ely Parker? He credits him explicitly on page two of *League of the Ho-De-No-Sau-Nee or Iroquois* (1851), dedicating the work in fact to Parker, "the materials of which are the fruit of our joint researches . . . in acknowledgment of the obligations, and in testimony of the friendship, of the author." Was Sara Winnemucca exploited by her editorial assistant Mary Mann, who aided in the preparation of *Life Among the Paiutes: Their Wrongs and Claims* (1883)? It hardly appears so. Francis La Flesche, the Omaha informant of, then collaborator with, then adopted son of Alice Fletcher became an author in his own right after years of her influence—exploitation in this case again was minimal. But James Murie's story differs sharply, in that major parts of his Pawnee research were never credited to him, by Ralph Linton especially; until recently, William Beynon's Tsimshian research went largely unrecognized.

The others would appear to have been exploited very little indeed. They include George Eastman, the prolific Santee physician-turned-author; George Bushotter, the first Lakota ethnographer, whose ten-month career under J. O. Dorsey produced thousands of pages of handwritten texts in his own language; Arthur Parker, the Seneca intellectual whose work ranged across half a dozen disciplines and careers, all devoted in some way to interpreting one way of life to another; and Richard Sanderville, the Blackfoot interpreter whose "deep and reasoned concern for preserving the knowledge of the Indian past" led to a major museum on the Blackfoot reservation and saved the Plains sign language for posterity. Nor was John Joseph Mathews, world traveler and scholar as well as author of five books including *The Osages* (1961) exploited—or exploitable; nor was the charismatic "Buffalo Child" Long Lance, movie actor, newspaperman and author of the 1920's and 1930's. Long Lance in fact (born of triracial background in the South, later adopted by the Bloods) was capable of doing some exploiting of his own; and the same has been suggested in very different veins for the Seneca and Oneida-Cayuga ceremonialists Jesse Cornplanter and Alexander General, Deskahe. The entrepreneurial Flora Zuni, hostess to and confidante of so many anthropologists, profited in several senses from their association. And William Shakespeare, the Arapaho historian with the whimsical and ironic name (given to him at Carlisle in 1881) whose life was surely touched with tragedy, appears to have benefitted from anthropologists as much as he lost in consequence of their acquaintance. Where anthropologists may have failed most significantly—as suggested in Hazel Hertzberg's paper—was in providing continuity and redefined identity for some of their Indian colleagues. This was at least partly due to their special task, in the assimilationist tenor of the period, of recording traditional culture while time remained—rather than concentrating upon "applied" questions of adaptation and adjustment of individuals, which concern came later (George W. Stocking Jr.'s discussion of "Romanticist" vs. "Progressivist" anthropological modes is relevant here; see Stocking 1976:31–37). For whatever reasons this emphasis prevailed, it is doubtless responsible in part for sentiments like those expressed by Indian singer Floyd Westerman: "Here come the anthros, better hide the past away—Here come the anthros, on another holiday; But there's nothing left to study and there's nothing left to see—still the anthros keep on searching, for the clue and for the key" (*Custer Died For Your Sins*, Perception Records).

In conclusion, I am reminded of another aspect of this complex and many-sided question. In July of 1959 the Northern Cheyennes, troubled over recent alleged mishandling of their Sacred Medicine Hat, sought to assure themselves of the safety of the contents of the medicine bundle in which it rested. There were rumors that the Hat itself might have been destroyed or damaged; and the bundle with its sacred wrappings had not been opened for many years. It was decided that it should be opened for inspection. I was present on that occasion with John Stands in Timber, historian for the tribe. Also present was an Anglo-Catholic priest equipped with a copy of George Bird Grinnell's 1910 article, "The Great Mysteries of the Cheyenne," which contains valuable early information on the Hat and its history. Fred Last Bull, in charge of the opening procedure, had had little personal experience with the Hat or its traditions, most of which have been forgotten. In a dramatic moment, praying for guidance, he turned to—and had read aloud—the account in Grinnell (Powell 1960; Liberty 1967; Stands in Timber and Liberty 1967; Powell 1969). The Hat and its associated regalia were found to be safe and in order, and they remain so today—carefully cherished—in the custody of the Tribe.

The moral should perhaps be obvious. Grinnell, a true "horse and buggy ethnographer" of the highest caliber, did useful service among the Cheyennes that day almost 20 years after his death. John Stands in Timber's own book, adding much by way of later perspective, has become a classic in his tribe. Fred Last Bull's opening statement in that work, made to me when he had briefly taken office as Keeper of the Sacred Arrows in 1957, remains politically useful at Lame Deer (Stands in Timber and Liberty 1967:v–vi; Tsistsistas Press II, No. 1, 1977:1). It would appear that what's past may yet be prologue—to some at least minimal degree—among present and future Native American peoples. And for whatever has been preserved to make this possible we can all—however oriented—be thankful.

LITERATURE CITED

Bahr, Howard M., Bruce A. Chadwick, and Robert C. Day
1972 Native Americans Today. New York: Harper and Row.

Barnouw, Victor
1963 Culture and Personality. Homewood, Illinois: The Dorsey Press.

Benedict, Ruth
1934 Patterns of Culture. Boston: Houghton Mifflin Co.

Burnette, Robert, and John Koster
1974 The Road to Wounded Knee. New York: Bantam Books.

Clemmer, Richard O.
1974 A New Perspective on Cultural Change and Resistance. Pp. 213–247 in Dell Hymes, ed., Reinventing Anthropology. New York: Vintage Books.

Darnell, Regna
1974 Readings in the History of Anthropology. New York: Harper and Row.

de Laguna, Frederica, ed.
1960 Selected Papers from the American Anthropologist: 1888–1920. Evanston, Illinois: Row, Peterson and Co.

Deloria, Vine, Jr.
1969 Custer Died For Your Sins. New York: Avon Books.

Eggan, Fred
1954 Social Anthropology and the Method of Controlled Comparison. American Anthropologist 56:743–763.

1966 The American Indian: Perspectives for the Study of Social Change. Chicago: Aldine.

Fiedler, Leslie A.
1968 The Return of the Vanishing American. New York: Stein and Day.

Fontana, Bernard L.
1973 Savage Anthropologists and Unvanishing Indians of the American Southwest. Indian Historian 6:5–8.

Grinnell, George Bird
1910 The Great Mysteries of the Cheyenne. Journal of American Folklore 20:542–575.

Hallowell, A. Irving
1960 The Beginnings of Anthropology in America. Pp. 1–103 in Frederica de Laguna, ed., Selected Papers from the American Anthropologist: 1888–1920. Evanston, Illinois: Row, Peterson and Co.

Harris, Marvin
1968 The Rise of Anthropological Theory: A History of Theories of Culture. New York: Crowell.

Hayes, H. R.
1960 From Ape to Angel: An Informal History of Social Anthropology. New York: Alfred A. Knopf.

Henry, Jeannett
1970 A Rebuttal to the Five Anthropologists on the Issue of the Wampum Return. Indian Historian 3:15–17.

1971 Anthropology and the American Indian. Indian Historian 4:10.

Hodge, F. W., ed.
1907, 1910 Handbook of American Indians North of Mexico, Bureau of American Ethnology Bulletin 30. Washington: Smithsonian Institution.

Hoebel, E. Adamson
1954 The Law of Primitive Man: A Study in Comparative Legal Dynamics. Cambridge: Harvard University Press.

1972 Anthropology: Its Growth, Methods, and Purposes. Pp. 55–79 in E. Adamson Hoebel, ed., Anthropology: The Study of Man. 4th Edition. New York: McGraw-Hill.

Howard, James H.
1955 The Pan-Indian Culture of Oklahoma. Scientific Monthly 18:215–220.

Hymes, Dell
1974 Reinventing Anthropology. New York: Vintage Books.

Kroeber, Alfred Louis
1939 Cultural and Natural Areas of Native North America. University of California Publications in American Archeology and Ethnology No. 38. Berkeley, California.

Lévi-Strauss, Claude
1966 Anthropology: Its Achievements and Future. Current Anthropology 7:124–127.

Liberty, Margot
1967 Narrative Account of the 1959 Sun Dance and Opening of the Sacred Medicine Hat. Plains Anthropologist 12:367–385.

1973 The Urban Reservation. Unpublished Ph.D. Dissertation, University of Minnesota, Minneapolis.

1977 Native American Studies and the White Man's Burden. Reviews In Anthropology 3:530–537.

Liberty, Margot, and William C. Sturtevant
1974 Prospectus for a Collection of Studies on Anthropology by North American Indians. Mimeographed.

Lowie, Robert
1948 Some Aspects of Political Organization Among the American Aborigines. Journal of the Royal Anthropological Institute 78:11–24.

Lurie, Nancy O.
1969 What the Red Man Wants in the Land That Was His. Saturday Review 52:39–41 ff. (October 4, 1969).

Maynard, Eileen
1974 The Growing Negative Image of Anthropologists Among American Indians. Human Organization 33:402–404.

McNickle, D'Arcy
1973 Native American Tribalism: Indian Survivals and Renewals. New York: Oxford University Press.

Mead, Margaret, and Ruth Bunzel
1960 The Golden Age of American Anthropology. New York: George Braziller.

Medicine, Beatrice
1971 The Anthropologist and American Indian Studies Programs. Indian Historian 4:15–18.

Morgan, Lewis Henry
1851 League of the Ho-De'No-Sau-Nee, or Iroquois. Rochester: Sage and Brother.

Murphy, Robert F. N. ed.
1976 A Quarter Century of American Anthropology. Pp 1–22 in Robert F. Murphy, ed., Selected Papers from the American Anthropologist 1946–1970. Washington: American Anthropological Association.

Murra, John V.
1976 American Anthropology: The Early Years. Pp. 3–5 In John V. Murra, ed., American Anthropology: The Early Years. 1974 Proceedings of the American Ethnological Society. St. Paul: West Publishing Co.

Officer, James E.
1971 The American Indian and Federal Policy. Pp. 8–65 in Jack O. Waddell and O. Michael Watson, eds., The American Indian in Urban Society. Boston: Little, Brown and Co.

Ortiz, Alfonso
1971 An Indian Anthropologist's Perspective on Anthropology. Indian Historian 4:11–14.

Powell, Peter J.
1960 Issiwun: Sacred Buffalo Hat of the Northern Cheyenne. Montana Magazine of Western History 10:36–40.

1969 Issiwun is Opened. Pp. 397–411 in Sweet Medicine: The Continuing Role of the Sacred Arrows, the Sun Dance, and the Sacred Buffalo Hat in Northern Cheyenne History. 2 volumes. Norman: University of Oklahoma Press.

Slotkin, Richard
1973 Regeneration Through Violence: The Mythology of the American Frontier. Middletown, Connecticut: Wesleyan University Press.

Stands in Timber, John, and Margot Liberty
1967 Cheyenne Memories. New Haven: Yale University Press.

Steiner, Stan
1968 The New Indians. New York: Dell Publishing Co.

Steward, Julian
1936 The Economic and Social Basis of Primitive Bands. Pp. 311–350 in R. H. Lowie, ed., Essays in Honor of Alfred Louis Kroeber. Berkeley: University of California Press.

Stocking, George W., Jr.
1976 Ideas and Institutions in American Anthropology: Toward a History of the Interwar Years. Pp. 1–54 in George W. Stocking, ed., Selected Papers from the American Anthropologist 1921–1945. Washington: American Anthropological Association.

Tax, Sol
1955 From Lafitau to Radcliffe-Brown: A Short History of the Study of Social Organization. Pp. 445–481 in Fred Eggan, ed., Social Anthropology of North American Tribes. Chicago: University of Chicago Press.

Tsistsistas Press
Lame Deer, Montana. (Tribal Newspaper.)

Voget, Fred W.
1975 A History of Ethnology. New York: Holt, Rinehart, and Winston.

Wallace, Anthony
1969 The Death and Rebirth of the Seneca. New York: Vintage Books.

Washburn, Wilcomb E.
1975 The Indian in America. New York Harper and Row.

Wax, Murray L.
1971 Indian Americans: Unity and Diversity. Englewood Cliffs, New Jersey: Prentice-Hall.

CHAPTER TWO

ELY S. PARKER[1]

Seneca, ca. 1828–1895

ELISABETH TOOKER

Near the end of his life, Ely S. Parker reflecting both on what he had achieved and what had been expected of him since his youth wrote:

> I was never "great" and never expect to be. I never was "powerful" and would not know how to exercise power were it placed in my hands for use. . . . But my days are not all peace and quiet. I am pursued by a still small voice constantly echoing, "thou are a genius, great and powerful." (E. S. Parker 1905:525–527)

According to one tradition, about four months before he was born, his mother had a dream which was interpreted by a prophet she consulted to mean that a son would be born to her

> who will he distinguished among his nation as a peacemaker; he will become a white man as well as an Indian, with great learning; he will be a warrior for the pale faces; he will be a wise white man, but will never desert his Indian people nor "lay down his horns" (his title as sachem) as a great Iroquois chief; his name will reach from East to the West—the North to the South, as great among his Indian family as the pale faces. (Converse 1897; see also A. C. Parker 1919:47–48)

But despite this prophecy—many years later Parker disclaimed any knowledge of or belief in it (A. C. Parker 1919:174), an account of Ely Parker's life must begin where Parker himself began it in a speech he prepared late in his life:

> that I am wholly unknown to you, an entire stranger, is the first difficulty confronting me in appearing before you. . . . But you, perhaps, are entitled to know to whom you are listening. . . . I am presented to you as General Parker? Well, who is General Parker? (E. S. Parker 1905:527)

In one sense, Ely Parker's life exemplifies the American dream, a venerable American success story of a rise from humble origins to a station of fame and some fortune. Born about 1828, as he said, "of poor, but honest Indian parents in Genesee County, in the western part of the State of New York (E. S. Parker 1905:528), he briefly attended Rensselaer Polytechnic Institute, talking a course in civil engineering. After leaving R.P.I., he became, as one biographer noted, "conspicuously successful, holding various important posts" (Yeuell 1934:219). In 1863 he joined the Union Army and became General Ulysses S. Grant's military secretary. He was with Grant at Appomattox and at Grant's direction made both the notes on and the final copies of the terms of surrender that ended the Civil War (A. C. Parker 1919:129–141, 320). After the war, he continued as Grant's military secretary and in 1867 was made brigadier-general (brevet) in the Regular Army. He resigned from the army in 1869 to become Commissioner of Indian Affairs in the Grant administration, a position he left in 1871. Going into business, he made and lost a considerable sum of money. Finally, he took a position with the New York City Police Department and remained with that Department until his death in 1895.

Ely Parker's life is also the story of a man who achieved this success in spite of difficulties he encountered as a member of a minority group and more particularly, an Indian. His people, the Seneca Indians, had not always been in such a situation. During the 17th century, the Senecas and other tribes of the Iroquois Confederacy had risen to a position of power in the Northeast, a position they maintained until the American Revolution. In that war, a number sided with the British and in 1779 General George Washington sent an expedition under the leadership of Generals John Sullivan and James Clinton against the Iroquois. This expedition destroyed a number of the villages the Senecas had abandoned as the American army advanced. The Seneca refugees fled west, many of them going to the British fort at Niagara. A few apparently decided to move to a settlement on the

Tonawanda Creek where Ely Parker was born almost a half century later. By this time, however, this land was part of the United States. The treaty of Paris that ended the Revolutionary War had so ceded it. But this agreement made no provision for the Indians and consequently the Iroquois had to make separate treaties with the United States. To further complicate matters, both the Commonwealth of Massachusetts and the State of New York claimed the region. The dispute was resolved by an agreement signed at Hartford in 1786 which gave sovereignty and jurisdiction of the territory to the State of New York and the preemption right (the right to purchase these lands) to Massachusetts. Massachusetts subsequently sold these preemption rights to a land company, who in turn bought from the Senecas the eastern portion of the land they then held. Finally, in 1797 Robert Morris, who then held the preemption rights, bought from the Senecas their remaining lands excepting six small tracts along the Genesee River and four large ones further west that came to be called the Buffalo Creek, Cattaraugus, Allegany, and Tonawanda Reservations. But the signing of this treaty did not end the attempts to buy the land the Senecas still held. In 1803 one of the tracts along the Genesee was sold and finally in 1826 the remaining Genesee lands and portions of the Buffalo Creek, Tonawanda, and Cattaraugus Reservations were also sold.

By the sale of these lands, the Senecas lost much of their hunting territory and although they continued to hunt in the area, the game declined as White settlers having bought land cleared it for farms. The Senecas were forced to turn to other means of earning a livelihood, notably by taking up White farming practices. One of the most successful at this occupation was Ely Parker's father, William Parker,[2] a veteran of the War of 1812 who owned a large farm on the Tonawanda Reservation and who was a member of the Baptist church that had been organized there in 1829.

As a young boy, Ely Parker was sent to the school associated with this mission where he was given the name Ely Stone, the name of a local Baptist elder who had been instrumental in establishing the school in the early 1820's. (It was not unusual at that time for Indian students to he named after some prominent White, and the missionaries had given Ely's older brother the name of a prominent Baptist minister—Spencer Cone. Ely Parker whose Indian name was Ha-sa-no-an-da—as he wrote it—later added his father's surname and adopted Samuel as a middle name.) This school located near the reservation was a boarding school run by the Baptist missionary and his wife with the help of one to three female teachers and assistants. The school had an average of 25 students, more attending some parts of the year and fewer at other times, and was supported by money provided by the Government and the Baptists. As Parker (1905:528) later described it, the school

> was conducted on the manual labor system, where boys were taught the rudiments of agriculture and the girls the elementary principles of housewifery. . . . We received board and clothing free, and also whatever merits and demerits the institution possessed. I aquired there all the rudiments of reading, geography and arithmetic; that is to say, I became reasonably familiar with Webster's spelling book, Lindley Murray's grammar, Olney's geography and Daboll's arithmetic.

Nevertheless, Parker also said that he graduated from the school with only a limited knowledge of English. As he observed,

> I understood [on graduation from the school] very little of the English language; as the school was composed of purely Indian pupils, they all would persist in speaking their native language when among themselves and the little English they required was not of an adhesive [i.e., lasting] character. (E. S. Parker 1905:530)

After he left school, young Ely then about 10 years old was taken to Canada where he spent a couple of years learning hunting and fishing (E. S. Parker 1905:530). It seems likely that he went with a group from the reservation that included a number of the most prominent members of the Baptist church including the interpreter (Annual Report of the Baptist Missionary Convention of the State of New York 1838:34). He returned to the Tonawanda Reservation when he was about twelve and on the trip had an experience which changed his life. As he later recounted it:

> At London, in Canada, two or three English officers were taken up at the fort there and brought on to the city of Hamilton at the head of Lake Ontario. It was natural that these officers should amuse themselves in some way to pass the time and tedium of travel. This they did at my expense, they all the time being under the impression that I did not understand or know the point of their jokes. The fact was that I did know just enough English to understand stand and know what they said and did, but I could not speak it well enough to enjoy their jokes. It was perhaps just as well that I could not. I was not injured and they had their fun, for nothing they said or did was laid in malice. In this solitary ride, I bethought myself that perhaps it might be good for me did I thoroughly

> understand and speak the English language as well as to be able to read English books. (E. S. Parker 1905:530)

Consequently, Parker returned to the Baptist mission school to qualify, as he said, "myself as well as possible to enter some advanced school among the whites" (E. S. Parker 1905:531). His command of English, however, was good enough for him to be given the job of interpreter at the school and church, a position that the Baptist mission had had considerable difficulty filling after the interpreter had gone to Canada (at the time few of the Tonawanda Senecas spoke English), much to the detriment of their work (Annual Reports of the Baptist Missionary Convention of the State of New York 1838:34; 1839:17; 1840:22–23; 1841:23).

In 1843 Parker left the mission school to attend Yates Academy at Yates in Orleans County. Some indication of the kind of instruction offered at Yates is given in Parker's (1845) account of his expenses for the first quarter of 1845 (expenses paid by the United States Government)

For ten weeks board from January 1st to March 12th	$12.50
For tuition one quarter	5.00
Ainsworth [Latin] Dictionary	2.25
Anthons Cicero	1.75
Coopers Virgil	2.00
Greek Reader	1.00
Greek Grammar	1.63
	$27.13

After almost two years at Yates, he transferred to Cayuga Academy in Aurora, New York in the fall in 1845. He remained there until the spring of the following year.

Two years later, anxious to learn a profession, Parker entered the law office of Angel and Rice in Ellicottville to read law. At the time, W. P. Angel was New York Indian sub-agent, a position he held from 1846 to 1848 and had had business with Parker in that capacity. But Parker was barred from the practice of law in New York State because he was not a White citizen, and he abandoned the study of law to take up civil engineering as a profession—a career he (E. S. Parker 1860) described in 1860 as follows:

> In 1849 I commenced the practice of Engineering on the Genesee Valley Canal at Nunda. I commenced as axeman and remained in Nunda 10 mos. I then removed to Rochester and entered the Canal Office there, and from axeman, I successively filled and discharged the duties of rodman, leveler, transitman, Asst. and Resident Engi-

neer. In June 1855, the State or Canal Board and myself differed. They wanted to make my office a political one, that is to demean the profession to subserve party purposes and ends. My Residency was the most important on the Erie Canal. I had about 35 young men under me, and I had charge of about $5,000,000.00 worth of work. The Canal Board insisted on their point and I resigned. The next week I went to Norfolk as Chf. Engr. of a new ship canal which we named the Chesapeake and Albermarle Ship Canal. Having located and staked out the line, and successfully commenced the work, and having done everything that I considered it my duty to do as an Engn, I, in the winter of 1856–7 resigned, went to Washington, obtained the appointment of Supt. of the Lt. House construction on the upper lakes, viz. Lks. Huron, Michigan and Superior. Feby. 1st 1857 I was living in Detroit, where the office for this Dist. was kept. But on the 1st of Mch. following I received another commission from the Hon. Secretary or the Treasurer, appointing me Supt. of the construction of a Custom House and a Marine Hospital at Galena. I immediately moved to Galena, and commenced my work the following April. I completed the two buildings last November and was immediately recommissioned as Supt. of the Construction of a Custom House in Dubuque. I removed here last winter, and here I am, building a very pretty Cus. Hos P.O. Court rooms etc.

Despite his success as an engineer, Parker was unable to obtain a commission in the Union Army when the Civil War broke out. The Governor of New York refused his request for a commission. So did the Secretary of War, William H. Seward, with the comment, Parker later wrote, "that the struggle . . . was an affair between white men and one in which the Indian was not called to act. 'The fight must be settled by the white men alone,' he said. 'Go home, cultivate your farm and we will settle our own troubles without any Indian aid'" (A. C. Parker 1919:106). And thus it is of some significance that at Appomattox, Parker later recounted, "After Lee had stared at me for a moment, . . . he extended his hand and said, 'I am glad to see one real American here.' I shook his hand, and said, 'We are all Americans'" (A. C. Parker 1919:133).

Ely Parker's achievements, however, were not merely those of a poor boy who made good or even of an Indian who attained distinction in the larger American society. Ely Parker was an Iroquois Indian, and it is as an Iroquois that he is best known to anthropologists, more particularly as Lewis H. Morgan's collaborator. Morgan later wrote *Systems of Consanguinity and*

Affinity of the Human Family (1871)—the monumental and seminal study of kinship terminologies—and *Ancient Society* (1877)—one of the most influential studies of cultural evolution, and became the leading American anthropologist of his time. Nevertheless, his first study, *League of the Ho-de-no-sau-nee or Iroquois* (1851) is also an extraordinary work; still the best single description of Iroquois culture, it was the first true ethnography to be written. Yet, this classic study was not a product of either Morgan's or Parker's mature years. Morgan was not yet 30 when he published his first extended description of the Iroquois as a series of letters addressed to Albert Gallatin in the *American Whig Review* (Morgan 1847), a description he later republished in substantially the same form in the *League* (Morgan 1851:37–146, 394–443). When the "Letters to Gallatin" including Morgan's famous account of Iroquois political organization first appeared, Parker was still a teen-ager.

Neither did either young man set out to write "the great American ethnography." Parker failed to mention the work in his few autobiographical writings—perhaps an indication of the importance he attached to it. And Morgan later noted that his "principal object" in writing the book which, he said, "exhibits abundant evidence of hasty execution, was to free myself of the subject" (White 1957:262). Morgan, who married his cousin, Mary E. Steele, later that year (1851) wanted to devote his time to his profession (Resek 1960:48–49; White 1957:262).

The development of Morgan's interest in the Iroquois is well-known. After graduation from Union College, Morgan returned to Aurora where he had been born in 1818, raised, and where he had attended Cayuga Academy—the school Ely Parker later attended on the advice and with the help of Morgan and his friends. In Aurora, Morgan became active in a literary club composed of young men called the "Gordian Knot." This club, subsequently reorganized into a society variously known as the "Grand Knot of the Iroquois," the "Order of the Iroquois," and the "New Confederacy," established chapters in other towns and cities in upstate New York and, as Morgan later recalled, began the work of studying out the structure and principles of the ancient League, by which they had been united for so many centuries. We wished to model our organization upon this, and to reproduce it with as much fidelity as the nature and object of our order would permit. This desire, on our part, led to the first discovery of the real structure and principles of the League of the Iroquois, which up to that time were entirely unknown, except in a most general sense. (White 1957:261)

That these young men of Aurora chose to base the ritual and organization of their secret society on an Iroquois theme is not surprising. Although

Cayugas no longer lived there, the region had been Cayuga territory not many years before (the Cayugas had sold these lands in a series of treaties signed between 1789 and 1807). As Morgan later wrote, "We finally concluded to . . . change our organization into an Indian society under the name of the 'Cayugas,' as we resided in the ancient territory of this Indian nation and quite near the site of their principal village" (White 1957:260–261).

It was also a time of great national pride and the struggling new country often turned to Indian symbols to express its national identity. Such feelings were not absent among the members of the Order and they saw their society as furthering national interest. As Morgan wrote at the time,

> We need somewhere in our Republic, an Indian Order which should aim to become the vast repository of all that remains to us of the Indians, their antiquities, their customs, eloquence, history, literature, indeed, everything pertaining to them which can be rescued from oblivion to which it is rapidly hastening. Another of its leading objects should be to beget and encourage a kinder feeling towards the Red Man, a disposition to appreciate and render a just tribute of admiration to the many virtues of the Indian character; and above all, when the Order thus instituted shall have reached its full maturity, it should make the whole Indian race the object of its benevolence and protection: to shield them in their declining fortunes from oppression, and to mitigate to some extent the misfortunes which are hastening their dissolution.
>
> Such an Order would have a vast and novel field of literary research, the romantic age of the western world; and surely the literary department of the Order would give ample range to the most gifted intellect. Indian life suggests ample materials for the philosophic, the poetic and the descriptive pen, and distant generations must look back to the Indian age for the fable, the antiquities and the romance of America. (Letter to William L. Stone dated June 10, 1844 quoted in Stern 1931:13–14.)

Morgan's genius, however, lay not in his role in the organization of a society whose members played at being Indian and wore Indian costumes at their meetings. This had been done earlier and with more verve by the Sons of Liberty, who had not only dressed as Indians for what came to be known as the Boston Tea Party but had also for a time celebrated May 12th as Saint Tamina's (Tammany) Day with festivities that often included Indian war dances (Stevens 1907:323–324). Nor was it in playing the modern anthropological equivalent—participant-observer. What records survive indicate that the amount of time Morgan spent in the field among the Iroquois may have totaled only a few months. Neither was it in being a successful advocate of Indian causes. Although Morgan was active throughout his life in the organization of groups of intellectuals (including the American Association for the Advancement of Science), he was a poor practical politician and his efforts to help the Iroquois were apparently few and of short duration. Other lawyers made a more significant contribution. Rather, Morgan's genius—I would suggest—lay elsewhere: in a deep commitment to understand how the system, particularly how the Iroquois system worked not only in the past but also at the time, for contrary to popular opinion the system was still functioning then as it still functions today on some reservations. It was this concern for understanding how the system worked that set the "Order of the Iroquois" apart from other fraternal organizations so popular in this country and that sets the *League of the Iroquois* apart from the run-of-the-mill ethnography. It was also the same concern that moved Morgan to write a quarter of a century after the publication of the *League* and five years before his death:

> It may be truly said, at this moment, that the structure and principle of Indian society are but partially known, and that the American Indian himself is still an enigma among us. The question is still before us, as a nation, whether we will undertake the work of furnishing to the world a scientific exposition of Indian society, or leave it as it now appears, crude, unmeaning, unintelligible, a chaos of contradictions and puerile absurdities. With a field of unequalled richness and of vast extent, . . . more persons ought to be found willing to work upon this material for the credit of American scholarship. It will be necessary for them to do as Herodotus did in Asia and Africa, to visit the native tribes at their villages and encampments, and study their institutions as living organisms, their condition, and their plan of life. (Morgan 1876:269)

Morgan himself had done this. When the young men of Aurora organized the Order of the Iroquois, they had turned to books on the Indians such as B. B. Thatcher's (1832) popular *Indian Biography* and William Stone's (1838; 1841) biographies of Joseph Brant and Red Jacket for information on the organization of the Iroquois Confederacy, but found little on this topic in them. Consequently, they turned to the Indians themselves including such knowledgeable Indians as the noted Onondaga chief, Abram La Fort, who like distinguished White authorities on Indians and Indian history were made members of the Order. But of all the Indian members of the Order that he met, Ely Parker proved to be of the most assistance.

Parker's reasons for helping Morgan understand how the system worked probably rested not so much on his knowledge or his identity as an Iroquois Indian—Parker was young, had spent much of his life in school, and was a Christian—as on his identity as an Iroquois from the Tonawanda Reservation. In 1838, when Parker was about 10 years old and about the time he went to Canada, the Iroquois had sold all their reservations in New York State and had agreed to move west. However, the circumstances under which this treaty was signed were so suspect and there was so much opposition to it that a new treaty was negotiated. Signed in 1842, this treaty, popularly known as the Compromise Treaty of 1842, provided for the sale of only two of the Iroquois reservations in the State—the large Buffalo Creek Reservation and the smaller Tonawanda Reservation. The residents of these two reservations were to move to one of the other two Seneca reservations in New York State—the Cattaraugus and Allegany Reservations—or to Kansas. Although those who had opposed the Treaty of 1838 and had forced its renegotiation felt this was the most they could get for the Iroquois, the Tonawanda Senecas objected to the agreement. They argued that the treaty was not binding on them as none of their chiefs had signed it and by bodily ejecting the two assessors from the reservation they prevented the provisions of the treaty from being carried out—an appraisal of the improvements being necessary before the money for them could be given and so the residents moved. Pursuing every course they could, the Tonawanda Senecas not only took their case into the courts, but they also sent a number of delegations to Albany and Washington to attempt to get the provisions of the treaty as it applied to them overturned.

It was while one such delegation was visiting Albany that Morgan met Ely Parker. Morgan, apparently in Albany on business, had taken the opportunity not only to look up treaties with the Indians, especially the Cayuga treaties, but also to visit a bookstore. Parker, in Albany as interpreter for a delegation of Tonawanda Senecas, also had taken advantage of his own opportunity to visit the same bookstore. As Morgan later said at the monthly council of Cayugas (the Aurora chapter) of the Order of the Iroquois on April 17, 1844:

> it was my good fortune to encounter at a Bookstore one afternoon, a young Indian of genuine extraction. He was about eighteen years of age [actually he was nearer 16], and of a pleasing and interesting appearance. To sound the war whoop, and seize the youth might

> have been dangerous, and to let him pass without a parley would have been inexcusable; accordingly your humble Prophet assumed a civil attitude, and accosted the young warrior in a friendly manner. He entered into familiar conversation at once, and before leaving him I learned that he came to the city with an Indian delegation, consisting of the old sachem of the Senecas, and two chiefs, from the Tonawanda Reservation; and that it would take them a week to transact their business. (Morgan 1844)

The "old sachem" Morgan mentioned he met in Albany was Jimmy Johnson (also known as Jemmy Johnson and as James Johnson), one of the two men leading the efforts of the Tonawanda Senecas to regain their reservation. The other leader in this effort was John Blacksmith, who in 1839 had been raised up as a League chief and given the name Donehogawa held by the Wolf clan in place of the deposed Little Johnson (A. C. Parker 1916:134), a leader of the pro-emigration party at Buffalo Creek. (In 1846 with about 200 other Iroquois, Little Johnson did migrate to Kansas where he and a number of others in the party died.) Unlike John Blacksmith, Jimmy Johnson was not a League chief, although his life had not been an undistinguished one. A grandson of the Seneca prophet, Handsome Lake, he had codified his grandfather's teachings and annually recited them at a council of the Iroquois held at Tonawanda. (Some years before a number of Handsome Lake's followers had come to live at Tonawanda as did Handsome Lake himself after he had been forced to leave the Allegany Reservation.) Among those who came to live at Tonawanda when Handsome Lake did were William Parker (Ely's father), his two brothers, and mother (A. C. Parker 1919:318). Jimmy Johnson was also a nephew of the famous Seneca orator, Red Jacket and after Red Jacket's death in 1831, had received the medal Red Jacket always wore, a medal given him by George Washington in Philadelphia in 1792.

Johnson was wearing this medal when Morgan called on the delegation after dinner, having made arrangements with Ely Parker earlier that day in the bookstore to do so. Parker acted as interpreter on this occasion and in succeeding interviews with Jimmy Johnson while Morgan was in Albany. Morgan seizing this opportunity to gain information about the Iroquois Confederacy spent, as he said, "hours each day until my return" conversing with Jimmy Johnson and Ely Parker.

Later that same year (1844) Morgan moved to Rochester to begin practicing law there. Rochester is considerably nearer the Tonawanda Reservation than Aurora, and this fact probably facilitated Morgan's work with Ely Parker. In the fall of 1845, having learned that a council of the Confederacy (the first in some years) was to be held at Tonawanda for the purpose of raising up chiefs, Morgan and three other members of the Order including two members of the "Turtle Tribe of Senecas" Morgan had helped found in Rochester, went to the reservation to see it. While he was there, he also interviewed some Iroquois, notably Abram La Port and Peter Wilson, on the organization of the *League* with Ely Parker again serving as interpreter. On Morgan's subsequent field trips, Parker also served as interpreter, but these trips were few and although documentary proof is sparse, it seems likely that Morgan also obtained some information from Parker in conversation with him in Rochester as well as through correspondence.[3]

All the evidence indicates this was a collaboration—a collaboration that Morgan who was unusually accurate in such matters acknowledges in his dedication to the League; that Parker was not only Morgan's interpreter but also provided him with information as he knew it and when he did not know it, inquired of knowledgeable people at Tonawanda, a task made relatively easy for him by his personal and family connections. It was also a task that interested both—Morgan for the reasons mentioned and Parker because of his role as one of the leaders in the effort of the Tonawanda Senecas to retain their reservation. And the collaboration proved advantageous to both; Morgan not only called on Parker for information and other aid, asking him to attend meetings of the Order, but also Parker called on Morgan for help, such as asking him to come to Washington in the spring of 1846 to testify on Iroquois political organization (E. S. Parker 1846).

But if Parker brought to this collaboration a knowledge of the Seneca language and customs, Morgan brought to it not only an interest in social organization, but also a knowledge of the law. Morgan's reliance on the interview for information rather than observation (Morgan did not include in the *League*, for example, an account of the council he attended in 1845 or an account of the council held at Tonawanda in 1848, given to him by Ely Parker except Jimmy Johnson's speech) resembles reliance on expert witnesses in courts of law, and his particular use of this material (the search for the principles of organization) the search of the jurist. At the time Morgan was studying Iroquois social organization (1844–46), Parker had not yet read law and Parker's description of Iroquois customs written late in his life (see especially his letters to Harriet Maxwell Converse in A. C. Parker 1919) show no such interest in the principles of Iroquois society. Parker himself wrote no extensive account of the Iroquois, and what he did write is only a kind of casual description of a rather ordinary sort. Morgan, however, both by training and inclination sought "the structure and principle" of Iroquois society.

In the years following their meeting in Albany, Parker became increasingly involved in the attempt of the Tonawanda Senecas to save their reservation. He left Cayuga Academy in the spring of 1846 to go to Washington with a delegation composed of three men: John Blacksmith, another Tonawanda chief, and himself. The reasons for his being asked to go were probably several. The two leading Tonawanda chiefs were getting old: Blacksmith was about 60 and Jimmy Johnson about 70 at the time. But probably more important was Parker's knowledge of English. He not only spoke English well (among his other talents, he was an excellent public speaker) and could act as interpreter, but also he wrote excellent English and—in the words of the day—wrote an excellent hand. This knowledge and his own ability led him to take an active role in the work of marshalling support for the Tonawanda case, "a great responsibility" Parker later wrote, "which was shouldered upon me when yet a mere youth, the weight of which I fear has left me prematurely old" (E. S. Parker 1860).

Something more of the responsibility Parker assumed when he began these negotiations, and the cost to him, is contained in a letter written to his brother while he was in Washington that year:

> If ever the Tonawandas were required to be united in their plans and purposes, it is now, in this our last struggle for the homes and graves of our honored dead. The interests of future generations hang upon the course we pursue. If we desire the happiness and increase of our posterity, we are the ones to lay the foundation for their success. We are struggling for our land . . . and if we succeed, most certainly we have the admiration and thanks of posterity for our wise policy. . . .
>
> . . . I have positively been made poor in serving them [the Tonawanda Senecas] so faithfully. I am now ragged, and I have no money to buy clothes with. . . . [But] I am so fargone in Indian business, that I shall have to stick to it be the consequences what they may. (E. S. Parker 1846)

And stick to it Parker did, making trips to Washington in the following years and doing what else he could for the Tonawanda cause.

After John Blacksmith died in 1851, the year the *League* was published, Parker, who like Blacksmith was a member of the Wolf clan, was raised up in Blacksmith's place and given his chiefly name. Symbolic of his role, he also received on that occasion the Red Jacket medal that had belonged to Jimmy Johnson. Finally in 1857, after the United States Supreme Court had ruled that because the treaty had been executed and ratified by the proper authorities, the treaty was binding on the Tonawanda Senecas even though their chiefs had not signed it, but that it did not provide for the forcible removal of the Indians from the reservation, a new treaty was negotiated and signed. This new treaty provided for the buying back of the reservation with monies granted to the Tonawanda Senecas for relinquishment of their claim to the lands to be given them in Kansas (Supreme Court of the United States, December term, 1856, no. 47: Kappler 1904:767–771).

During the period (1842–57) the Tonawanda Senecas were engaged in the fight to save their reservation, the Iroquois on the other two Seneca reservations in New York State—the Allegany and Cattaraugus Reservations—overthrew their chiefs and instituted an elected council (Abler 1967). The Tonawanda Senecas did not join in this 1848 "revolution." They could hardly have done so. One of their arguments was that their chiefs had not signed the Compromise Treaty of 1842 and to abrogate the authority of the chiefs would weaken their case. However, after the reservation had been bought back, Ely Parker was instrumental in making some changes in the Tonawanda form of governance—principally the election of a clerk, treasurer, marshal, and three peacemakers (the reservation continued to be governed by a council of hereditary chiefs) and was in part responsible for setting the New York State Legislature to enact this and other laws governing the Tonawanda Senecas (A. C. Parker 1919:287–292; New York State 1861:645–654).

By this date, Ely Parker had fulfilled part of the prophecy contained in his mother's dream before his birth. But it brought him neither peace nor contentment. As he later remarked about himself:

> I am an ideal or a myth and not my real self. I have lost my identity and I look about me in vain for my original being. . . .
>
> All my life I have occupied a false position. As a youth my people voted me a genius and loudly proclaimed that Hawenneyo [the Creator] had destined me to be their Saviour and gave public thanksgiving for the great blessing they believed had been given them, for unfortunately just at this period they were engaged in an almost endless and nearly hopeless litigated contest for their New York homes and consequently for their very existence.

> . . . I pleased my people in eventually bringing their troubles to a successful and satisfactory termination. I prepared and had approved by the proper authorities a code of laws and rules for the conduct of affairs among themselves and settled them for all time or for so long as Hawenneyo should let them live.
>
> They saw all this and that it was good. They no longer wanted me nor gave me credit for what had been done. A generation had passed and another grown up since I began to work for them. The young men were confident of their own strength and abilities and needed not the brawny arm of experience to fight their battles for them, nor the wisdom brought about by years of training to guide them any longer. (E. S. Parker 1905:525)

In 1856, after a lapse of five years, Morgan's interest in Indian studies was renewed as a consequence of attending the A.A.A.S. meeting in Albany (White 1957:262–263) and the following year, the year that the fate of the Tonawanda Reservation was finally decided, he presented a paper at the A.A.A.S. meeting in Montreal on the "Laws of Descent of the Iroquois" (Morgan 1858). With this paper, he began the comparative study of kinship terminologies and social organization—subjects that were to engage his attention for the remainder of his life. In 1859 he took the first of what became annual trips to the West to collect information. But at the end of his trip in 1862, which he had continued even after learning of the illness of his two daughters, he learned of their deaths and wrote:

> Our family is destroyed. The intelligence has simply petrified me. I have not shed a tear. It is too profound for tears. Thus ends my last expedition. I go home to my stricken and mourning wife, a miserable and destroyed man. (White 1959:200)

He went on no further field trips to collect ethnographic information, but devoted much of his time first to writing *Systems of Consanguinity and Affinity of the Human Family* (1871) which he regarded as a memorial to his daughters, and then to *Ancient Society* (1877) and *Houses and House Life of the American Aborigines* (1881), the latter published the year of his death.

In light of these accomplishments, it is of some significance that as a young man Morgan, who had wanted to understand how the Iroquois system worked, and Parker, who was learning how such political systems functioned in order to save his people's land, met in a bookstore. For the result of their collaboration, what Morgan (1851: Dedication) called "the fruit of our joint researches" was to be published seven years later as a book. But perhaps of even greater significance was a matter Morgan mentioned only obliquely when he wrote in the Preface to the *League* that Ely Parker's "intelligence and accurate knowledge of the institutions of his forefathers, have made his friendly services a peculiar privilege" (Morgan 1851:xi); that in that Albany bookstore, the two young men undoubtedly recognized something in each other which set them apart from most others—extraordinary ability.

NOTES

1. I am indebted to the American Philosophical Society library in Philadelphia, Pennsylvania, the Henry E. Huntington Library in San Marino, California, and the University of Rochester Library in Rochester, New York for the many courtesies they have extended to me in the course of my research on Lewis H. Morgan and Ely S. Parker, of which this paper is a part. I am also indebted to the libraries of the University of Rochester and the American Philosophical Society for permission to quote from documents in their collections.

2. Ely was the second child of William and Elizabeth Parker. The eldest was Spencer Cone, who for a time was virtually the only Tonawanda Seneca in favor of removal west. Ely had three other brothers (Nicholson, Levi, and Solomon) and a sister. The youngest, Solomon died in 1846. Nicholson moved to the Cattaraugus Reservation and married Martha Hoyt, a niece of Laura Wright, wife of the noted missionary to the Senecas, Asher Wright. (One of Nicholson's grandsons was Arthur C. Parker, who in 1919 published a biography of his great-uncle Ely.) Levi remained on the Tonawanda Reservation. Their sister, Caroline married John Mount Pleasant, a widowed Tuscarora chief and moved to the Tuscarora Reservation. Ely himself married Minnie Sachett, a White woman, by whom he had a daughter.

3. Unfortunately, it is not possible to ascertain from the extant manuscript materials how much ethnographic data Morgan obtained in conversation with Parker and how much by letter. Nor is it possible to ascertain how often or in what manner Morgan checked his description with Parker before he published it. There is little in the Parker papers in the American Philosophical Society Library, the Huntington Library, or the University of Rochester Library that indicates the nature of the collaboration. More useful for this purpose are the Morgan papers in the University of Rochester Library. However, a number of Morgan's papers were destroyed

either by Morgan himself before his death or by his wife shortly after he died; only those not so destroyed were given to the University of Rochester (Resek 1960:viii). Some examination of these papers suggests that Morgan intended to preserve for the use of future scholars at least some field and other data he and others had collected but which had not been published. But either he or his wife (or both) did not intend to preserve for such future use his personal letters. There are relatively few personal letters and virtually nothing on business affairs in the papers given to the University of Rochester. Morgan also seems to have been that kind of writer who destroys his drafts after the work has been published. There are few drafts in the Rochester collection, and of these almost none related to the *League* or to the publications—the *Letters to Gallatin* (1847) and the *Reports to the Regents* (1848–52)—Morgan republished in the *League*. Further, although there are field notes and comparable materials in this collection, Morgan apparently did not save all such materials. There is information in the *League* that Morgan undoubtedly obtained from Parker which is not to be found in these papers, and this information includes not only the type of material customarily omitted in field notes (the omissions that make such field notes so difficult for others to use), but also words and lists Morgan must have written down and some of Parker's written translations. Something of the nature of these gaps in the Morgan papers can be seen by comparing Morgan's letter to Parker asking for information that is dated January 29, 1850 and Parker's reply dated February 12, 1850 (Fenton 1941:151–158) with the section in the *League* (Morgan 1851:198–205) on the Green Corn ceremony—one of the subjects mentioned in both Morgan's and Parker's letters. In his letter, Morgan asks for a description of the proceedings of this ceremonial as well as others and mentions that he has not seen it (apparently he is even uncertain as to the number of days it requires). Parker's description of this ceremonial in his reply is fairly general although he does mention that it usually lasts three days. However, in the *League* there is a day-by-day description of it. It seems most likely that sometime after Parker wrote Morgan in February and before the *League* was published Morgan obtained a detailed account of the proceedings. Yet, a manuscript record of this description is not preserved although Morgan did preserve Parker's letter and even included it in his "Manuscript Journals" which he himself had had bound. The existence of this letter and more importantly Parker's statement in it that "I have at many different times written to you upon the subjects concerning which you now ask further information" (Fenton 1941:153) might suggest that Parker provided Morgan with much ethnographic data via letter. Parker's skimpy answers, however, suggest that this medium was not wholly satisfactory; Parker simply did not provide the detail Morgan had asked for. Thus, one suspects that Morgan asked him again for it—perhaps after Parker moved to Rochester in 1850. One also suspects that Parker inquired about the proceedings, perhaps of Jimmy Johnson. Further, one suspects that Parker explained what he learned in a conversation with Morgan who (and this is more conjectural) wrote a rough draft during that conversation, a draft he did not keep after the *League* was published. This procedure would also explain other gaps in the Morgan papers. There is one piece of evidence suggesting that Parker did not read Morgan's drafts before they were published: in a letter Parker (1847) wrote Morgan from Washington in February, 1847, Parker says that he has read Morgan's *Letters to Gallatin* in the *Whig Review* and notes that there is an error in the second letter—that the League council was held not just for exigencies but annually at Onondaga "as" Parker wrote, "I told you last fall, and now repeat to you."

LITERATURE CITED

Abler, Thomas S.

1967 Seneca National Factionalism: The First Twenty Years. In Elisabeth Tooker ed., Iroquois Culture, History and Prehistory: Proceedings of the 1965 Conference on Iroquois Research (Albany: New York State Museum and Science Service).

Converse, Harriet Maxwell

1897 A Prophecy Fulfilled: The Remarkable Vision Seen by Gen. Ely S. Parker's Mother, and How It Has Been Verified. Buffalo Express for January 24, 1897.

Fenton, William N.

1941 Tonawanda Longhouse Ceremonies: Ninety years after Lewis Henry Morgan. Bureau of American Ethnology Bulletin 128:139–165.

Kappler, Charles J.

1904 Indian Affairs: Laws and Treaties. Vol. 2. Washington: Government Printing Office.

Morgan, Lewis H.

1844 An Address Read by Schenandoah Before the Gue-u-gueh-o-noh, Aurora, April 17, 1844. (Manuscript in the University of Rochester Library.)

1847 Letters on the Iroquois, by Shenandoah, Addressed to Albert Gallatin, President, New York Historical Society. The American Review: A Whig Journal 5:177–190, 242–247, 447–461; 6:477–490, 626–633.

1849–1852 Reports. Annual Report of the University of the State of New York 2:81–91; 3:59–95; 5:67–117.

1851 League of the Ho-de-no-sau-nee, or Iroquois. Rochester: Sage and Brother.

1858 Laws of Descent of the Iroquois. Proceedings of the American Association for the Advancement of Science 11(2):132–148.

1871 Systems of Consanguinity and Affinity of the Human Family. Smithsonian Contributions to Knowledge 17. Washington.

1876 Montezuma's Dinner. North American Review 122:265–308.

1877 Ancient Society. New York: Henry Holt.

1881 Houses and House-life of the American Aborigines. Contributions to North American Ethnology 4. Washington.

New York State

1861 Laws of the State of New York, Passed at the Eighty-fourth Session of the Legislature, Begun January First and Ending April Sixteenth, 1861, in the City of Albany. Albany: Munsell and Rowland.

Parker, Arthur C.

1916 The Constitution of the Five Nations or the Iroquois Book of the Great Law. New York State Museum Bulletin 184.

1919 The Life of General Ely S. Parker: Last Grand Sachem of the Iroquois and General Grant's Military Secretary. Buffalo Historical Society Publication 23.

Parker, Ely S.

1845 Expenditures for the First Quarter of 1845, Dated Yates Academy, Yates, Orleans Co., N.Y., March 31, 1845. (Manuscript in the American Philosophical Society Library.)

1846 Letter to Nicholson H. Parker, Dated Washington, June 21, 1846. (Manuscript in the American Philosophical Society Library.)

1847 Letter to Lewis H. Morgan, Dated Washington City, February 13, 1847. (Manuscript in the University of Rochester Library.)

1860 Letter to Benjamin Wilcox, Dated Dubuque, Sept. 10, 1860. (Manuscript in the University of Rochester Library.)

1905 Writings of General Parker: Extracts from his Letters, and an Autobiographical Memoir of Historical Interest. Proceedings of the Buffalo Historical Society 8:520–536.

Resek, Carl

1960 Lewis Henry Morgan, American Scholar. Chicago: University of Chicago Press.

Stern, Bernhard L.

1931 Lewis Henry Morgan, Social Evolutionist. New York: Russell and Russell.

Stevens, Albert C.

1907 The Cyclopaedia of Fraternities. Revised ed. New York: E. B. Treat.

Stone, William L.

1838 Life of Joseph Brant—Thayendanegea. 2 vols. New York: Alexander V. Blake.

1841 The Life and Times of Red Jacket, or Sa-go-ye-wat-ha. New York and London: Wiley and Putnam.

Thatcher, B. B.

1832 Indian Biography. New York: J. and J. Harper. (Republished in many editions.)

White, Leslie A.

1957 How Morgan Came to Write *Systems of Consanguinity and Affinity*. Papers of the Michigan Academy of Science, Arts and Letters 42:257–268.

1959 Lewis Henry Morgan: The Indian Journals, 1859–62. Ann Arbor: University of Michigan Press.

Yeuell, Donovan

1934 Ely Samuel Parker. In Dumas Malone, ed., Dictionary of American Biography, vol. 7, pt. 2, pp. 219–220. New York: Charles Scribner's Sons.

CHAPTER THREE

SARAH WINNEMUCCA

Northern Paiute, ca. 1844–1891

CATHERINE S. FOWLER

Sarah Winnemucca is a historical figure whose life and works have had more direct impact on the course of 19th century United States Indian policy than on the discipline of anthropology. In the latter half of the 19th century, she wrote a book (Hopkins 1883: *Life Among the Piutes: Their Wrongs and Claims*) and at least one article (Winnemucca 1882) detailing the harried course of Northern Paiute-White relations to that time. She also lectured extensively in the far West and in the East on reservation conditions, inequities in federal Indian policy and government agent corruption. Her book and speeches lent direct support to the passage of the controversial "lands in severalty" legislation, then before the Congress. Sarah Winnemucca also established and operated for two years her own school for Northern Paiute children near Lovelock, Nevada—an early attempt at self-determination in Indian education.

Sarah Winnemucca is a controversial figure, and herein lies some of her historical interest. Robert Heizer (1960:3) suggests that her "selfless motives and tremendous energies and high purpose make her a person to admire in the history of our far West." Omer Stewart (1939:129) on the other hand, described her as "ambitious, educated . . . , trying to attain self-aggrandizement by exalting her father." Sarah's ethnographic and ethnohistoric contributions are rarely cited by Great Basin ethnographers beyond some cursory statement to the effect that she wrote a book that was probably little read in her native state of Nevada.

In this paper, I will briefly examine the life of Sarah Winnemucca, some of the controversy that surrounds her and some of her ethnohistoric and ethnographic contributions. The events of her life suggest clearly some of the motives that led her to speak for Indian rights at a time when a Native American woman would hardly be respected for doing so. I would like to suggest in the light of 20th century ethnohistoric and ethnographic hindsight that Sarah's position on assimilation, perhaps more than any other single factor, has led scholars, and to a certain degree her own people, to diminish her contributions to Native American scholarship.

Sarah Winnemucca was born about 1844 near the Sink of the Humboldt River, in what is now western Nevada. She came from a family that from the time of first contact with Whites had advocated peaceful coexistence—a position that did not gain the members favor among all segments of the Northern Paiute population. Sarah's maternal grandfather, Truckee, had been favorably disposed toward early explorers, and settlers, interpreting their advent as the reuniting of the Northern Paiutes with their lost White brothers and sisters, as foretold in the Northern Paiute creation cycle (Hopkins 1883:6). Truckee served as a guide to various emigrant parties traversing the Sierra, fought in California with John C. Fremont in his Mexican campaigns and continually befriended White families and individuals throughout northern Nevada and California. There is good evidence that Truckee and several other Northern Paiutes spent as many as half of the years between 1842 and 1860, the year of his death, in the settlements of California. He spoke both Spanish and English in addition to his native Northern Paiute, making him an effective go-between when present in Nevada. He also continually related the wonders of developing California to his people. Sarah (Hopkins 1883:18) describes how she and some of her people learned to sing what she later identified as soldiers' roll calls and the Star Spangled Banner long before they could understand the words.

Sarah's father, Old Winnemucca, was also generally on the side of peace and coexistence, although several specific events from the mid 1860's through the 1870's made him cautious and wary. During this time, partly as a result of the massacre of members of his band on the shores of Mud Lake in 1865 (Hopkins 1883:77; Angel 1881:170), Winnemucca became sullen and withdrawn, choosing a path of avoidance rather than accommodation. Sarah continually stressed that her father was "chief" of all the Paiutes, a point of controversy for latter-day ethnographers and ethnohistorians.

Sarah's brother, Naches, also acted as a go-between in relations between Indians and Whites in western Nevada. Naches was convinced of the utility of agriculture and for several years operated a cooperative farm on 160 acres of land near Lovelock, Nevada. He obtained the land partly through cash purchase and partly by convincing railroad magnate Leland Stanford that he intended to put the land to good use. (The land was a railroad section.)

Thus, the Winnemuccas were what would be labeled today "Whitemen's Indians" at least from outward appearances. However, there is also a strong current of self-determination that runs through their attitudes and activities that is less often stressed. Again, hindsight may clarify this position as we proceed.

When Sarah was approximately 10 years of age, she and her mother and siblings spent part of a year with Truckee near San Jose, California. She describes in detail in her book (Hopkins 1883:27 ff.) her impressions of this strange land, its strange goods, and even stranger people. She had an almost pathological fear of Whites as a child, in spite of her grandfather's continual reassurances concerning their kindly nature and good intentions. She was greatly impressed by the material possessions and wealth of the foreigners, attributing their success to industry in agriculture and ranching.

In 1858, Sarah and her sister went to live in the home of Major William Ormsby in Carson Valley. She learned English rapidly under these circumstances (Hopkins 1883:58). In 1860, upon the death-bed request of Truckee, Sarah and her sister were returned to friends in California and there entered a school run by the Sisters of Charity in San Jose. They were there only a short while when pressure from the local White citizenry forced their removal. Upon her return to Nevada, Sarah continued her education on her own while working as a domestic in and around Virginia City. One newspaper (*Helena Daily Herald* 11/4/1891) account notes that she spent a goodly portion of her meager earnings on books, a reasonably scarce commodity on the frontier at the time. She states candidly, however, that she always had trouble with reading (Hopkins 1883:58).

Sarah began to take an active interest in Indian affairs in 1866, when with her brother, Naches, she was requested to go to Fort McDermitt to discuss scattered depredations in the region. They were also requested by the army to try to convince Old Winnemucca and his band to come to Fort McDermitt to be settled on a reservation. At this time, Sarah began a series of run-ins with agents in the vicinity over a number of inequities, including the meager provisions being given the people. She spoke openly against the policy of the agent at Pyramid Lake, which required that the people turn over ⅔ of their produce and then feed themselves and take their next year's seed from the remainder. Sarah's hostilities extended to the missionaries who by this time were taking over agent positions in the Indian Service. She notes that these "so-called Christians" were mainly concerned with money and had few truly benevolent feelings toward the people. She vividly describes the issue of clothing to the Shoshones near Battle Mountain by Colonel Dodge, on which occasion she acted as interpreter:

> Oh such an issue! It was enough to make a doll laugh. A family numbering eight persons got two blankets, three shirts, no dress goods. Some got a fishhook and a line; some got one and a half yards of flannel, red and blue.
>
> . . . In the morning some of the men went around with only one leg dressed in red flannel. . . . And this man called himself a Christian, too. (Hopkins 1883:86–7)

In the ensuing years to 1875, Sarah worked periodically as an interpreter for the military at Ft. McDermitt and Camp Harney. She remained convinced throughout her life that her people fared better under the military than the Indian Bureau. In fact, a subtle, but interesting picture of the value of being "prisoners" of the military can be drawn from her accounts. At one point, for example, Old Winnemucca even pleaded with the commander at Ft. McDermitt that he and his band be taken prisoners instead of being sent to Malheur Reservation (Hopkins 1883:121). Regular rations, clothing of better quality, and protection from White depredations far outweighed the inconvenience of confinement.

There was to be one notable exception to Sarah's rule about agents, and the association with him was of major importance in her life. His name was Samuel Parrish, recently appointed agent at Malheur, Oregon. Parrish offered Sarah a position as interpreter in 1875, and later a post as teacher's aid. He immediately put the people to work at agriculture, with the following admonition:

> I have not come here to do nothing; I have no time to throw away. I have come to show you how to work, and work we must. I am not like the man who has just left you. I can't kneel down and pray for sugar and flour and potatoes to rain down as he did. I am a bad man; but I will teach you all how to work, so you can do for your selves by-and-by . . . I will build a school house and my brother's wife will teach your children how to read like the White children. I want 3 young men to learn to be blacksmiths and 3 to learn to be carpenters. I want to teach you all to do like White people. (Hopkins 1883:1060)

Parrish kept his promises and the first year the agricultural venture was a success. The people kept all of the produce for themselves with the exception of items sold to Parrish and his employees. Unlike previous agents, Parrish paid for his needs at a labor rate of one dollar per day per man. His staff did likewise.

But all came to naught in the following year when Parrish was dismissed—he was not a good Christian—and replaced by William Rinehart. Rinehart's policies precipitated trouble almost from the beginning. Most importantly, he changed Parrish's policy on land and labor. He also discharged Sarah when she reported his misdeeds to the military, an action for which she did not blame him.

In his opening speech to the people at Malheur, Rinehart stated clearly that "the land you are living on is government land. If you do well and are willing to work for the government, the government will give you work" (Hopkins 1883). Egan, spokesman for one group of Paiutes on the reservation answered:

> Our father, we cannot read; we do not understand anything; we don't want the Big Father in Washington to fool with us. We are men, not children. He sends one man to say one thing and another to say something else. The man who just left us told us the land was ours, and what we do on it was ours. And you say it is government land and not ours. You may be right. We love money as well as you. It is a great deal of money to pay. There are a great many of us and when we work, we all work. (Hopkins 1883:124)

Not understanding Rinehart's labor policy, and expecting that work done would bring one dollar per day per man, everyone reported for work and then for pay. Rinehart's answer came not in cash, but in issues, labeled conveniently, "blankets - $6, coats - $5, pants - $5, shoes - #3," etc. The Bannock War of 1878 was in part an aftermath of troubles that began at Malheur. Angry and bitter Paiute farmers were easily encouraged to join Bannock hostiles, and they left the reservation *en masse.*

During the Bannock War, Sarah again went to work for the military as an interpreter in the command of General Oliver Otis Howard. Howard described her conduct during the campaign as excellent, and "especially compassionate to women and children who were brought in as prisoners" (Howard 1883:1). Sarah remained for several months at Vancouver Barracks and later at Yakima Reservation where the Paiute prisoners were detained, working as an interpreter and teacher. Yakima was a nightmare of overcrowding, abject poverty and intertribal hostilities. There was barely enough support for the Yakima, let alone 534 Paiute aliens (Wilber 1879).

With the cessation of hostilities, Sarah's position was abolished. At that time, she began to lecture in San Francisco and in Nevada, dramatizing the problems at Malheur and Yakima, and pleading for the return of Leggins' band of Paiutes unjustly detained at Yakima. She spoke against Indian agents and called specifically for the resignation of Rinehart and the restoration of Malheur to the people. On November 25, 1879, she delivered her first lecture at Platt's Hall in San Francisco. According to newspaper accounts of the lecture, she was attired in native dress and spoke eloquently and without notes. According to the account in the *San Francisco Call*:

> There was little left of the redoubtable Christian agent when she finished him. She described him as having a right arm longer than his left, and while beckoning them to be kind and good and honest with one hand, the other was busy grabbing behind their backs. She wound up with a summary of Mr. Rineharts character with a bit of mischievous sarcasm that brought down the house. (Daily Silver State 11/28/79)

Word of Sarah's success on the lecture platform spread, and it was only a month before she and Naches, along with Old Winnemucca and Captain Jim were summoned to Washington to meet with various government officials. After several rounds of discussion, they succeeded in obtaining a document from then Secretary of the Interior, Carl Schurz, granting the release of Leggins' band at Yakima, and specifying that they and other Paiutes who so wished were free to return to the Malheur reservation,

> "whereupon, at this their primeval home, they and others heretofore entitled, are to have lands allotted to them in severalty at the rate of one-hundred and sixty acres to each head of a family, and each adult male. Such lands they are to cultivate for their own benefit. As soon as enabled to do so, this department is to give to the Indians patents for each tract of land conveying to each occupant the fee-simple in the lot he occupies." (Hopkins 1883:224)

With an apparent victory won, Sarah and the three men returned to Nevada, where they waited at Lovelock for supplies to help the people go to Malheur (it was February, the dead of winter). They did not come. After a perilous ride to Yakima, Sarah also found that the agent there would provide neither provisions nor an escort for Leggins' band to go to Malheur (Wilber 1880). The grant by the Secretary of the Interior was for nothing, as it provided no basic support.

Also at this time, largely at the instigation of Rinehart, an intensive campaign to discredit Sarah ethically and morally was begun. Files in the Office of Indian Affairs (United States Bureau of Indian Affairs 1965), brought together under the title, "The Case of Sarah Winnemucca," contain many damaging letters. She did retain a few staunch supporters, however, among them General Howard and several citizens of Lovelock. In all fairness to her detractors, Sarah was short tempered, particularly in the context of offenses to her people, and she was known to take a drink and to scream and swear on occasion. She also had three husbands, two of them White men.

In 1883, Sarah went East on a lecture tour. On May 9, she appeared in Boston before an audience consisting of General Howard, and several other military figures (*Daily Mountain Democrat* 3/9/1883). She again spoke of the corruption of the agents, misappropriations, poor government policies and the missionaries. At the end of her speech, a letter from Senator Henry Dawes, currently sponsoring the "Lands in Severalty" legislation before the congress, was read to the effect that he was "in perfect accord with the object of the meeting, which was looking at the abolishing of the so-called Indian Agents." Mr. Dawes' plan to grant Indians title to their lands in severalty, which in effect would accomplish this end, must have seemed inspired.

Between April, 1883, and August, 1884, Sarah gave nearly 300 lectures from Boston and New York to Baltimore and Washington D.C. From newspaper accounts, the lectures were well received. Sarah spoke continually of inequities and called for restoration of lands in severalty to the Paiutes. While in Boston, she became fast friends with Elizabeth Palmer Peabody, noted pioneer in kindergarten education and her sister, Mary Tyler Mann, widow of Horace Mann. Under their direction, she also spoke in the homes of Ralph Waldo Emerson, John Greenleaf Whittier and those of several distinguished congressmen, among them Senator Dawes. Sarah also completed her book at this time, through the encouragement and under the editorship of Mary Mann. She earned many supporters and at the same time, her lectures and book lent support to the passage of SB48, the "Lands in Severalty" bill. Its eastern advocates found their shining example of the effects of education and self-determination in Sarah. There is, in fact, more than a hint of usury in their efforts on Sarah's behalf. She wanted the restoration of lands at Malheur. They favored general allotment. In the concluding note to Sarah's book, Mary Mann states that the plan was to present the following petition to the Congress in the hope that it "will help to shape aright the new Indian policy, by means of the discussion it will receive" (Hopkins 1883:247).

Then follows the text of a petition requesting the grant of lands in severalty to the Paiute at Malheur Reservation, where "they may enjoy said lands without losing their tribal relations, so essential to their happiness and good character, and where their citizenship, implied in this distribution of land, will defend them from the encroachments of the white settlers, so detrimental to their interests and their virtues" (Hopkins 1883:247).

Although the general lands in severalty legislation finally passed both houses of Congress in 1887, the grant of lands at Malheur apparently died in the Committee of Indian Affairs. On at least six occasions from December, 1883, to April, 1884, petitions with previous text and more than 4,000 signatures were presented to the Congress personally by Sarah and other delegates (Congressional Record 1883–1884). But Malheur was already in the hands of White squatters and little action seemed possible.

Discouraged, Sarah returned to Nevada in August of 1884 to begin preparations for founding her own school for Paiute children with the partial financial support of Miss Peabody and with money earned from the sale of her book and her lectures. The school was to be at Pyramid Lake, but contrary to promises made to Sarah and Elizabeth Peabody by the Commissioner of Indian Affairs (Peabody 1884) the position of teacher was given to the agent's wife. To raise money on her own to build the school on Naches' farm near Lovelock, Sarah again went on a lecture tour, speaking in Reno, Carson City and San Francisco. In a lecture delivered in San Francisco in February, 1885, Sarah proposed her most novel solution to the Indian problem. She stated that:

> if she had the wealth of several whom she named, she would place all the Indians of Nevada on the ships in the harbor, take them to New York and land them there as immigrants, that they might be received with open arms, blessed with the blessings of universal suffrage, and thus placed beyond the necessity of reservation help and out of reach of the Indian agents. (*Daily Silver State* 2/6/1885)

With great financial difficulty, Sarah succeeded in operating her school for a little over two years. In a published report of the school's first year, Elizabeth Peabody (1886) summarizes Sarah Winnemucca's "practical solution to the Indian problem" as one involving Indian controlled education, Indians' right to run their own lives, and the full privileges of owning land in severalty. Naches' farm and Sarah's school are used repeatedly as examples. The second annual report (Peabody 1887) pleads for funds to carry on this "new departure." Funds were not forthcoming, and in ill health and despondent over marital problems, Sarah was forced to close the school in 1887. Soon thereafter, she went to Henry's Lake, Idaho, to be with her sister. She died there in 1891.

Sarah Winnemucca's desire to see lands issued in severalty to the Paiute without inducing the effects of tribal disintegration was not realized in her lifetime. And, by 1895, the effects of the passage of the general allotment legislation in 1887 were already apparent. Dawes himself, in the Proceedings of the Lake Mohonk Conference of the Friends of the Indian (1896), conceded that clauses he had to add for political reasons allowing the sale of surplus lands once allotments were made, as well as the assignment of allotments on poor lands by unscrupulous agents, had already taken their toll. Dawes (1896:49) states: "The law has fallen among thieves and there are not enough good Samaritans to take care of it." Sarah's "so-called Christians" had won again.

Sarah Winnemucca's known publications include her book (Hopkins 1883) and one article titled "The Pah-Utee" (Winnemucca 1882). The latter may have been an excerpt from one of her speeches. Sarah's book is principally an autobiographical and historical account of the period 1844 through 1883, while her article is essentially a statement on pre-contact ethnography. The coverage of cultural data in Sarah's article parallels in many ways the ethnographic paradigm in early anthropology. She provides data on Northern Paiute subsistence patterns, trade, shamanism, puberty observances, courting and marriage customs, death and burial practices, and more. Some of these topics are also given expanded treatment in her book. Sarah's description of antelope charming and hunting is particularly detailed, perhaps because her father, Old Winnemucca, had antelope power and she witnessed the procedure several times (Hopkins 1883:55 ff.).

Both Sarah's book and her article also contain valuable data on her perceptions of the cultural and attitudinal changes she felt were occurring during this period. For example, she suggests that less stability exists in Northern Paiute marriages than existed formerly:

> They take a woman now without much ado, as white people do, and leave them oftener than of old . . . an indulgence taken advantage of to abandon an old wife and secure a younger one. They argue that it is better for them to do so than to leave their young women for the temptation of white men. (Hopkins 1882:255)

In another example, she notes that native doctors are beginning to "know their value," to have more political power and to extract money fees from patients in emulation of White doctors. There are numerous suggestions of other changes as well.

Subtle courtesies, assumptions and values are also portrayed in Sarah's materials. For example, she speaks of always making a place for a weary guest to sit, making a fire to warm him or her and offering the person something to eat (Hopkins 1883:12). She also describes the decision-making process by which everyone gets an opportunity to speak and think about matters before deciding on an issue (ibid., 27). Differences in values held by Whites and Paiutes are also discussed; for example, Sarah's attempt to make Old Winnemucca understand that it is often the sincere custom of Whites to give gifts to friends when they depart. Old Winnemucca was very hesitant to take Agent Sam Parrish's gifts when Parrish was relieved at Malheur because they would be painful reminders of his absence. Similarly, Old Winnemucca reasoned, one keeps nothing that belongs to the dead (ibid., 52). In another passage, Sarah also explains to the people the peculiar White custom of hanging clothes on a line to dry. This did not mean, she adds, that they were being thrown away and were free for the taking. Indians had been shot in Virginia city for "stealing" laundry (ibid., 120).

From all accounts, Sarah's speeches also contained considerable ethnographic material. In fact, one might speculate that perhaps more was known about Northern Paiute ethnography by the general public in the 1880's partly through Sarah's efforts than has been known at any time since.

One of the most interesting features of Sarah's book, and, I suspect one of the most important for interpreting it, is its narrative style. Her tale is told with numerous quotes from participants, although, quite obviously by reconstruction. I suspect that this may be the same quotative style that is a major feature of Northern Paiute narratives. Sarah's book is, perhaps, her narrative tale, her view of the history of her family and the difficulties of her people—her ethnohistory. As such, from our point of view, it contains some errors of historical fact (although considering the many names and dates, and the amount of detail, it is remarkably accurate). In line with this reasoning, it is interesting to compare Sarah's account with those by other authors in the same period. Examples of the detail she gives: 1) a thorough description of the townsite of Genoa, Nevada, with the location of houses and businesses and the names of occupants; and 2) an account of the supposed murder of two White men, McMullen and Mac Williams in 1858 at the hands of the Washoe. The former is verified by early plat maps of the settlement. Thompson and West's account (Angel 1881:334) of the latter lists their names as McMarlin and Williams and the date as 1857. From the academic perspective, her book lacks the balance of historical evaluation that scholarly models would suggest. However, placed in the more appropriate context of Northern Paiute oral tradition, her account would be balanced by those of other narrators—a context that it loses in print. Accusations of bias and error may result from attempts to judge her work according to another model.

The book's narrative style, as well as some of its ethnographic subtleties, lead me to conclude that while some of Sarah's contemporaries questioned the fact, the book is primarily her effort and not that of Mary Mann. Although Mann undoubtedly edited the book for sentence structure, spelling and punctuation, as she freely states in her preface, it could only be Sarah's detractors that would suggest that she were not capable of the achievement. There are enough of Sarah's original letters, as well as the testimony of her speeches, to demonstrate that she had good command of English. Sentences in her letters do contain errors in spelling and punctuation. They are also frequently conjoined. But on the whole, her letters are generally well written. Internal features in the book, like the conjoining tendency, and a number of what I suspect are "pronunciation spellings," like "Acotrass" for "Alcatraz," "Carochel" for "Churchill" and "shut off the postles" for "shoot off the pistols" indicate that Mann may not have caught everything. However, in the absence of a manuscript for either book or article, we cannot be sure of the nature and extent of author/editor collaboration.

In conclusion, Sarah Winnemucca attempted through accommodation and selective assimilation to bridge the gap between two cultures. She was firmly convinced that with education, agricultural land and freedom from outside intervention, the Paiutes could and should manage their own lives. She was not shy and retiring as might have been her prescribed behavior given her identity. She was a fighter, quick to learn, and an astute observer of the customs of the Whites as well as those of her own people. In one sense, she is Stewart's (1939:129) ambitious, educated and self seeking woman. In another she is also Heizer's (1960:3) person of "selfless motives, tremendous energies and high purpose, making her a person to be admired in the history of our far West."

LITERATURE CITED

Angel, Myron, ed.
1881 History of Nevada, With Illustrations and Biographical Sketches of Its Prominent Men and Pioneers. Oakland, Calif.: Thompson and West.

Congressional Record
1883–1884 Petitions Presented. Congressional Record, Dec. 10, 1883; Dec. 14, 1883; Jan. 17, 1884; Jan. 24, 1884; March 10, 1884; April 9, 1884. Washington.

Dawes, Henry L.
1896 The Severalty Law. Proceedings of the Thirteenth Annual Meeting of the Lake Mohonk Conference of the Friends of

the Indian, 1895. Pp. 48–52. Boston: The Lake Mohonk Conference.

Heizer, Robert F.

1960 Notes on Some Paviotso Personalities and Material Culture. Nevada State Museum Anthropological Papers, No. 2.

Hopkins, Sarah Winnemucca

1883 Life Among the Piutes: Their Wrongs and Claims. Boston: Cupples, Upham and Co.

Howard, Oliver O.

1883 Letter, To Whom It May Concern, April 3, 1883. In Life Among the Piutes: Their Wrongs and Claims, by Sarah Winnemucca Hopkins. P. 249. Boston: Cupples, Upham and Co.

Peabody, Elizabeth P.

1844 Letter, to Commissioner of Indian Affairs, April 10, 1884. National Archives, RG-75, Washington.

1886 Sarah Winnemucca's Practical Solution of the Indian Problem: A Letter to Dr. Lyman Abbot of the "Christian Union." Cambridge: John Wilson and Son.

1887 The Piutes: Second Report of the Model School of Sarah Winnemucca 1886–87. Cambridge: John Wilson and Son.

Stewart, Omer C.

1939 The Northern Paiute Bands. University of California Anthropological Records, Vol. 2, No. 3, pp. 127–149.

United States Bureau of Indian Affairs

1965 The Case of Sarah Winnemucca. "Special Files of the Office of Indian Affairs, 1807–1904," No. 268. National Archives Microfilm Publication, No. 574. Washington.

Wilber, James H.

1879 Letter, to Commissioner of Indian Affairs, January 30, 1879. In "Letters Received by the Office of Indian Affairs, 1824–81: Washington Superintendency." National Archives Microfilm Publications, No. 234. Washington.

1880 Letter, to Commissioner of Indian Affairs, June 29, 1880. In "Letters Received by the Office of Indian Affairs, 1824–81: Washington Superintendency." National Archives Microfilm Publications, No. 234. Washington.

Winnemucca, Sarah
1882 The Pah-Utes. The Californian, 6:252–6.

ACKNOWLEDGMENTS

Research for this paper and a forthcoming biography of Sarah Winnemucca was supported by a grant-in-aid from the American Council of Learned Societies. Margaret M. Wheat assisted in all phases of the research. The support of the Council and Ms. Wheat is gratefully acknowledged.

CHAPTER FOUR

FRANCIS LA FLESCHE
THE OSAGE ODYSSEY

Omaha, 1857–1932

MARGOT LIBERTY

Francis La Flesche was the first professional American Indian anthropologist. A son of the last Omaha head chief, Estamaza or Iron Eye, he was born on a Nebraska reservation in 1857, and died there 75 years later, after a lifetime of scholarship devoted to preserving the Indian record. His father, Estamaza or Iron Eye, half French, had been a progressive in favor of adopting White ways—his village was known as that of the "Make Believe White Men"—and his children were altogether extraordinary. Susette La Flesche, for example, born in 1854, became famous as "Bright Eyes," already memorialized in two biographies (Crary 1973; Wilson 1974); and a younger sister Susan (born in 1865) became an M.D. who served as a physician to the Omaha tribe (Green 1969: 56–81, 97–162). No biography as yet has been attempted of Francis, although his claim to distinction (if somewhat less romantic on the whole) is at least as great as that of his sisters. The complexity of his life and its achievements can only be suggested here.

The Omaha Reservation, established on the west bank of the Missouri River in 1854, three years before Francis was born, was important politically: a "first" under the new Reservation Policy which replaced previous Federal policy of removing Indians from their native areas to a common Indian Territory further west or south (Officer 1971:27). It was also important as the scene of the first effort to allot tribal lands to individual Indians "in severalty," which would give each family possession of its own acreage, and theoretically hasten assimilation into wider American society: a belief which was to dominate the thinking and the action of American

Indian policy makers for many years. The Omaha tribe was also peaceful, in the United States' view—it had never taken up arms against encroaching White settlers. Located for close to 300 years in the same general region of the eastern Great Plains, it had experienced long contact with French fur traders, and later, U. S. explorers utilizing the Missouri; soon thereafter it saw an influx of missionaries and fledgling anthropologists and reformers. All of these things were important to the development of Francis La Flesche (Vestal 1945:139–148; Mead 1932; Lurie 1966 a and b; Liberty 1973).

Despite its mixed-blood heritage, the La Flesche family remained close in some ways to tribal traditions (Francis was later to support new Indian institutions, particularly Pan-Indian political organization and the Native American Church). Susette and probably most of the others underwent the early-childhood ceremony known as "The Turning of the Child"; Francis acted the role of the Sacred Child in the Wawan or pipe ceremony before he was ten, and he served as runner on one of the last tribal buffalo hunts before he was twenty (Green 1969:46–47; Fletcher and La Flesche 1911: 376–401; Alexander 1933:328; Hertzberg 1971:266, 304–305). He was thus not unacquainted with traditional institutions when he accompanied Susette to Washington with the Ponca chief Standing Bear and others on a political speaking tour in 1879–1880, on which he met Alice Fletcher and J. O. Dorsey, each of whom was to affect his future. By June of 1881, after a brief unhappy marriage on the reservation, he accepted an appointment in Washington as a copyist in the Office of Indian Affairs (through the assistance of Senator S. J. Kirkwood of Iowa, newly Secretary of the Interior)—a position he was to retain until he shifted to the Bureau of American Ethnology in 1910 from which he did not officially retire until 1929 (Jackson 1881:186–217; Green 1969:64). The first year that Alice Fletcher visited the Omaha reservation was 1882. As is well known, she became involved in the question of land allotment very quickly; and associated with La Flesche very soon as well. His training in linguistics under J. O. Dorsey is of tremendous significance to his later work; but it was Fletcher who primarily utilized him, first as field assistant, informant and interpreter, and then as full collaborator in work over many years which culminated in the classic 27th Annual Report of the Bureau of American Ethnology (1911), *The Omaha Tribe*. His other work encompassed a series of articles published between 1885 and 1926 (see bibliography), many of which were utilized in the 1911 volume; a personal book of reminiscences about Presbyterian Mission schooling ca. 1864–1875, *The Middle Five*, published in 1900 (cf. Liberty 1976), and his Osage work, which appeared in six Smithsonian volumes dated 1914 through 1939 (some of these after his death). Masses of notes and documents in manuscript form also remain at the National Anthropological Archives of the Smithsonian Institution in Washington. La Flesche was also active during these Washington years in Pan-Indian political affairs (Hertzberg 1971:24). He continued the brief formal education received in Nebraska (cf. *The Middle Five*) all the way through an L.L.B. degree obtained in 1892 and an L.L.M. degree in 1893; and he was given an honorary doctorate by the University of Nebraska in 1926. He was also involved, with the composer Charles Wakefield Cadman, in the writing of an American Indian grand opera in three acts! Completed in 1912 and called "Da-Oma, The Land of Misty Waters," it was never apparently published or produced (Green 1969:200–202). He was also active in the Washington scientific scene, serving as president of the Anthropological Society of Washington in 1922. Among all of these things it is La Flesche's Osage work, as the most extensive as well as the most independent of his achievements, which I wish to consider here.

The Osages were closely related to La Flesche's own people: one of the five cognate tribes known collectively as the Dhegiha Siouans. Included are the Osage, Omaha, Kansa, Ponca, and Quapaw; more distantly related are the Chiwere Siouans: lowa, Oto, and Missouri. The Osage and Omaha languages are close enough to permit conversation—a factor that proved vital in La Flesche's Osage research. This research began officially in 1910 after his transfer to the Bureau of American Ethnology, when the Omaha work for the 27th Annual Report was complete. For many years his training had proceeded under Alice Fletcher—years of work in Nebraska with Fletcher and alone, collecting numerous Omaha relics and traditions. By 1891, after ten years, Fletcher had legally adopted him as her son, and they shared a house in Washington for more than thirty years thereafter until 1923, giving rise to a certain amount of gossip—although Fletcher was more than twenty years older than her protegé, and during much of this period, crippled as well. She died in 1923 at more than eighty years of age, leaving him a considerable estate (Green 1969:176, 182, 202 ff.). He had already learned from her the disciplined standards of scholarship which he put to work among the Osages in Oklahoma and elsewhere between 1910 and 1923. His own health failed in 1927. His remaining time was spent on the Omaha dictionary which was not to be completed before he died at his brother's home on the reservation, to which he had recently retired, in 1932.

The Osage work, then, spanned more than eighteen years (see Smithsonian Institution Annual Reports 1911–1929 and Smithsonian Institution Miscellaneous Collections 1914–1926, cited in bibliography). It was published by the Bureau of American Ethnology in four Annual Reports (two of which contain other material) and two Bulletins, including an Osage dictionary, with dates ranging through the quarter century 1914–1939. (Actual publication often ran several years late; for cxample, the 36th Annual Report, dated 1915, did not actually appear until 1922.) Its focus is upon ceremonial life and ritual which were literally vanishing before the eyes of early twentieth century observers, spurred by the growing influence of the Native American Church. Many of the ritual sequences recorded had not been performed for twenty years and many of their performers were aging rapidly, caught between the fear of improper disclosure of sacred material on the one hand, and the dread of its actual loss, on the other. Haunted by the realization "that the sheet water of oblivion might wash their moccasin prints from the earth" (Mathews 1961:xii) they began to talk, often under the shadow of severe personal peril, to La Flesche. They continued to do so despite death and disaster to a number of them: some of which can be explained by the vicissitudes of old age, but some of which (as in the case of La Flesche's beloved informant and ceremonial father, Saucy Calf) cannot (Smithsonian Institution Annual Reports for 1913:49; 1917:59; 1919:49; 1922:62; Smithsonian Institution Miscellaneous Collections, 1914:78–81; 1918:110). In addition to the fear of supernatural punishment for improper disclosure lay the problem of traditional exorbitant payment for ceremonial knowledge (Annual Reports for 1914: 52–53 and for 1917:60).

Nonetheless, La Flesche's prodigious labor continued. The material in the four Reports, known collectively as *The Osage Tribe* (1914–1928), appeared finally in three sequential forms: free translation, Osage text, and literal translation. It comprises a massive body of more than 2000 pages which have been described as "the most complete single record of the ceremonies of any North American Indian people" (Alexander 1933:329). It has been widely quoted in anthologies of Indian literature (e.g. Astrov 1945:96–104; Day 1951:104–111; Brandon 1971:73–78; Rothenberg 1972:342–346, 464; Levitas et al. 1974:35–38) by authors who to date have not yet begun to comprehend its complexities. It has been little utilized by John Joseph Mathews, the present chronicler of the tribe, himself Osage (Mathews 1961:792, citing only three of six volumes), possibly because of the extreme difficulty of interpretation of much of the material included. *The Osage Tribe* is intricate in the extreme. Let us at this point examine its component parts and then attempt an overview of the whole.

In general, the material focuses primarily on the Nonhonzhinga Ieta, Sayings of the Nonhonzhinga (Seers, or "Little Old Men"), which formerly comprised seven long degrees of ritual associated with warfare. Osage social organization like that of other Dhegiha tribes is based on patrilineal descent; and it features named descent groups known in the literature as gentes or clans. Each of these—twenty-one in the Osage case—has specific ritual duties and its own version of each of the long ritual recitations and songs. Since inter-tribal warfare was outlawed in the 1870s the function of much of this war ritual ended before 1900—although the Osages for a while utilized the ruse of a hireling White man who acted the part of the necessary fallen enemy! (La Flesche 1939:143). The new Native American Church provided an additional deterrent to the continuation of the old religion: appearing among the Osages in the early 1890s (La Barre 1959:113), it rapidly became their major religious force, and its influence against the older tribal rites was strongly felt by the early twentieth century. Thus many of La Flesche's informants after 1910 had not performed the ritual they gave him for twenty odd years, and he concentrated all his energies toward recording what they could remember: as one informant (Saucy Calf) said, "It is a long time since there has been any occasion for me to recite any of these rituals. The words and the songs are like birds, they fly away for a time but they come back again" (La Flesche 1927:533).

The Osage materials included in *The Osage Tribe* (1914–1928; the 36th, 39th, 43rd, and 45th Annual Reports of the Bureau of American Ethnology) contain several "degrees" of the Nonhonzhinga Ieta (some in two versions each, representing one gens from each of the Earth and Sky moieties). They also include two versions of the Child Naming Rite (1925). The subsequently published Bulletin 101, *War Ceremony and Peace Ceremony of the Osage Indians* (1939) contains an additional war rite as well as the famous pipe or calumet ceremony. Bulletin 109 (1932) is *A Dictionory of the Osage Language.*

The 36th Annual Report (1915) presents two major blocks of ritual—*The Rite of the Chiefs* (Gahige Okon) chronicling the development of tribal institutions; and *The Sayings of the Ancient Men* (Nikinonkon), the seventh and most important degree of the Nonhonzhinga Ieta. *The Rite of the Chiefs* (92 printed pages of free translation alone) is not a part of that series. It begins in allegory, following the people through their early military period into a civil period which gave them new, peacemaking leaders. During one component, *The Ceremony of Sending* (Wathethe) the members of each gens recite simultaneously their own memorized "wigie"(s) concerning the meanings and origins of major life symbols: e.g. the notched-tailed turtle, the mussel, the female red cedar, the deer, the otter, the beaver, and the buffalo. Since twenty-one of these groups were represented by several members apiece, and since the twenty-one separate recitation groups were not coordinated in any way, the effect was one of pandemonium "expressive of individual devotion to the task in hand" but marked by a "confused sound of words" (La Flesche 1914:92). Clearly, this is something of an understatement. Modern students of Indian poetry (e.g. Jerome Rothenberg 1972) have been impressed with the aesthetic problems of presentation of such a corpus, as well as its potential possibilities.

Also in the 36th Annual Report, *The Sayings of the Ancient Men* (Nikinonkon) occupy 150 pages of free translation of abstract tribal beliefs concerning Wakonda, the creative force which moves in the reaches of space as well as on earth. In essence the material constitutes a creation myth, in which the people descend to earth from the heavens. The Sun and Moon, Morning and Evening Stars are addressed, as is the young Golden Eagle, the Water Spider, the Water Beetle, the White Leech, the Great Elk, the Crayfish, and various boulders and stones and wild plants (all creatures great and small!). Black coloration symbolic of charcoal from the "relentless fires of warfare" is seen upon the bodies of particular animals: specifically the Mountain Lion, the Black Bear, and the Great White Swan, who all claim rights to power and to the giving of personal names (see below). Adventures are told concerning the strange man Watsewaga's missions to obtain such ceremonial items as black and red flint knives; and his journey to many valleys to locate an enemy people. The material is difficult to interpret, but its poetic power is evident in numerous passages, for example:

> Verily at that time and place, it has been said, in this house
> The people came together as bidden
> The people of the Wazhashe
> And those of the Tsizhu
> And those of the Honga spake, saying: Our younger brother
> Has travelled to four valleys in the far-off lands, O, Wazha'zhe
> In the fourth valley
> He beheld seven bends of a great river
> Enwrapped in a cloud of white smoke from many fires.
> Seven villages he saw among the seven bends of the river
> Enwrapped in a cloud of white smoke from many fires.

This particular version ends abruptly; but in another, mysterious arrows are bestowed "to make these people fall" (La Flesche 1914:211, 219).

The 39th Annual Report (1918: 329 pages of free translation) gives two versions of *The Rite of Vigil* or Fasting Rite drawn respectively from the Earth Moiety's Mountain Lion gens and the Sky Moiety's Peacemaker gens. *The Rite of Vigil* varies in position in the Nonhonzhinga Ieta recitations of the different gentes, i.e., sometimes it is spoken second, and sometimes fourth; but of the seven degrees of war ritual it is next in length and importance to *The Sayings of the Ancient Men* (universally spoken last). It involves the fasting of a war leader to obtain supernatural power, including many forms and images widespread throughout Osage religion. An intricate succession of ritual is presented, including the so-called Seven Songs containing sixteen sets, and the Six Songs containing seventeen sets. During 1914 and 1915 when La Flesche was struggling to assemble his voluminous notes on this material he was interrupted twice by Osage informants visiting Washington or his own reservation, who dictated more than 100 pages of additional data for this and another ceremony. Several of these informants were literally fearing for their lives, in consequence of giving this material, and several actual deaths were attributed to this cause during this period (cf. sources cited above).

The 43rd Annual Report (1929: 131 pages of free translation) gives two versions of the evocative Osage *Child-Naming Rite* drawn again from the Earth Moiety's Mountain Lion gens and the Sky Moiety's Peacemaker gens. The theme of this rite refers to the desire for supernatural power to obtain a long, peaceful life, and a never-ending line of descendents. The first three sons and the first three daughters in each Osage family were addressed by special kinship terms (i.e., Ingthon, Kshonga, and Kazhinga for the first three sons, and Minon, Wihe, and Ci'ge for the first three daughters) and each also received a special name, drawn from specific gens traditions. Such "gentile birth names" included, for the first three boys, Child of the Sun, Giver of Clear Speech, and Arrow Maker; and for the first three girls Sacred Arrowshaft, Woman Who Travels Over the Earth, and Beloved Child of the Sun. Fourth and subsequent sons and daughters were in a residual category, although the fourth were also given special names—Dark Eyes for boys and The Favorite for girls. An eligible child not named in this ceremonial fashion had no place in the tribe and could command no future respect as an adult; parents were thus careful to see that proper observances took place. Ceremonial phases included decoration of a Master of Ceremonies (with red paint, plumes, buffalo-fat hair dressing, and a shell gorget necklace); the sending of specific gifts as fees to the heads of gentes designated to give major recitations; and also the use of bowls of shelled corn and cedar-scented water in the actual naming of the child. Sky and star imagery is strong in the recitations of both moieties. Appeals are made to celestial bodies grouped in male and female pairs: the Sun and Moon; the Morning and Evening Star; the Big Dipper and the

Pleides (Deer-Head, in Osage); the Pole Star and the Dog Star; and Three Deer and Stars-Strung-Together (two aspects of the group we call Orion). In one passage, the Stranger from the Stars (Watsegitsi) speaks forth:

> I am a sacred man, O elder brothers
> . . .
> I am The Young Chief
> I am the Star Chief
> I am the Star Radiant
> I am the Travelling Star
>
> The Young Chief shall be your name, as you travel the path of life
> The Star Radiant shall also be your name, as you travel the path of life. . .
>
> (La Flesche 1926:48 ff.)

The difficulty of translating and transmitting in any way, the material involved here, is considerable: it all seems to dissolve under scrutiny like a swirl of smoke. A constant refrain in Osage ritual, for example, concerns the "little ones" who "have nothing of which to make their bodies." The response from the supernatural animals who serve as life symbols is, consistently, "When the little ones make of me their bodies, they shall live to see old age, as they travel the path of life." In one final typical refrain appear the lines:

> There comes a time
> When a calm and peaceful day comes upon me
> So shall there come upon the little ones a calm and peaceful day,
> As they travel the path of life.
>
> (La Flesche 1926:84)

The 45th Annual Report (1927: 188 pagcs of free translation) contains material from the *Waxobe Awathon* or Hawk Ritual, the first degree of the seven War Rites (Nonhonzhinga Ieta) as well as material from the Shrine Degree, in which a sacred covering of rushes is woven for the Hawk and other holy relics. The Hawk, child of the Sun and Moon, was adopted in ancient times as a tribal symbol by a people who admired its overwhelming and fatal descent upon enemies, from the wide blue sky. Hawk ritual expresses belief that continued existence of the people depends upon the courage of their warriors, here associated with Hawk courage through an intricate series of recitations and songs. (Again, we have Seven Songs, this time with 26 sets; and Six Songs, this time with 16 sets.) Some beautiful imagery appears in such sequences as the Buffalo Songs, Deer Song, and

Black Bear Song; also Songs of the Waters, Songs of the Stars, The Great Evening Songs, the Little Evening Songs, the Snake Songs, the Great Rain Songs, the Little Rain Songs, and Songs of Releasing the Arrows. The subsequent Shrine Degree concerns preparation of a suitable series of wrappings for the Hawk, designed to incorporate symbols of its Sky and Earth domains, and appeal to Wakonda for numerical increase in, as well as for prosperity of, the Tribe. (In view of subsequent Osage oil development in Oklahoma, Wakonda must have been listening at some point in the proceedings: see Bailey's paper elsewhere in this volume.)

La Flesche observed parts of the Hawk Ritual on an early field trip to Oklahoma in 1910. His major informant Saucy Calf was murdered and his house burned during the following year. La Flesche did not write of this directly: speaking in his introduction to this volume of the old man's sensitivity and kindness, he tells us only that "in February 1912, he suddenly died" and that "the voice of the old man, though he had been dead many years, is still held captive by the dictaphone, and can be heard today singing the songs and reciting the rituals of the Waxobe tribal rites as they were taught him by the Ancient Nonhonzhinga of the Thoxe gens" (La Flesche 1927:538). He had however been adopted as Saucy Calf's ceremonial son; and must have felt his loss very keenly (La Flesche 1927:533). La Flesche however was able to use a number of other Osage informants. Among many were Kuzhisie, utilized in recording plant usages and gentile personal names; Shongemonin, in recording Tzizhu Peace gens fasting ritual, child naming ritual, and *Sayings of the Ancient Men*; Wanonshezhinga, in recording plant usages; Washonshe and his wife, in recording Shrine ritual; Waxthuxage, (d. May 1915) in recording *Tzizhu Peace Gens Hawk Ritual*, as well as fragments of *The Sayings of the Ancient Men*; Watsemonin, in recording Honga Black Bear Gens fasting ritual; Wasthizhi, in recording the *Honga Puma Gens Rite of Chiefs*, fasting ritual, *The Sayings of the Ancient Men*, child-naming ritual, and the Washabe Athin or War Ceremony; and Xutha Watonin (d. September 1915), in recording *Tzizhu Sun Gens Sayings of the Ancient Men* as well as further War Ceremony ritual (Smithsonian Annual Reports and Miscellaneous Collections as cited in Bibliography). A part of La Flesche's access to these sources (by no means always rapid or easy) was due to his cognate Indian descent and familiarity with the language; but he was also a supporter of the Native American Church (Hertzberg 1971:174, 226) and thus more acceptable on the reservation generally than might otherwise have been the case.

Overall, La Flesche's Osage work is totally different from the volume co-authored with Alice Fletcher (1911), *The Omaha Tribe*. In some ways it is one of the most confusing bodies of ethnography in the whole American

Indian record, which is saying a good deal. Whereas *The Omaha Tribe* provides an orderly topical overview of all the recognized cultural categories of early twentieth century anthropology, *The Osage Tribe* in four volumes (1914–1928) concentrates upon vanished or vanishing ritual to the exclusion of all else. La Flesche was working against time in a situation of overwhelming complexity, including staggering problems of sheer volume alone; and time ran out for him before he could attempt a comprehensive overview (if he had so desired). The Osage endeavor entailed more than twenty years (half of his whole professional life) and doubtless contributed to the physical breakdown in 1927 which prevented any major work thereafter, including completion of the Omaha dictionary to which he had been devoted.

To explain the volume problem: there were seven degrees of the Nonhonzhinga Ieta or War Rites alone, and each gens had its own version of each of the seven. (These are not well defined or known except for the first, second, and seventh: having varied in order of recitation among the various gentes; and a majority having—despite La Flesche's best efforts—rolled under "the sheet waters of oblivion" long ago.) Those collected by La Flesche, who tried to get one from at least one gens in each of the two main tribal divisions or moieties (the Tzizhu or Sky division had seven gentes, and the Honga or Earth division fourteen gentes: the latter being split into the Honga and the Wazhazhe or Osage subdivisions, of seven gentes each) ran about 100 pages each of free translation. This yielded approximately a ten percent sample of the total corpus retained in Osage memory of the War Rites alone (La Flesche also published, as noted, the *Child-Naming Rites*, the *War and Peace Ceremonies*, etc.). By simple arithmetic (twenty-one gentes times seven degrees times 100 pages per degree) the literature of the *War Rites* alone if complete would total some 14,700 pages of free translation, a figure which would be at least doubled by the inclusion of Osage text and free translation (as provided in all four volumes of *The Osage Tribe*). And then there is the other stuff. I am suggesting here that the Osage ceremonial record if reasonably complete in all versions of everything would run to some 40,000 pages of print, from fifty to eighty volumes of the dimensions of the typical 500–800 page Annual Report of the Bureau of American Ethnology (of which 48 main volumes were actually published between 1879 and 1933: Judd 1967:78–95). We may find food for some thought here upon the nature and dimension of the ritual inventory traditionally retained in the memories of preliterate peoples.

It is my view that proper analysis and interpretation of this body of material will require something close to the twenty-odd years La Flesche put into recording it, if adequate understanding of the interplay between specific cultural form (e.g., kinship and clan or gens structure) and the oral literature of Osage religion is ever to be achieved. Meanwhile, what can be said about the significance of this body of work, and about La Flesche's role in preserving it? I will offer some general points of consideration, in no particular order.

1. La Flesche (as most other subjects of this volume) represented the primary keystone element of early American anthropology, in bridging the gap between Native American peoples and their alien invaders from the East. The collaboration between representatives of such native peoples (often called "informants") and of such alien peoples (usually classified as "anthropologists") has led with all of its heartbreaks, inanities, and frequent comic relief, not to mention occasional leaps of true creative brilliance, to one of the great scientific and humanistic traditions of the Western world. The importance of this collaborative effort with all its ups and downs should not be underestimated, either in terms of its contributions to Western thought, or its preservation of elements at least of a priceless cultural heritage for native American peoples of past and future generations.

2. La Flesche was originally a "country Indian": well born, of partially White ancestry, the eldest son of the last ranking Omaha tribal chief. He took part as a youth in what remained of Omaha ritual, but his traditional world held no place of honor for him in the degeneration of the twentieth century reservation (cf. Mead 1932) so he left it, in the assimilationist value system of the times, for employment in the super-White bureaucratic world of Washington, D.C. He nonetheless never lost touch with his own Omaha people, returning home to Nebraska on every vacation, retiring there in 1929, and dying there at the home of his brother Carey in 1932. He appears to have become something of a classic Victorian gentleman, as indicated in his early book *The Middle Five* (cf. Liberty 1976). His sisters were true Victorian ladies: Susette or "Bright Eyes," the political crusader, a national heroine by 1880; Susan an M.D. educated in the same posh Eastern school as Susette (and another sister Marguerite) who served her people on the reservation for an extended period soon thereafter; and a third sister Rosalie Farley, married to a White rancher-farmer, whose involvement in early allotment activity has left a small Nebraska town named on latter day maps in her honor. The role of such mixed-blood elites of American Indian society has never been adequately examined (although Norma Kidd Green's important book *Iron Eye's Family* provides vital back ground on this particular family).

3. Of the wide range of roles played by American Indians in American anthropology (see Appendix) La Flesche moved through nearly the entire sequence: from informant, interpreter, and field assistant to co-author and eventually, independently published author and scholar. The relative influences upon his career derived frotn James Owen Dorsey (cf. Dorsey 1883) and Alice Cunningham Fletcher (cf. Fletcher and La Flesche 1911; La Flesche 1923; Lurie 1966 a and b; and Green 1969) have yet to be assessed. It seems nevertheless that La Flesche began moving effectively from an early period in his career within a world of intellectual achievement in Washington and elsewhere which was considerably brightened by his own contributions. Examples exist at least of flashing wit (La Flesche 1904) as well as ad-lib verbal talents characteristic of the better class of traditional American Indian orators (Green 1969: 196).

4. La Flesche worked at a time critical in the fortunes of any preliterate people faced with steamroller forces of acculturation: a time during which old restraints and restrictions upon the divulging of sacred traditions becomes—in the stark awareness of impending cultural loss—pitted against the value of preserving something at least for posterity (it is here that Mathews' "sheet waters of oblivion" statement, cited above, retains its most perfect relevance). I am indebted to John C. Ewers' observation some years ago (in a personal conversation, with reference to Blackfoot ritual) that just when things seem irretrievably lost and gone, *someone* comes forward, having decided it is better to transfer a part of the heritage of centuries however unorthodoxly to *somebody*, than to have it all vanish permanently forever. The surviving Osage ceremonialists working with La Flesche were responding in this way, despite very real and genuine fears for their own safety. The new peyote (or Native American Church) religion had decreed that whatever traces were left of the old religion should be abandoned completely; its medicine bundles and relics in fact burned in the new religion's own new fireplaces (Floor discussion, Garrick Bailey, in Liberty, Sturtevant et al. 1976:148). There existed also very probably the fear of sorcery, the dimensions of which were not reported among La Flesche's own Omaha tribe (and certainly not by La Flesche) until years later (Fortune 1932). Conversely, there may have been also some aspect of relief among certain ritualists in transferring ceremonial data out of their own personal possession: the fear of supernatural punishment for mishandling it being very widely felt. In short, a sense of almost unbearable urgency may have affected La Flesche as well as many of his informants, a number of the most important of whom died almost immediately after working with him

(Smithsonian Institution Annual Reports for 1913:49; 1922:62; Smithsonian Institution Miscellaneous Collections, 1914:78–81; 1918:110).

5. La Flesche himself was caught between the crossfires of many worlds. He deserves extensive biographical treatment, far beyond what has been possible here. The conflicts of his own position were considerable and they continued throughout his life: his own father Iron Eye, for example, having died very suddenly almost at once after the 1888 transfer of the Omaha Sacred Pole out of tribal hands at La Flesche's instigation (Fletcher and La Flesche 1911:224; Liberty 1976:102). In the general context of reservation and Pan-Indian grapevines and/or moccasin telegraphs it required a strong person to continue in the way of anthropology after that: and La Flesche, whatever else he may or may not have been, was strong in his own chosen dimensions (see Green 1969:176–178 for indications of the kind of gossip and criticism he was constantly subjected to among his own people).

6. In conclusion, I would like to reemphasize the magnitude of La Flesche's Osage achievement: not only in the volume of material he preserved, but also in its unique and special character. This body of material (with the exception of parts of the Child Naming Ritual) has vanished without a trace from modern Osage memory (Garrick Bailey to author, 1977, and in 1976 transcript cited above). What future use may be made of it time alone will tell. Hopefully some of the present day "little ones" will rediscover its beauty "as they travel the path of life" (La Flesche 1914: 277–292).

ACKNOWLEDGMENTS

I would like to thank Jamie McIntyre and Amy Masters for research and editorial assistance in the preparation of this paper. I am also grateful to Paul Riley of the Nebraska State Historical Society, and to Jim Glenn of the National Anthropological Archives of the Smithsonian Institution. John V. Murra first made me aware of the full range and significance of Francis La Flesche's Osage work. And John C. Ewers has in this endeavor and many others lent invaluable support, for which I am deeply and permanently grateful.

LITERATURE CITED

Alexander, Hartley Burr
1933 Francis La Flesche. American Anthropologist 35:328–331.

Astrov, Margot, ed.
1962 American Indian Prose and Poetry "The Winged Serpent": An Anthology. New York: Capricorn Books.

Brandon, William
1971 The Magic World: American Indian Songs and Poems. New York: William Morrow and Co.

Crary, Margaret
1973 Susette La Flesche: Voice of the Omaha Indians. New York: Hawthorn.

Day, A. Grove
1951 The Sky Clears: Poetry of the American Indian. New York Macmillan Co. Reprinted 1964, Lincoln, Nebraska: University of Nebraska Press.

De Laguna, Frederica, ed.
1960 Selected Papers from the American Anthropologist: 1888–1920. Evanston, Illinois: Row, Peterson and Co.

Dorsey, J. O.
1884 Omaha Sociology. Annual Reports of the Bureau of American Ethnology 3:205–370.

Fletcher, A. C.
1911 The Omaha Tribe. Annual Reports of the Bureau of American Ethnology 27:17–654. Reprinted 1967, Lincoln, Nebraska: University of Nebraska Press.

Fortune, Reo
1932 Omaha Secret Societies. Columbia University Contributions to Anthropology No. 14:1–193.

Green, Norma Kidd
1969 Iron Eye's Family: The Children of Joseph La Flesche. Lincoln, Nebraska: Johnson.

Hertzberg, Hazel W.
1971 The Search for an American Indian Identity: Modern Pan-Indian Movements. Syracuse, N.Y.: Syracuse University Press.

Jackson. Helen Hunt
1881 A Century of Dishonor: A Sketch of the United States Government's Dealings with some of the Indian Tribes. New York: Harper and Brothers. Reprinted 1965 as A Century of

Dishonor: The Early Crusade for Indian Reform. New York: Harper Textbooks.

Judd, Neil
1967 The Bureau of American Ethnology: A Partial History. Norman: University of Oklahoma Press.

La Barre, Weston
1959 The Peyote Cult. Hamden, Connecticut: The Shoe String Press.

La Flesche, Francis
1885 The Sacred Pipes of Friendship. Proceedings, American Association for the Advancement of Science 33:613–615.

1889 Death and Funeral Customs among the Omahas. Journal of American Folklore 2:3–11.

1890 The Omaha Buffalo Medicine-Men. Journal of American Folklore 3:215–221.

1900 The Middle Five: Indian Boys at School. Boston: Small, Mayard and Co. Reprinted 1963 as The Middle Five: Indian Schoolboys of the Omaha Tribe. Madison: University of Wisconsin Press.

1904 Who was the Medicine Man? Fairmount Park Art Association, Annual Report 32:3–13.

1912 Osage Marriage Customs, American Anthropologist 14:127–130.

1914–1928 The Osage Tribe, Annual Reports of the Bureau of American Ethnology 36:35–604; 39:31–630; 43:23–164; 45:529–833. See separate entries for 1914–1915, 1917–1918, 1925–1926, and 1927–1928.

1914–1915 Rite of the Chiefs; Sayings of the Ancient Men. Part One of The Osage Tribe (published in four parts 1915–1928), pp. 43–597 in 36th Annual Report of the Bureau of American Ethnology, 1914–1915. Smithsonian Institution: Washington, D.C.

1915 Omaha and Osage Traditions of Separation. Proceedings, International Congress of Americanists 19:459–462.

1916 Right and Left in Osage Ceremonies. In Holmes Anniversary Volume: 278–287. Washington, D.C.: Smithsonian Institution.

1917–1918 The Rite of Vigil. Part Two of *The Osage Tribe* (published in four parts 1915–1928), pp. 37–630 In 39th Annual Report of the Bureau of American Ethnology, 1917–1918. Washington, D.C.: Smithsonian Institution.

1920 The Symbolic Man of the Osage Tribe. Art and Archaeology 9, No. 2:68–75.

1922 Omaha Bow and Arrow Makers. Proceedings, International Congress of Americanists 20:111–116.

1923 Alice C. Fletcher (obituary). Science LVII:115–116.

1925–1926 Two Versions of the Child-Naming Rite. Part Three of *The Osage Tribe* (published in four parts 1915–1928), pp. 29–820 In 43rd Annual Report of the Bureau of American Ethnology, 1925-1926. Washington, D.C.: Smithsonian Institution.

1926 Omaha Bow and Arrow Makers. Annual Reports of the Smithsonian Institution: 487–494. Washington, D.C.: Smithsonian Institution.

1927–1928 Rite of the Waxobe and Shrine Degree. Part Four of *The Osage Tribe* (published in four parts 1915–1928). Pp. 529–833 In 45th Annual Report of the Bureau of American Ethnology, 1927–1928. Washington, D.C.: Smithsonian Institution.

1932 A Dictionary of the Osage Language. Bulletin 109, Bureau of American Ethnology. Washington, D.C.: Smithsonian Institution.

1939 War Ceremony and Peace Ceremony of the Osage Indians. Bulletin 101, Bureau of American Ethnology. Washington, D.C.: Smithsonian Institution.

Levitas, Gloria, Frank R. Vivelo and Jaqueline C. Vivelo

1974 American Prose and Poetry: We Wait In the Darkness. New York: G. P. Putnam's Sons.

Liberty, Margot

1973 The Urban Reservation. Unpublished Ph.D. Dissertation, University of Minnesota, Minneapolis.

1976 Native American "Informants": The Contribution of Francis La Flesche. Pp. 99–110 in John V. Murra, ed., American Anthropology: The Early Years. 1974 Proceedings of the American Ethnological Society. St. Paul: West Publishing Co.

Liberty, Margot, William C. Sturtevant et al.
1976 Transcript of Papers and Floor Discussion, 1976 Spring Symposium, American Ethnological Soceity. Typewritten manuscript, Oral History Program, University of Pittsburgh, Pittsburgh, Pa.

Lurie, Nancy Oestrich
1966a The Lady From Boston and the American Indians. American West 3:31–33, 81–85.

1966b Women in Early American Anthropology. In Pioneers of American Anthropology: The Uses of Biography. June Helm, ed. Seattle: University of Washington Press.

Mathews, John Joseph
1961 The Osages: Children of the Middle Waters. Norman: University of Oklahoma Press.

Mead, Margaret and Ruth Bunzel
1960 The Golden Age of American Anthropology. New York: George Brazilier.

Nebraska State Historical Society
n.d. Manuscript Record, La Flesche Family Collection, Papers 1859–1933. MS2026. Typewritten manuscript, 3 pp. Lincoln: Nebraska State Historical Society.

Officer, James E.
1971 The American Indian and Federal Policy. In Jack O. Waddell and O. Michael Watson, eds., The American Indian in Urban Society, pp. 8–65. Boston: Little, Brown and Co.

Rothenberg, Jerome
1972 Shaking the Pumpkin: Traditional Poetry of the Indian North Americas. New York: Doubleday and Co.

Smithsonian Institution
n.d. Manuscripts by Francis La Flesche in the National Anthropological Archives (Extracted from the Catalogue of Siouan Manuscripts by Raymond De Mallie). Typewritten manuscript, 21 pp. Washington, D.C.: Smithsonian Institution.

Smithsonian Institution Annual Reports, Smithsonian Institution, Washington, D.C.
1911 Annual Report* for 1910: 46, 53 (*Hereinafter cited as AR)

1912 AR for 1911: 38, 39, 41
1913 AR for 1912: 40–51, 54, 56, 108
1914 AR for 1913: 52–53
1915 AR for 1914: 53–55
1916 AR for 1915: 44–45
1917 AR for 1916: 59–60, 71
1918 AR for 1917: 50–51
1919 AR for 1918: 48–50
1920 AR for 1919: 43–44
1921 AR for 1920: 64
1922 AR for 1921: 62
1923 AR for 1922: 20, 62–63, 68
1924 AR for 1923: 21, 71
1925 AR for 1924: 22, 71
1926 AR for 1925: 22, 70, 71
1927 AR for 1926: 27, 69–70
1928 AR for 1927: 73–74
1929 AR for 1928; 19, 66

Smithsonian Institution Miscellaneous Collections

1914 Ceremonies and Rituals of the Osage. Pp. 66–69 In Explorations and Fieldwork of the Smithsonian Institution (hereinafter cited as EFWSI) in Smithsonian Institution Miscellaneous Collections 63 (hereinafter cited as SI-MC).

1915 Osage Songs and Rituals. Pp. 78–81 In EFWSI in 1914, SI-MC 65, No. 6. Washington, D.C.

1916 Osage War Rites. Pp. 107–109 In EFWSI in 1915, SI-MC 66, No. 3. Washington, D.C.

1917 Work Among the Osage Indians. Pp. 118–221 In EFWSI in 1916, SI-MC 66, No. 17. Washington, D.C.

1918 Tribal Rites of the Osage Indians. Pp. 84–90 In EFWSI in 1917, SI-MC 68, No. 12. Washington, D.C.

1919 Researches Among the Osage. Pp. 110–113 In EFWSI in 1918 SI-MC 70, No. 2. Washington, D.C.

1920 Osage Tribal Rites, Oklahoma. Pp. 71–73 In EFWSI in 1919, SI-MC 72, No. 1. Washington, D.C.

1924 Ethnology of the Osage Indians. Pp. 104–107 In EFWSI in 1923, SI-MC 76, No. 10. Washington, D.C.

1926 Ethnological Work Among the Osage of Oklahoma. Pp. 117–119 In EFWSI in 1925, SI-MC 78, No. 1. Washington, D.C.

Vestal, Stanley
1945 The Missouri. New York: Holt, Rinehart, and Winston. Republished in 1964, Lincoln: University of Nebraska Press.

Wilson, Dorothy Clarke
1974 Bright Eyes: The Story of Susette La Flesche, An Omaha Indian. New York: McGraw-Hill.

CHAPTER FIVE

CHARLES ALEXANDER EASTMAN, THE "WINNER": FROM DEEP WOODS TO CIVILIZATION

Santee Sioux, 1858–1939

DAVID REED MILLER

Charles Alexander Eastman (Ohiyesa) was born in 1858 near Red Wood Falls, in a village on the small Santee reservation, along the banks of the Minnesota River. As the tensions mounted between settlers and the Santee over hunting rights, delayed annuities, an increasing scarcity of game animals, and impending starvation, Eastman's relatives in August of 1862 found themselves suddenly refugees as the tensions climaxed in the Minnesota Sioux Uprising. Ohiyesa (meaning "winner"), a boy of four, was taken by his grandmother and uncle, White Foot Print, onto the prairies of present day North Dakota, and by 1864 into Manitoba. Isolated once again from contact with Whites other than occasional traders or visits to trading posts, young Ohiyesa experienced a life dependent on a harmonious relationship with nature, and a lifeway and culture that he thought were all that he would ever need or have. Eleven years later Ohiyesa was surprised one day upon returning from a hunt to discover that his father, Jacob Manylightnings Eastman, had returned after having been assumed lost in the many skirmishes between the Sioux and the military in 1863–64. Jacob Eastman, a new homesteader at Flandreau, Dakota Territory, came to Manitoba in search of his son, in hopes of bringing him to his new home and way of life. Jacob believed that education was the vehicle of Indian survival, and wanted Ohiyesa to accept this new "warpath."

Knowing no English and little of the ways of White cultural existence, Charles Alexander Eastman began his new life.[1] During the next seventeen years Eastman attended Santee Normal School, Beloit College Preparatory

School, Knox College Preparatory School, Kimball Union Academy, Dartmouth College, and, finally, Boston University Medical School to emerge at age thirty-two a physician. Upon his graduation he was presented to the 1890 Lake Mohonk Conference, and was held up as an example of what education could do for the American Indian (Eastman 1916:1–61; Miller 1976:1–96).

Armed with optimism and a belief in goodness and charity instilled in him by his years of education in New England, Eastman set forth to help his people. Thanks to the influence of his benefactor in college and medical school, Frank Wood of Boston, he was appointed to the post of Agency Physician at Pine Ridge Agency, South Dakota. Arriving in November 1890, delayed by his appearance at the Lake Mohonk Conference, he observed the increasing tensions of the Ghost Dance movement among the Lakota.

By January first, he was tending the wounded survivors of the Wounded Knee Massacre in the Episcopal Church at Pine Ridge which had been converted into a hospital. In the midst of the excitement Charles met and became engaged to marry Elaine Goodale. Miss Goodale, had taught for several years in schools on the Great Sioux Reservation and had recently been appointed Superintendent of Indian Education for the Dakotas. Charles and Elaine, well liked by the Lakota at Pine Ridge, then began to encounter difficulties with the Indian agent. In the crisis situation of 1890–91, military officers were appointed as agents in an effort to show the Indians the severity with which any repeated "rebellion" would be met. By 1892 in a controversy over the details of a special payment to "loyal" agency Indians for property lost in the recent outbreak, Eastman opposed the Indian agent, Captain George LeRoy Brown. Brown in the end won by harassing him into resignation[2] (Eastman 1916:92–135; E. Eastman 1945:26–42; Miller 1976:97–155).

Out of a job, with a wife and young daughter to support, Eastman moved his family to St. Paul, where he struggled to open a private medical practice. Elaine encouraged him to speak and to write, expressing his views about contemporary Indian issues as well as the values of his Indian heritage. Elaine was a talented poet and an accomplished writer, already contributing occasional stories to magazines and newspapers.[3] In late 1894 Eastman was approached by the YMCA to be an International Secretary charged with establishing chapters among American Indians. Having been active with the organization while in college and medical school, he accepted. But after a year and a half of travel and recruitment Charles felt he needed to find a more effective way to help his people. Encouraged by his brother, John, a Presbyterian minister in Flandreau, he set out for

Washington to lobby for restoration of Santee treaty rights abolished after the 1862 Uprising. But American Indians without citizenship or suffrage were not politically important constituents in the minds of most Congressmen. By 1899, in debt and personally unfulfilled, Eastman accepted a temporary position as Outing Agent for Captain R. H. Pratt at Carlisle Indian School in Pennsylvania while he awaited word on his request to reenter the Indian Health Service.

Since 1893, Eastman had been writing stories and remembrances of his childhood, primarily for his own children, which his wife polished and submitted to magazines like *St. Nicholas and Harpers*.[4] Soon he began to gain a literary reputation, and to think of writing books. In 1900, he was appointed Agency Physician at Crow Creek Reservation, South Dakota, and in 1902 his first book, *Indian Boyhood*, was published. But due to political problems in 1902 he became the center of a controversial investigation, with his personal reputation at stake. He remained in government service only through the aid of Hamlin Garland, who was attempting to obtain standard surnames for Indians as a means of protecting their property rights. Garland, convinced Eastman was the man to rename the Sioux, obtained his transfer from Crow Creek to this special project (Miller 1976: 190–239). Although Eastman was occasionally lecturing and writing articles, which he assembled later as books, he worked as Renaming Clerk through 1909.

By 1910, at fifty-one years of age, Eastman remained in many ways a frustrated and disillusioned man, still not having found his "place" in life. In his restlessness, he sought some sort of renewal of identity:

> Early in the summer of 1910 the 'call of the wild' in me became very insistent, and I decided to seek once more in this region (northern Minnesota) the half obliterated and forgotten trails of my forefathers. I began to see the vision of real camp fires, the kind I knew in my boyhood days. So I hastily prepared for a dive into the wilderness, and on a morning in June found myself upon the pineclad shores of Leech Lake, impatient to reach a remote camp of Indians on Bear Island, twenty five miles away. (Eastman 1911b:236)

Funded by the University of Pennsylvania Museum to conduct several months of fieldwork collecting folklore texts and museum artifacts, Eastman encountered the Ojibways of the lakes of Northern Minnesota, the hereditary enemies of his Sioux forefathers (Dartmouth College Alumni Magazine, December 1910). Yet in visiting the north woods which he described as the "only one region left in which a few roving bands of North American Indians still hold civilization at bay," Eastman found the new sense of identity and spiritual renewal as an "Indian" that he was seeking (Eastman 1912:19). Eastman's writing upon his return from the wilderness became more philosophical, reflecting the depth of his experience in his reunion with nature. Although he wrote several articles about the events of the trip to the north country, the fall of 1910 was spent writing *The Soul of The Indian* (Eastman 1911a). In this, his most expressive and articulate essay, Eastman created a text for understanding himself:

> Long before I ever heard of Christ, or saw a white man, I had learned from an untutored woman the essence of morality. With the help of dear Nature herself, she taught me things simple but of mighty import. I knew God. I perceived what goodness is. I saw and loved what is really beautiful. Civilization has not taught me anything better!
>
> As a child, I understood how to give; I have forgotten that grace since I became civilized. I lived the natural life, whereas I now live the artificial. Any pretty pebble was valuable to me then; every growing tree an object of reverence. Now I worship with the white man before a painted landscape whose value is estimated in dollars! Thus the Indian is reconstructed, as the natural rocks are ground to powder and made into artificial blocks which may be built into the walls of modern society.
>
> The first American mingled with his pride a singular humility. Spiritual arrogance was foreign to his nature and teaching. He never claimed that the power of articulate speech was proof of superiority over the dumb creation; on the other hand, it is to him a perilous gift. He believes profoundly in silence—the sign of perfect equilibrium. Silence is the absolute poise of balance of body, mind, and spirit. The man who preserves his selfhood ever calm and unshaken by the storms of existence—not a leaf, as it were, astir on the tree; not a ripple upon the surface of shining pool—his, in the mind of the unlettered sage, is the ideal attitude and conduct of life. (Eastman 1911a:87–89)

In *The Soul of the Indian* Eastman created his own ideal of Indianness, very different from White American society. But Eastman was not unaware of "social evolutionism" as espoused by Spencer and Sumner. He examined the Indian in light of the inevitability of "civilization" over the "savage." In his writing Indians were referred to as "they," never "we." Eastman saw himself as set apart from his own people by education and life experiences. He subscribed to the notion that the "noble savage" with the "natural" virtue of close proximity to nature was on a low, simple, and pristine rung of the ladder of evolution to "civilization." In a sense he was scarred by western science and philosophy. As a marginal Indian and a marginal member of White society, Eastman felt uncomfortable with his status and sought in some way to resolve the ambiguity of his position. He believed that if his White readers could only understand the beauty and truth of the Indian way of life and learn to emulate the quality of truth found in it, a higher, more sensitive morality would eventually prevail in the larger American society.

However in all of Eastman's writings, many of them published repeatedly, first as articles and then as chapters in his books, he sought to teach and explain details about the native American way of life. In most of his early work he attempted to relate for young children the tales and stories of his childhood and the general folklore and woodlore of the Sioux. But were these stories or details intended to be ethnographic? For example, in the account from Indian Boyhood (Eastman 1902) entitled "Hakadah's First Offering," Eastman was careful to avoid potential criticism by omitting the ethnographic detail that the dog which he had to give up to his grandmother was to be eaten. Eastman, in explaining the sacrifice of his playmate, implied that its only function was to deny the importance of material possessions and to appease the Great Mystery. He thus misled his reader by censoring an important ethnographic detail from his description. On the other hand, his 1893 address "Sioux Mythology," delivered before the World Columbian Exposition in Chicago and reprinted in abbreviated form in Popular Science Monthly in 1894 (Eastman 1894:88–91; Bassett and Starr 1898:221–226), was very important because it was Eastman's first scholarly presentation before a professional audience, in which he offered a succinct description of the key concepts of reasoning important to the Sioux in their view of the world. Included were the roles of death, religion, health, and medicine, and the behavior of animals as a model for proper human behavior. Among his first attempts to relate cultural values and concepts, this article remains his most ethnographically insightful.

Eastman conceived of himself as a "rememberer" much like his childhood teachers, his grandmother, and Smokey Days, the story teller. In this sense he saw himself to be a folk historian or recorder rather than an academic. In the foreword to *The Soul of the Indian* he says:

> My little book does not pretend to be a scientific treatise. It is as true as I can make it to my childhood teaching and ancestral ideals, but from the human, not the ethnological standpoint. I have not cared to

> pile up more dry bones, but to clothe them with flesh and blood. So much as has been written by strangers of our ancient faith and worship treats it chiefly as matter of curiosity. I should like to emphasize its universal quality, its personal appeal! (Eastman 1911a:XVI)

During the twenty five years of his literary career, an increasing tone of anti-intellectualism emerged. He rejected the intellectual and academic aspects of anthropology and history. He sought "human" and "personal" explanations. For example, in January of 1907 in St. Louis, Eastman contended that in all his childhood no word existed for an arrow-head made of flint. Because he had never heard the practice of flint knapping discussed and had never seen flint worked in his childhood, he rejected the idea that flint "arrowheads" were ever made by Indians. In the same address he denied that the Mound Builders had ever existed, maintaining that mounds were really battlefields, formed by the accumulation of dirt and sand over time. He also contended on the basis of his own knowledge of Sioux tradition that many theories of ethnology and archaeology could not be true (Deland Papers). Although recognizing various ethnologists as contributors to knowledge, nowhere in print does he discuss adequately his opinion of the validity of anthropology or its study of the American Indian.

The most historically oriented article of Eastman's career appeared in *The Catauquan* in July 1900, and was entitled "The Story of the Little Big Horn (Told From the Indian Standpoint by one of Their Race)." Writing the article while he was Outing Agent at Carlisle Indian School, Eastman contended that most accounts have exaggerated the number of Dakota and Cheyenne that were needed to engage and defeat Custer. Although the article was undocumented, his account appears to include the reminiscences of many of the warriors mentioned in the article.

> The battle of the Little Big Horn was a Waterloo for General Custer and the last effective defense of the Black Hills by the Sioux. It was a fair fight. Custer offered battle and was defeated. He was clearly out-generaled at his own stratagem. Had he gone down just half a mile farther and crossed the stream where Crazy Horse did a few minutes later, he might have carried out his plan of surprising the Indian village and taking the Indian warriors at a disadvantage in the midst of their women and children.
>
> Was it a massacre? Were Custer and his men sitting by their campfires when attacked by the Sioux? Was he disarmed and then fired upon? No. Custer had followed the trail of these Indians for two

> days, and finally overtook them. He found and met just the Indians he was looking for. He had a fair chance to defeat the Sioux, had his support materialized, and brought their entire force to bear upon the enemy in the first instance.
>
> I reiterate that there were not twelve thousand to fifteen thousand Indians at that camp, as has been represented: nor were there over a thousand warriors in the fight. It is not necessary to exaggerate the number of the Indians engaged in the notable battle. The simple truth is that Custer met the combined forces of the hostiles, which were greater than his own, and that he had not so much underestimated their numbers as their ability. (Eastman 1900:358)

In many of Eastman's writings, including *Red Hunters and the Animal People* (Eastman 1904), *Old Indian Days* (1915), and *Indian Heroes and Great Chieftains* (1920), he gives much detail about the Sioux and their Algonquian neighbors and enemies. His sources must have included more than simple childhood memories. He apparently utilized interviews such as the ones conducted with the Ojibway in the summer of 1910. These interviews apparently were carried on with Indians of note whenever and wherever the opportunity arose. For the Little Big Horn article he undoubtedly had collected data for a number of years. While at Pine Ridge Agency in 1891–92, he and his wife had invited many Indians in for evening suppers and long sessions of story telling. Among those who visited from time to time were George Sword and American Horse, and possibly, Red Cloud. In 1896, Eastman visited the Oak Lake Reserve near Brandon, Manitoba, and saw many of the relatives he had left behind in 1873 (Miller 1976: 166–167; Eastman 1916:143–145). He was able to see the elder of his two uncles again. Both these uncles had been at the Battle of the Little Big Horn. Joseph White Foot Print Eastman undoubtedly filled Charles in on the history of his people since 1873, and details of the battle were surely included (Eastman 1900:354). Later, during his period as Renaming Clerk (1903–1909), he talked with many old warriors including Rain-in-the-Face, whom he met and interviewed two months before the old man's death on Standing Rock Reservation (Eastman 1920:132–151). By such interviews he gained additional information that eventually was blended with the memories of his childhood. But his "fieldwork" methods were unsystematic and disorganized, as was his writing method itself.

One of Eastman's nieces related that while writing *Red Hunters and the Animal People* (1904), he would walk the woods alone in the mornings beside Bald Eagle Lake, Minnesota, where the family lived during the summer of 1903. Carrying a small note pad, he would jot notes of ideas as inspirations came to him. Returning around noon, he would explain his ideas to his wife, who then, under Charles' supervision, developed the ideas into prose, typing a draft for additional corrections and polishing. Elaine was indispensable to her husband's writing: after his separation from her in 1921, he published nothing new (Grace Moore Interview 1971; Miller 1976:271, 318).

Because he was neither an intellectual nor an academic, Eastman blurred and distorted much of the data he presented. He contributed little new ethnographic information. The redeeming value of writings such as *The Soul of the Indian* (1911a) and *Indian Scout Talks* (1914) was that an attempt was made in them to describe what it meant to be an Indian when the historical and environmental backdrop of the frontier wilderness was disappearing. Undoubtedly Eastman's relatives had been among the first to assimilate trade goods and new ideas such as literacy and settled life from the Euro-Americans. But Eastman saw the need to redefine the essence of Indian identity and, thus, a type of moral character. He joined the ranks of Americans who between 1900 and 1920 were turning to the out-of-doors for relaxation and inspiration. Many of the national parks were being established, summer camps for children and adults were appearing, and conservation measures were developing to maintain and cultivate "America the Beautiful." Groups such as the Camp Fire Girls, and the Boy and Girl Scouts, as well as increasing numbers of Indian hobbyists and enthusiasts, turned to the Heritage of the American Indian to learn moral and practical lessons about the out-of doors (Nash 1967; Miller 1976:262–263).

Eastman heartily endorsed the outdoor movement. He wrote articles such as "Education Without Books" (1912b) and "What can the Out-of-Doors Do for Children" (1921). During the summer of 1914, he was employed as the camp director of a large Boy Scout camp near Chesapeake Bay in Maryland. Throughout the summer he compiled ideas for chapters to his book *Indian Scout Talks* (1914) which he dedicated as a guide for Boy Scouts and Camp Fire Girls. His essay, "At Home with Nature," suggests the extent of his feeling for the natural life:

> To be in harmony with nature, one must be true in thought, free in action, and clean in body, mind, and spirit. This is the solid granite foundation of character.
>
> Have you ever wondered why most great men were born in humble homes and passed their early youth in the open country? There a boy is accustomed to see the sun rise and set every day; there

> rocks and trees are personal friends, and his geography is born within him, for he carries a map of the region in his head. In civilization there are many deaf ears and blind eyes. Because the average boy in the town has been deprived of close contact and intimacy with nature, what he learns from books he soon forgets, or is unable to apply. All learning is a dead language to him who gets it second hand.
>
> It is necessary that you should live with nature, my boy friend, if only that you may verify to your own satisfaction your school room lessons. Further than this you may be able to correct some error, or even to learn something will be a real contribution to the sum of human knowledge. That is by no means impossible to a sincere observer. In the great laboratory of nature there are endless secrets yet to be discovered.
>
> We will follow the Indian method, for the American Indian is the only man I know who accepts natural things as lessons in themselves, direct from the Great Giver of Life. (Eastman 1914:1–2)

The Eastmans soon decided to take advantage of the national fascination with the out-of-doors and to begin a camp of their own. It would be a camp specializing in introducing Indian-lore to children, with Charles as the main drawing card. In the spring of 1915, drawn by the beauty of the region of Mount Monadanock remembered from his college days at Dartmouth, he came to Keene, New Hampshire looking for a site for the camp. It opened in July of 1915 on the northwest shore of Granite Lake. Called "A School of the Woods," it catered to girls recruited from as far away as Boston and as near as the Keene countryside. The Eastmans set out to create in their campers a sense of appreciation for the out-of-doors and the folk and woodlore of the Native American. The first promotional brochure stated:

> It is desired to secure for each member not only the largest possible gain in physical health and vitality, but its finest womanly development in the direction of a broad and genuine outlook upon nature and life. It is hoped to fill their lives for nine happy weeks so full of novel and wholesome and absorbing interests, that there will be no room for the clash of personalities, for undue self-consciousness, or unhealthy fancies. (Eastman collection, Jones Library, Amherst, Massachusetts)

The summer was a success due to the enthusiasm and hard work of Charles and Elaine and the five Eastman children. In the promotional brochure for the summer of 1916 Charles expressed a new sense of contentment and self confidence:

> . . . we come from nature, we must eventually return to her, and we depend upon her absolutely for harmonious development of body and soul. We must continually replenish our blood with fresh supplies of air, food, and water. Why not, then live with nature while we can, and thus purify and replenish our whole being? This is our plan for the boys and girls. (ibid.)

At the same time, Charles was involved in assuming leadership in the increasingly popular and yet ineffective Society for American Indians. Having been interested in Indian claims since his Washington years as a lobbyist from 1897 to 1899, Charles saw participation in SAI activities promoting Indian citizenship as the first step in helping Indian people enforce the honoring of promises made in their treaties (Hertzberg 1971:172–209). But the bureaucratic and legislative entanglements of Washington, and the increasing complexity of issues concerning American Indians were finally so overwhelming to him that he periodically escaped to Granite Lake, to his family, and his own piece of wilderness. Between 1915 and 1920 Charles, aided by Elaine, produced many articles, as well as *Deep Woods to Civilization: Chapters in the Autobiography of an Indian* (1916), the sequel to *Indian Boyhood* (1902), and *Indian Heroes and Great Chieftains* (1920).

By the summers of 1918 and 1919 Eastman was leaving the running of camp Oahe (meaning "Hill of Vision") to Elaine and his daughters, while he travelled to Washington and elsewhere on other business. Owing to the war years, the camp was not a financial success; by the summer of 1921 the Eastman's debts were serious. Difficulties had plagued their marriage for several decades. With all of the children grown, their reasons for remaining together became fewer. Charles then lost his favorite daughter, Irene, in the influenza epidemic of 1917. Under the name Taluta (meaning "Red Deer"), she had accompanied him on many lecture tours, singing"Indian Melodies" which she had adapted to her beautiful soprano voice (Eastman Collection, Jones Library, Amherst, Massachusetts; Miller 1976:337–338). Because of Irene's burial in an unmarked grave on a hill near the camp, Granite Lake became a place of sorrow for the Eastmans. The break in their marriage finally occurred in the summer of 1921. Charles left for Detroit to live with a son who had returned from the war in Europe, leaving the camp to Elaine and their daughters (Miller 1976:265–270).

In the next decade Eastman found himself forced again and again to use his "Indian-ness" for financial survival. He threw himself into controversies such as the Sioux Black Hills claim, and claiming his share of lawyer's fees in the successful Santee compensation settlements in 1922, which he had first advocated as early as 1898 (Miller 1976:273–274). In 1923 at age sixty-five, Eastman entered the government service for the third time. The sudden death of Major James McLaughlin in August of 1923 prompted the Coolidge administration to appoint him to McLaughlin's vacated inspectorship. For the next two years travel and the writing of tedious reports occupied his time.

In his term of office as U.S. Indian Inspector, Eastman participated in several memorable events. In the fall of 1923 he assisted in David Lloyd George's visit to the United States. Later praised by President Coolidge, he assembled a group of "traditional" Indians from Cheyenne River Reservation, South Dakota, to greet the British statesman with a name giving ceremony and the presentation of a warbonnet, pipe, and pipebag. In December of 1923, he took part in Herbert Work's grand conference of the Committee of One Hundred to advise the government of potential improvements to be made in the U.S. government's relationship to American Indians.

After a year of traveling, making inspections, and conducting investigations, Charles received the most controversial assignment of his career as inspector. Because of an evolving historiographical debate about the role and longevity of Sacajewea or "Bird-woman," the "guide" of the Lewis and Clark expedition of 1804–1806, Commissioner of Indian Affairs Charles Burke ordered an investigation. Predominantly because of Wyoming's prosuffragette historian, Grace Raymond Hebard, who had interviewed many older Shoshoni people on the Wind River Reservation, many believed that Sacajewea had not died in 1812 at Fort Manuel on the Missouri River, but had instead lived into her eighties on the Wind River Reservation. Attempting to canonize Sacajewea as the symbol of unsung frontier womanhood, members of the Wyoming congressional delegation made efforts through Congress to erect a national monument on her supposed gravesite in Wyoming. The choice of this grave was supported on the basis of Hebard's interpretation (Tabor 1967:6–10; Anderson 1973:2–17). Eastman was charged with collecting the facts of the controversy. In January of 1925, he visited Ft. Washakie, Wyoming, and Fort Berthold, North Dakota. His investigation focused only upon material that was immediately accessible to him. Hebard, who was eager for official endorsement and recognition of her theories concerning Sacajewea's longevity sent him drafts of chapters of her forthcoming book (Hebard Papers, Center for Western Studies, University of Wyoming, Laramie, Wyoming; Miller 1976:301–309; Hebard 1832). Unfortunately, her opponents did not supply Eastman directly with their own versions, although their conclusions were readily available in print

(Robinson 1924; Drumm 1920). Consequently Eastman simply reiterated Hebard's idolization of Sacajewea as the foremost female character in American history. His report summarized her story in his then familiar romantic tone: "It is the Ben Hur of the Indians, a most remarkable life of any age, fate compelled and forced her all the time, but in the end she defeated them—she defeated the fates" (Eastman, 1941:187).

While a U.S. Indian Inspector, Charles was expected to submit weekly typewritten reports on his activities. But his reporting became so irregular that he was sent various reprimands. He explained his tardiness by relating the manner in which he approached report writing. During investigations and inspections he would make notes, and then prevail upon someone to type up a final report. Of course many reservations had no stenographer, and so Eastman would simply wait till he found one who could be pressed into service. Reprimands for these and other failures continued; in addition, he took sick with recurring bronchitis. Reluctantly he resigned his inspectorship on March 20, 1925, using the summer months to recover and to attempt to write again. Although Hebard had asked him to write the introduction to her book, Charles finally answered her note in October of 1925: "I am now preparing a true story of Sacajewea's life. I think the whole of her life bears out the spirit and heroism in her." (Hebard Papers, University of Wyoming) In November of 1925, Eastman decided to move to Chicago to be near the collections of the Newberry Library, but distractions arose in several forms. While at the Newberry, he found a portrait done by Frank Blackwell Mayer of his mother in 1851 (Mayer 1932). Thrilled with the find, he turned to tracing details of his family geneology (Hitchcock letters, Newberry Library; Eastman 1946). But once again lacking financial resources, he was forced onto the lecture circuit. Although he continued to attempt to produce new manuscripts, never again did he do so. He turned his energies to selling foreign publishing rights to his existing nine books, and their domestic reissue.

In 1925 Charles invested his modest savings in a small piece of wooded property near Desbarats, Ontario, on the north shore of Wilson's Channel. Here he had a cabin erected. His neighbors across the channel recalled him fondly, but noted his frustrations as a writer: ". . . he did not express himself easily on paper, and he never finished the reminiscences he worked on up here" (Wallace n.d.: 5; Bennett Collection). Matotee Lodge meaning "the bear's den" (as Charles named his cabin) became a symbol of his return to the "Indian" and thus "natural" roots of his identity.

In his last decade of life, Charles became a "show" Indian in the mold of those he had harshly criticized decades earlier. He became the central inspiration for many Indian hobbyists and the thrilling attraction for many a YMCA camp or Boy Scout Troop. Without financial resources, he depended on several generous friends, and lived into his eightieth year.

Many of the Indian enthusiasts of the Detroit area grew fond of old "Doc" Eastman. Milford Chandler, noted student of the American Indian, and Roy Nichols, ornithologist at Cranbrook Institute, organized summer campouts for the area hobbyists on Chandler's land. With several tipis erected and hobbyists dressed in fine regalia, the encampments were very festive. Undoubtedly memories of his boyhood were recaptured, and as the summer drew to a close, Charles was reluctant to leave. Chandler agreed to let Charles live throughout the fall in his tipi. He checked on Charles in the evenings, and they spent the weekends in intense conversations about Indian things. But one day as the cold weather was upon the lodge, while they were building a fire, the fire went out of control. As Eastman and Chandler battled the flames, smoke inhalation overtook the old man. His recurring lung problems were severely aggravated. Within several weeks he contracted pneumonia and a heart condition, and was dead January 8, 1939, in a Detroit hospital. On January 11, 1939, he was buried in Grand Lawn Cemetery in a grave that is unmarked to this day (Pohrt 1976).

Neither an intellectual nor a great scholar, Charles Alexander Eastman tasted both success and failure. His readers, especially children, loved his stories and he was seen by many as an interpreter of one way of life to another. Whether he was an ethnographer is dubious. He sought a different level of meaning in terms of "personal appeal." He attempted to define ideals, moral codes, sex roles, mythology and cosmology; and finally, he attempted to influence White civilization by his version of the contribution of his Indian heritage. By teaching and even helping to invent a new conception of the American Indian, Eastman wanted American society to learn about itself using the mirror provided by the first Americans

NOTES

1. Apparently while attending his first year at Santee Normal School, Santee Agency, Nebraska, Ohiyesa selected his new name.

2. For a detailed discussion of the confrontation between Brown and Eastman see Miller 1976:97–155.

3. For a detailed bibliography of the writings of Elaine Goodale Eastman see Miller 1976:374–379. A number of unpublished manuscripts are in the collections of the library at Smith College, Northampton, Massachusetts, including a biography of Helen Hunt Jackson, and an autobiographi-

cal accounting of her experiences in the Dakotas before 1890. Ironically Charles's name is conspicuously absent. There are no Eastman papers, and there is no mention at all of Charles in the Elaine Goodale Eastman Papers.

4. Discussions of the writings of Charles Eastman can be found in Miller 1976; McLaird 1968; and Wilson 1975. A comprehensive bibliography is presented in Miller 1976:370–373.

LITERATURE CITED

Anderson, Irving

1973 Probing the Riddle of the Bird Woman. Montana Magazine of Western History 23:2–17.

Bassett, Helen Wheeler, and Frederick Starr, ed.

1898 The International Folklore Congress of the World Columbian Exposition, Chicago, July 1893. Volume 1. Chicago: Charles H. Sergel Company.

Drumm, Stella, ed.

1920 John C. Luttig's Journal of a Fur Expedition on the Upper Missouri, 1812–1813. St. Louis: Missouri Historical Society

Eastman, Charles Alexander

1894 Sioux Mythology. Popular Science Monthly 46:88–91.

1898 Sioux Mythology. In the International Folklore Congress of the World Columbian Exposition, Chicago, July 1893. Volume 1:221–226. Chicago: Charles H. Sergel Company.

1900 The Story of the Little Big Horn. Chautauquan 31:353–358.

1902 Indian Boyhood. New York: McClure Phillips and Company.

1904 Red Hunters and the Animal People. New York: Harpers and Brothers.

1907 Old Indian Days. New York: McClure Phillips and Company.

1910 Smokey Days Wigwam Evenings: Indian Tales Retold. Boston: Houghton Mifflin.

1911a The Soul of the Indian. Boston: Little Brown.

1911b A Canoe Trip Among the Northern Ojibways. The Red Man 4:236–244.

1912a Last of the Algonquins. Travel 18:19–21.

1912b Education without Books. Craftsman 21:372–377.

1914 Indian Scout Talks. Boston: Little Brown.

1915 The Indian Today: The Past and Future of the First American. Garden City: Doubleday and Page.

1916 Deep Woods to Civilization: Chapters in the Autobiography of an Indian. Boston: Little Brown.

1920 Indian Heroes and Great Chieftains. Boston: Little Brown.

1921 What Can the Out-of-Doors Do for Children. Education 41:599–605.

1941 Supplement B, Special Report of Sacajewea to the Commissioner of Indian Affairs. Annals of Wyoming 13:187–193.

1946 Additional Geneological Notes Regarding the Ancestry of Dr. Charles A. Eastman, A Minnesota Mdewakanton Dakota. Minnesota Archaeologist 12:7–11.

Eastman, Elaine Goodale

1945 The Ghost Dance War and Wounded Knee Massacre of 1890–91. Nebraska History 26:26–42.

Hebard, Grace Raymond

1932 Sacajewea, a Guide and Interpreter of the Lewis and Clark Expedition, with an Account of the Travels of Troussant Charbonneau and of Jean Baptiste, the Expedition Papoose. Glendale: Arthur H. Clark.

Hertzberg, Hazel W.

1971 The Search for an American Indian Identity: Modern Pan-Indian Movements. Syracuse: Syracuse University Press.

McLaird, James D.

1968 From Deep Woods to Civilization: Charles Alexander Eastman, Dakota Author. Dakota Book News 13:1–13.

Mayer, Frank Blackwell

1932 With Pen and Pencil on the Frontier in 1851: The Diary of Frank Blackwell Mayer. Bertha L. Heilbron, ed. St. Paul: Minnesota Historical Society.

Miller, David Reed

1976 Charles Alexander Eastman: One Man's Journey in Two Worlds. M.A. Thesis, University of North Dakota, Grand Forks.

Moore, Grace

1971 Interview held at Flandreau, South Dakota, March 12, 1971.

1973 Interview held at Flandreau, South Dakota, October 27, 1973.

Nash, Rodrick
1967 Wilderness and the American Mind. New Haven: Yale University Press.

Pohrt, Richard
1976 Interview held at Flint, Michigan, May 24, 1976.

Robinson, Doane
1924 Sac-a-jawe vs. Sa-kaka-wea. South Dakota Historical Collections 11:71–84.

Smith, Marjorie Whalen
1968 Historic Homes of Cheshire County, New Hampshire. Brattleboro: Griswold Offset Printing.

Tabor, Ronald W.
1967 Sacajawea and the Suffragettes. Pacific Northwest Quarterly 58:6–10.

Wilson, Raymond
1975 The Writings of Ohiyesa—Charles Alexander Eastman, M.D., Santee Sioux. South Dakota History 6:55–73.

ARCHIVAL COLLECTIONS CITED

Baker Archives, Dartmouth College
Clipping Files and Dartmouth Alumni Magazine Clippings, Eastman File.

Edward Bennett, Jr.
Eastman Collection, Lake Forest, Illinois. Mrs. Malcolm Wallace Mss. u.p., "Desbarats History" (circa 1943).

Charles Deland Papers
South Dakota Historical Society, Pierre.

Eastman Collection
Jones Library, Amherst, Massachusetts.

Grace Raymond Hebard Papers
Center of Western Studies, University of Wyoming, Laramie.

Hirim Melville Hitchcock Letters
Aryer Collection, Newberry Library, Chicago.

CHAPTER SIX

JAMES R. MURIE
PAWNEE ETHNOGRAPHER

Pawnee, 1862–1921

DOUGLAS R. PARKS

Major ethnographic descriptions written by Indians themselves are rare. Even rarer, though, are instances in which the bulk of the primary ethnographic materials on a particular tribe was collected and written by a member of that tribe. Such an instance, however, is James Rolfe Murie, a Pawnee whose anthropological career spanned some three decades from the 1890s to the 1920s—a career which has been and continues to be largely unrecognized by anthropologists. The only ones who seem to have appreciated his work, save those with whom he worked collaboratively, are a small group of Pawnee and Arikara specialists, and even some of these seem not to be fully aware of all that he accomplished. Certainly no one to date has exhaustively utilized all of the data which he collected. Nevertheless anthropologists today must be forever grateful to this man who painstakingly salvaged an enormous amount of ethnographic detail from a tribe which had an unusually complex and elaborate religious life, and whose religious leaders tenaciously guarded their knowledge.

This paper will present some background of Murie's life and his anthropological career, then briefly review his Pawnee and Arikara work, and finally appraise his contributions as an ethnographer. The source material on Murie's life and his professional work is meager. In large part it must be reconstructed from correspondence and reminiscences. There is no single published source that gives any detail on either topic. Therefore it is impossible to give as detailed a picture as might be desirable. Yet sufficient material exists to enable construction of an overall view of the man and the methods he employed in his anthropological work.

BACKGROUND

James Murie was born in Grand Island, Nebraska in 1862. At that time the Pawnee were still living in their traditional territory and much of their old culture remained intact. Only recently, by the treaty of 1857, had they ceded most of their land to the government and confined themselves to a small reservation. When Murie was born their removal to Indian Territory (now Oklahoma) was still a decade away. During that period the Pawnee were, with few exceptions, still living in earthlodges and tipis, following the old subsistence pattern of long winter and summer buffalo hunts, practicing native agriculture in which the work was done by women, and maintaining their native religion—all this in spite of government and missionary attempts at changing their lifeways from as early as 1830.

Information on Murie's parents and his early childhood is meager. His mother, whose English name was Anna Murie, was a full-blooded Pawnee, a member of the Skiri band. His father, James Murie, was White—a Scot who was a captain under Major Frank North and commanded a battalion of Pawnee scouts. The elder Murie abandoned his family shortly after his son's birth and went west to California. When he left, young James (whose childhood Pawnee name was *ri•tahkacihari'* "Young Eagle") and his mother went to live with her brother who, we are told, "lived like a White man" (*Southern Workman* March, 1880). The only other source for his life in Nebraska is a group of several personal recollections which he later shared in a newspaper letter written during his student days at Hampton Institute. In that letter he related,

> In 1869 I went on a hunting with the Pawnees and Puncas we went on about three days they found some bufflos so all the men got their best horses and fixed them up and than took their bows and arrows and guns they went all around them and than they just run after them and see who'll get there first one man would kill two or three sometimes four and eight, and they skin them, and take them home, skin and all. the skins are used for moccasins and men legends once I went swimming while the men went after bufflos. while I was in the water, I seen a bufflo coming towards where I was, frighten me, to. I had to climbed upon a tree. it was mad some men were after him

> and had some arrows in him. they killed him and than I got down. from the tree. and I seen them skin it. we had lots bufflo meat we camp same place. the Indians were drying their meat so it well less long. after while we went on again. we want on till sun was at. next morning they seen some more bufflos. they killed many more they had to stay there till their meat was dry. we stayed there and the Indian women got their things and worked on. with their skin. they finished them. and had lots of meat and skins, and return home again. I just use to eat dry meat all the time no towns around nor near, to buy some bread and sugar. I use to get hungry, for bread. I use to cry. for some bread my stepfather had to take me where their was some Pawnees that did not go on hunting we got there. I had all the bread I want I was glad then the next day we went on and got to a town and went in the cars and went on we got to another town we got out and went home. (*Southern Workman* March, 1880)

Before leaving Nebraska for Indian Territory in 1874, Murie attended for four months a day school at the agency in Genoa. "My mother was willing for me to come to school and be among the White people," he later reminisced (*Southern Workman*, March, 1880). After moving to the new Pawnee reservation in the Territory, he attended day school for a year and then spent a year at the boarding school at the agency. Here he had a room of his own next to the agent's office and boarded at the school. Being around the agency and thereby mingling with Whites most of the time, he soon learned sufficient English that he was able to be an interpreter for the agent. One day in 1879 he was asked if he wanted to go to school in the East. He responded affirmatively, and so he was outfitted and started off to Hampton Normal and Agricultural Institute in Virginia.

Murie was 16 years old when he entered Hampton in October 1879. School records there credit him with one year of previous schooling and speaking some English. He enrolled in the primary school and during the first year worked on the school's farm, the routine at that time being farm work in the morning and classes in the afternoon. The next year he began work in the printing office.

> I thought that I would try and learn the printers' trade, as I saw that one of the Pawnee boys at Carlisle was learning the trade. I thought that I would learn it so that both of us would have the same trade, so we may be able to start the same trade out in the Territory. . . . I work two days every week. And now I can set types for the *Southern Workman*. I like this trade very well, but then I

> will not say that I will start this trade out in the Territory; I don't know whether circumstances will permit or not, for my tribe need education, and I expect to be a teacher among them. I like this trade very well and wish to learn as much as I can while here. (*Southern Workman* March, 1881)

The basic educational goals for Indian students at Hampton seem to have been threefold: developing their use of English, teaching them a trade, and providing Christian training. All were goals aimed at making them productive citizens not unlike contemporary Whites. In Murie's case the program met with success. He quickly showed academic aptitude and seems to have done quite well as a student, even though, as he once complained, he was troubled by geography. While working in the printing office, he edited and did most of the writing and type-setting for the column "From the Indians" on the Students' Own page of Hampton's *Southern Workman.* And in this endeavor he took a great deal of pride, according to Booker T. Washington, one of his teachers (Harlan 1973, II:98). In his religious instruction, too, there was success: he was confirmed in the Episcopal church while in school, and later after leaving Hampton he wrote, "I want them (the Pawnee) to put their superstitious ideas aside, and believe in the White man's Great Spirit. I am working for the Indian people and for 'the Father above the skies'" (Hampton Institute 1893:198).

Four years after entering Hampton, Murie left, having completed all classes and having received a diploma in the Normal Department. At that time Hampton did not have a College Department as it does now, so he could go no higher. He returned home, the first of his tribe to do so from an Eastern school, destined to be perhaps Hampton's most distinguished Indian graduate (Harlan 1973, II:100). His reaction to his homecoming is in part contained in a letter to Capt. S. G. Armstrong, principal at Hampton:

> When I went away the Pawnees were not on their farms but were in villages. On my way home from Arkansas city, I saw farms on the sides of the road owned and worked by Pawnees. They had log houses as well as the mud lodges to live in, and very comfortably fixed. I was pleased to see what they had done in such a short time. Many had some wheat and were harvesting when I arrived. Many made money from it, which encourages many and many have already sown some four or five acres apiece. Pretty near all the Pawnees are farmers, with the exceptions of those that are employed by the government and those that own cattle. (*Southern Workman* December, 1883)

His interest now was to put to good use the education that he had received by becoming a teacher.

First, though, he took a job as a clerk in the store of Mattock and Bishop which was near the agency. He did the bookkeeping as well as clerking and was apparently well thought of. However, when the new Pawnee Agency boarding school opened in the fall of 1883, he quit the job and took a position as assistant teacher at the school. Here, in addition to teaching, he had charge of the boys and their dormitory. His students were six and seven year-olds who knew no English; his task was to teach them the language. The next fall he resigned from his job at the agency school and

> took twenty-one of the largest children to Haskel Institute, and on arriving there found we were the first lot to arrive. I took my largest boys and fixed up the rooms in good order for others who were coming. I acted (as) Disciplinarian and Drill-master for three months, but no salary. By the first of January I was appointed Assistant Disciplinarian and Drill-master at $15.00 per month. (Hampton Institute 1893:347)

After two years at Haskell he resigned and went east, hoping to study for the ministry. In Washington he visited the Commissioner of Indian Affairs, who told him that he had received sufficient education and promised him an appointment as a teacher at the Pawnee school. Satisfied with this commitment, he returned home; but the agent at Pawnee claimed that he had never received any instructions for such an appointment and refused Murie the job. Murie waited; still there were no instructions, so he gave up his more ambitious plans and lived for a period in the Skiri camp, of which time he says, "Had I been weak in heart I should this day have been wearing Indian clothes" (ibid., 348). He then settled down on a tract of land and began to farm. Writing back to Hampton in 1890 he related:

> I have a farm on the Arkansas River bottom, with 12 acres in cultivation. I have bought some wire and will soon have a fence around it. I also have my logs laid up for a house, and as soon as the portable saw-mill goes to running I will have boards for sheathing and rafters sawed. I bought fourteen bundles in Arkansas City. As soon as my house is complete I shall move over there to stay. I am not in the government service and, therefore, do not get any salary.
>
> I am married, and we have one little boy who is now six months old. We call him Fred Wallace Murie, and not *Le-coots* or *Tah-Kah*.

> I want my little boy to grow up in white man's ideas and become educated so he can help his people; and also be a good citizen of this country.
>
> Every day we are showing our people what 'Lands in Severalty' would bring us, and what good it would do us. They see that it's coming on to them, and they are scattering out on claims, improving their places so they can be as near ready for it when it comes. I am doing all I can to help them start farms, especially the young men. These young men should be encouraged.
>
> I am helping my people in any way I can, whether in Government service or not; I am always ready to help an Indian man with his machinery or an Indian woman with her sewing machine; or telling my people the story of Christ. I care not where I may be just so I am working for the Indian people, and for 'Our Father.' (ibid., 348)

Thus we see Murie, educated and with his plans to become a teacher thwarted, falling back on farming, the occupation and lifestyle most favored by the government for advancing the Pawnee. His stint in the country was not long, however, for within a year or two he was back at the Pawnee agency living in a log cabin that was built on agency land, located on the spot now occupied by the Tribal Community House. Here he became variously involved in tribal and agency matters, among them serving as an interpreter, recording names on the censuses, and working with the land allotment of 1893 when all Pawnees became citizens and each family received a farm. In 1896 he began work as a clerk in the bank in the new town of Pawnee, a job at which he was to continue off and on for most of the next twenty years.

PAWNEE WORK

Murie's anthropological career began in the mid 1890s when Alice Fletcher, who had been studying the Omaha, came to Pawnee to begin a study of Pawnee ceremonialism and particularly the Calumet Ritual. Fletcher, who had known Murie from his student days at Hampton, enlisted his aid as a collaborator in her work. Murie agreed, and on this and two of Fletcher's subsequent field trips he accompanied her to ceremonies and to the homes of informants to whom he introduced her. He also transcribed and translated songs and other textual material, and assisted her in various other ways. When Fletcher was back in Washington, she and Murie corresponded extensively over a five year period from 1898 to 1902 (see Acknowledgments), Murie answering questions that came up in her work and providing her with additional material. On several occasions during this period he also visited her in Washington. Twice, in 1898 and in 1900, he brought the Chawi informant who provided the data for the book *The Hako: A Pawnee Ceremony* (Fletcher 1904) so that the three of them could work on the description of that ceremony; in 1902 Murie again visited her for a final review of the manuscript. In addition he made several trips to Washington on tribal business with older Pawnees, and on such occasions he and his party would visit Fletcher and provide her with an opportunity to collect information (see Fletcher 1899, 1900, 1902, and 1903). In 1902, though, he ended his work with her when be began full time work for George A. Dorsey.

Murie's work with Fletcher had been that of an assistant. His work under Dorsey's guidance was to improve and develop. Credit must, however, be given to Fletcher for awakening Murie's interest in Pawnee culture and religious life, and its preservation by himself and anthropologists; for before he met Fletcher he seems to have taken no significant interest in the traditions of his people, preferring instead to be like a White man as he so often said, and consequently sharing many White attitudes.

Dorsey, who was then Curator of Anthropology at the Field Museum of Natural History in Chicago, began his Pawnee work in 1899. This study was part of a larger project, begun by the Field Museum and then funded by the Carnegie Institution, aimed at compiling a systematic and extended study of the mythology and ceremonies of the Caddoan tribes. The Pawnee work became by far the most extensive, owing to collaboration. Before 1902 Dorsey made several brief trips to Pawnee during which he laid the groundwork for his later efforts. In 1902 he made another trip there, purchased some cultural specimens, collected some traditions, and most importantly hired Murie as a full time assistant. Up to this time Murie had worked with him while he was in Pawnee, taking him to informants and generally assisting him; but now he was given full responsibility for collecting what was to be the bulk of the traditions that formed the two volumes of Pawnee mythology that were published under Dorsey's name (Dorsey 1904a; 1906c). During the summer of 1903 he also worked among the Arikara of North Dakota.

Murie's work with Dorsey extended through 1909. For several years he and his family lived in Chicago where he worked at the Field Museum, but for most of the period he lived in Pawnee where he acted as a field researcher. The procedure that he and Dorsey worked out was for Murie to collect and write out the ethnographic data and for Dorsey then to edit it and have it typed. In this manner Dorsey not only obtained Pawnee and Arikara traditions but also built up a large body of notes and manuscripts on Skiri ceremonial and social life and on Arikara ceremonialism as well. Some of this material was incorporated into Dorsey's numerous articles on the Pawnee; some went into the posthumously published monograph on Skiri society that was authored by Dorsey and Murie and prepared for publication by Alexander Spoehr; some of it was published, in parts *verbatim*, by Ralph Linton in four leaflets on Pawnee religion as well as an article on the Morning Star sacrifice; and a great quantity remains unpublished.[1] The latter notes and manuscripts are currently in the archives of the Department of Anthropology of the Field Museum. In the course of his field work, Murie also recorded Pawnee texts and songs as well as Arikara songs on cylinders. Originally in the collections of the Field Museum, the cylinders are now housed in the Archives of Traditional Music at Indiana University.[2] In addition, Murie also collected specimens from the field for Dorsey and was instrumental in the Field Museum's acquisition of several important Skiri sacred bundles (viz., the Pahukatawa and the Big Black Meteoric Star bundles) as well as a large collection of material culture items. Thanks then to Dorsey's interest and Murie's efforts, the museum has today one of the two significant Pawnee collections in the country (the other important collection being that of the American Museum of Natural History).

An interesting but unfortunately obscure aspect of Murie's work with Dorsey was an apparent venture into linguistics. In the Chilocco *Indian School Journal* in 1909 [9(9): 34] there is a brief note stating that Murie and his family had visited the school and that Murie was currently engaged in making a dictionary and grammar of the Pawnee language. To my knowledge, no partial or complete manuscript of a grammar or a dictionary exists (or perhaps survives). But among the Murie papers in the Field Museum there is a notebook entitled *Skiri Pawnee Texts* that in part corroborates the newspaper note. The bulk of the notebook consists of two long texts written out in the Skiri dialect but with no accompanying English translation, and in the back are some 30 pages filled with verb paradigms and the principal parts of many irregular verbs as well as a partial paradigmatic chart for kinship terms. The orthography for the material is the best of Murie's extensive transcriptional work, for he wrote vowels and consonants consistently and correctly throughout (in many instances, although not consistently, he also marked vowel length). In addition he indicated final voiceless vowels and stress. It is lamentable that more such material, if it in fact ever existed, has not survived.

After 1906 Murie's work with Dorsey seems to have been sporadic; at other times he worked at the bank in Pawnee as cashier and interpreter. As Dorsey's work took him more and more away from the Pawnee, he seemingly would have liked to continue his partnership with Murie, for he asked that he accompany him on an expedition to Borneo as his assistant. Murie demurred, however, stating that he had no desire to lose his head to the headhunters. In 1910 he became a part-time field researcher for the Bureau of American Ethnology, no doubt because of his previous experience with Dorsey and Fletcher, and in the *32nd Annual Report* of the Bureau he is listed as being involved in ethnological research on the Pawnee. The Bureau, then headed by F. W. Hodge, engaged him over a five year period to write up descriptions of surviving Pawnee ceremonies, particularly medicine rites. This time he was working independently. The Bureau furnished him with various items of equipment—a graphophone for recording songs, a typewriter, a camera, and several tents—as well as providing for field expenses and a small salary. Murie's procedure was to camp with the Indians when the ceremonies were being performed and so observe all of the proceedings. Then at their conclusion he returned home to write out in full what he had observed and taken notes on. He also recorded the songs during the actual performance of the ceremonies and later wrote them out, too. When he completed parts of a manuscript, he mailed them to the Bureau; likewise the cylinder recordings were sent there.[3]

In all Murie completed extensive, minutely detailed descriptions of three ceremonies of the South Bank Pawnee: what he called the White Beaver Ceremony (or what is perhaps better known as the Doctor Dance) of the Chawi band; the Bear Dance of the Pitahawirata band; and the Buffalo Dance, also of the Pitahawirata. The Bear Dance that he witnessed and described was the last one to be performed.

Beginning in 1912 Clark Wissler, Curator of Anthropology at the American Museum of Natural History, began editing a series of descriptive papers on the societies of the Plains tribes, hoping to work out a detailed distribution of the various types. He had information for all of the tribes but the Pawnee; and to fill that lacuna Wissler wrote to Hodge early that year to ask him for permission to get information from Murie. Actually Wissler hoped that Murie would contribute a short monograph on the subject. Hodge replied that he should feel free to work with Murie so long as the work would not duplicate that which Murie was doing for the Bureau. That summer Robert Lowie, who was also with the American Museum at that time and who had just finished work among the Arikara on their societies, visited Murie in Oklahoma to compare notes, since Murie too had previously worked among the Arikara. At the same time he wanted to propose that Murie work with Wissler. Murie agreed to the outlined proposal, and subsequently Wissler arranged with him to write up separate descriptions for each of the societies that the Pawnee formerly had, including accounts of the origin and ceremony or dance of each society. Wissler also submitted a list of questions to him that he should follow. Murie then sought out the old men who were knowledgeable about each society and interviewed them, generally at his own home at night. He and the old men would sit on the floor, and the latter told what they knew while he listened and took notes. Afterwards during the day he would work at his roll top desk writing out from his notes and from memory what they had told him. Later he would bring back various ones individually to his home to answer specific questions and flesh out what he had previously put together. Once he completed a description, he would once more bring the old men together at his home, feed them, and then again at night record the songs of that society. As soon as he completed a section he sent it to Wissler, who would edit it and send it back to him for revision. This procedure continued for a year, and then in the summer of 1913 Wissler visited Murie for several weeks in Pawnee to work up the developing manuscript. Over the next year the same *modus operandi* obtained, until in 1914 the manuscript was ready for publication. When it appeared in print, Murie was listed as author, while in the introduction Wissler explained that Murie had prepared the paper under his direction.

During 1913 while he was working on the societies paper for Wissler, Murie also collected related specimens for the American Museum and simultaneously worked on the Buffalo Dance manuscript for the Bureau. Then the next year when he was nearing the end of the paper for Wissler, he suggested to his collaborator that he write out in full the rituals for the important sacred bundles of the Skiri band, a project that he had always wanted to do. Wissler agreed, and after *Pawnee Indian Societies* was finished told him to go ahead on the work and that they would follow the same procedure as before. At the same time Wissler arranged with the Bureau of American Ethnology for a jointly-sponsored project whereby the American Museum would direct Murie's work and would receive the sacred bundles and other cultural items collected, while the Bureau would get the resulting manuscript and publish it.

Work on the ambitious new project began in 1914 and continued up through 1921, when it culminated in the manuscript *Ceremonies of the Pawnee*. Murie as before collected material from the old priests and doctors, wrote it up, and sent it to Wissler, with whom he periodically met.

Generally the meetings were in the summer, either at Wissler's family farm in Hagertown, Indiana or in the East, when Wissler would work out organization and form for the subject and go over in detail with Murie what he had collected. All the while, of course, Murie was also engaged in collecting bundles and other specimens for the Museum. Finally in 1921 the manuscript was completed when Murie met with Wissler, who was in Washington with the National Research Council. Before leaving Pawnee, he wrote to his collaborator: "Now, Doc, I want you and me to do good work on [the] Pawnee stuff so we can get [a] fine work out—better than any that's been out on Indians" (December 22, 1920, American Museum of Natural History correspondence files). In June, after they had spent a month together and Murie had returned home, Wissler replied: ". . . you can enjoy the satisfaction of having done a good piece of work, the like of which has not been done before" (ibid., June 22, 1921). The project was finished; and Murie had completed his *magnum opus*, totaling nearly 1600 pages. On November 18, 1921, while Wissler was trying to arrange to bring him to the American Museum in New York to lecture and show films on the Pawnee, he died of apoplexy while chopping wood in his front yard. He was buried in the Indian cemetery north of Pawnee.

The *Ceremonies* manuscript is a combination of two sets of material. The first is a detailed presentation of the ritualistic cycle and ceremonies of the Skiri and is a result of Murie's work with Wissler. The second part consists of the unusually detailed descriptions of the three South Band ceremonies done for the Bureau. As a whole the work is a massive collection of field data, both ethnographic and linguistic, that is unique on at least two counts: first, it contains what is probably the largest collection of accurately transcribed and translated ceremonial song texts ever recorded for a North American tribe;[4] and secondly, it contains a vast collection of vision stories that underlie the songs in the South Band ceremonies. But more importantly it is the foremost source on the rituals of a tribe that, of all the tribes on the Plains, developed its religious philosophy and ceremonialism to the fullest extent.

The *Ceremonies* manuscript was to have been published in 1921, but for unclear reasons failed to be printed. Again in the 1930s it was to be published, but on two occasions it was put aside because of other priorities. It has remained in the archives of the Bureau of American Ethnology (now the National Anthropological Archives) ever since, and today is once again being considered for publication.

From the preceding discussion, it should be clear that Murie was only a marginal participant in Pawnee culture. After moving to Oklahoma he lived all his life in Pawnee, except for his school years and the brief period in Chicago while working for Dorsey. He married into the tribe and identified himself as a Pawnee; and because Pawnee is a small town it would have been impossible for him to divorce himself from Indian society. Yet his childhood and his educational experience put him to a large extent outside traditional Indian society and fitted him more properly for White society. As were so many young Indians in similar circumstances in that period, he became a part of the progressive, non-traditional element of the tribe, straddling both cultures, Indian and White. He attended Indian ceremonies and dances as an observer, or at most a participant observer, but not as full participant (although this changed somewhat later in life), and wherever he went he always wore a suit, never Indian clothing. He never owned a set of Indian clothing, in fact. He and his wife did, however, have several trunks in which they kept blankets, shawls, and goods for give-aways when other tribes came to Pawnee for a *kuskeha:ru'* (i.e., a friendship visit). But his attitude towards and view of Pawnee religion—in fact, life in general—were basically that of a White. And so in his anthropological work we must realize that his accounts were derived primarily from observation—from what he witnessed and what native practitioners told him—and not from the introspection of a believer—although of course he could not have failed to have a cultural empathy, if not an underlying predisposition for native Pawnee religion that an alien would not have. In his early years when he worked with Fletcher and Dorsey and even in his early work for the Bureau and with Wissler, he expressed surprise in his letters at many of the ceremonies about which he had not known, and his reactions when he witnessed those ceremonies were again surprise and awe. Later in life he tried to embrace his Pawnee identity more fully. After the old priests had died, he led a number of ceremonies in which he had been instructed in the course of his work and seemingly would have been a priest himself; in fact, he reputedly attempted to have a vision but failed; and so he continued to the end to share in both cultures which had produced and sustained him.

ARIKARA WORK

While working for Dorsey and the Field Museum, Murie spent two summers in North Dakota among the Arikara. He was particularly well suited for doing field work there since he had established friendships with several Arikara students while at Hampton and, according to Dorsey, had learned to overcome the differences between Pawnee and Arikara speech at that time. Furthermore, because the Arikara and Skiri Pawnee have always recognized a close relationship to one another and have had mutual visiting, Murie's acceptance into the community was assured.

His first trip, about which the most is known, and which apparently yielded the most material, was in 1903. He arrived at Fort Berthold on May 26 and remained there through August, for a period of three months. During this time he stayed with the family of Strikes The Enemy, a tribal priest and doctor who adopted Murie and also inducted him as a priest. During this summer in the field, Murie attended 16 ceremonies—those of various doctors' societies and the openings of various sacred bundles. On most of these occasions he took notes of varying length and detail. In addition he wrote out nearly 100 stories and collected specimens for the Field Museum. In 1905 he again spent the summer in North Dakota, this time concentrating on collecting material on Arikara ceremonial life. It is not clear, however, precisely what resulted from this field trip.

Murie's Arikara work, like the Pawnee work for Dorsey, consisted primarily of three sorts of data collection: (1) mythology, (2) ceremonial organization and ritual, and (3) specimens for the museum. Only one publication resulted, the extensive and excellent collection of Arikara traditions that Dorsey published under his own name in 1904. However, Murie also left with the Field Museum a collection of 22 sets of notes, which vary in length: some are only a half or a single (legal sized) page description of a specimen, name, or ceremony, while others run up to 10 or more pages describing in considerable detail the ritual or origin of a ceremony or bundle. Two of the manuscripts are notes on societies and dances. As a collection the notes are uneven in quality; some do not give enough detail to be of much use, but others provide rich detail on ritual practices. The largest manuscript, *Societies and Dances*, is not impressive, showing quite clearly that Murie did not fully understand Arikara socio-religious structure. However, the notes are valuable because of the ethnographic "pieces" he recorded. For example, Murie corroborates the existence among the Arikara of several societies that had been reported in earlier accounts but which Lowie (1915) was unable to confirm. The same assessment holds for the entire collection: as a self-contained entity they do not provide a coherent description of Arikara socio-religous structure, but as material supplementing other accounts they are invaluable. The reason for this, of course, is that the Arikara received scant attention from modern ethnographers. (The only individuals to contribute significantly to the study of Arikara culture have been Edward Curtis, Melvin Gilmore, Robert Lowie, and George Will; and of these only Gilmore did extensive field work. All, however, including Gilmore, published only on selected topics.) Hence Murie, because of his collection of myths as well as the unpublished ethnographic notes, must be recognized as one of the major contributors to the study of this tribe, as well as his own.

CONCLUSION

Throughout his adult life in Oklahoma, Murie was active in both tribal and community affairs. He accompanied Pawnee delegations to Washington on tribal business, and he was, as we have indicated above, usually involved in various tribal matters. In 1915 he was elected president of the Indian Farmers' Institute in Pawnee. In addition to being a member of the Episcopal Church, he was also a faithful member of the local Masonic Lodge and was a Noble of the Mystic Shrine in Tulsa.

Little is known about Murie, the man, or what he was like personally. Most of those who knew him intimately are deceased now. However, in the course of my own field work in Oklahoma during the past decade, I have discussed Murie with older Pawnees, several of whom are related to him. In these reminiscences he was clearly perceived by them as an educated man who had served his people—one who had compiled a record of Pawnee life and religion as experienced over a century ago and now long forgotten. One elderly lady also fondly remembered him as "a big tease." He liked to joke and laugh. His daughter-in-law, who had lived in the Murie household for several years, has added that he had a distinctively attractive personality—that, in fact, "he could charm a snake off a hot rock."

In 1887 he married Mary Esau. They had eight children; but only four survived to be adults, the others dying in infancy or childhood. In 1919, after nearly 30 years with Mary, he divorced her to marry Josephine Walking Sun, daughter of Old Lady Washington, keeper of one of the Morning Star bundles. He moved into the Washington home and lived there until his death. He had two children by Josephine, one of them a girl named Viola Wissler Murie after the wife of Clark Wissler, who died before she was two years old.

Murie's work is both unpublished and published, the latter under his own name as well as that of others. The published work included three volumes of mythology published by Dorsey (1904a, 1904b, 1906c), the *Notes on Skiri Society* edited by Spoehr (1940), and the paper on societies done with Wissler (1921). The unpublished material, which is extensive, includes the collection of ethnographic notes at the Field Museum and the Smithsonian's *Ceremonies* manuscript. In addition, Murie is in part responsible for many of the Pawnee ethnographic notes of Alice Fletcher that are in the National Anthropological Archives.

Murie's education was minimal, and his analytic work insignificant. Yet he collected a massive corpus of data over three decades upon which all students of Pawnee and Arikara ethnology have relied heavily—and of which full advantage has not yet been taken. The unpublished notes, together with the other materials (published and manuscript) on Pawnee religion and ethnography, constitute a rich source for further, more sophisticated work—for what one might reasonably term "ethnographic philology"—as well as related topics. Viewing this work as a whole one can only conclude that Murie's contribution was monumental; and that it is time he received the recognition he deserves.

ACKNOWLEDGMENTS

The primary sources for Murie's early life are newspaper articles by and about him. These appear in various issues of the *Southern Workman* (Hampton Normal and Agricultural Institute, Hampton, Virginia), beginning in 1883 and extending through 1903. Two short biographical sketches appear in *Twenty-two Years' Work of the Hampton Normal and Agricultural Institute* (Hampton, 1893). Another sketch appears in Volume 2 of *The Booker T. Washington Papers*, Louis R. Harlan, ed. (Urbana 1973). Short clippings of varying value about activities of Murie during his school years and later in life appear in the following publications: *American Missionary*, *Indian Leader*, *Red Man and His Helper*, *The Indian Friend*, *Native American*, *Arrow*, *Indian School Journal*, and *Carrier Pigeon*.

For the period of his work with anthropologists, information has come primarily from correspondence. The Field Museum of Natural History has various ethnographic notes, and a small set of letters between Murie and George A. Dorsey. The American Museum of Natural History has an extensive file of Murie-Wissler correspondence as well as letters between Wissler and the Bureau of American Ethnology dealing with Murie's work and the manuscript. The National Anthropological Archives, Smithsonian Institution, has various ethnographic notes, and important sets of correspondence between Alice C. Fletcher and Murie, and Murie and the Bureau. In addition, it has copies of letters between the Bureau and Gene Weltfish, while the latter had the manuscript in the field and was retranscribing the linguistic material in it.

The following *Annual Reports* of the Bureau of American Ethnology contain brief mention of Murie's activities while he worked under the Bureau's auspices: 32nd (1910–1911); 34th (1912–1913); 36th (1914–1915); 37th (1915–1916); and 41st (1919–1924).

An obituary for Murie appeared on the front page of the *Pawnee Democrat* (Pawnee, Oklahoma), November 24, 1921. Additional information on his life came from his daughter-in-law, Mrs. Constance Murie, Pawnee, Oklahoma, during an interview in October 1973.

My interest in Murie's life and anthropological work began when I was editing his manuscript *Ceremonies of the Pawnee* in preparation for its publication. Work on the manuscript and his biography was pursued during 1973–74 while I held a post-doctoral fellowship at the Smithsonian Institution. I wish to express my appreciation to the staff of the Department of Anthropology at the Smithsonian for a stimulating environment and innumerable services during my tenure there. In addition to the sources given above, I have profited from discussions with Dr. John C. Ewers, Dr. Alexander Lesser, and Dr. Waldo Wedel. Mrs. Constance Murie graciously provided me with biographical information on and reminiscences of her husband's father, giving above all a human touch to the man. The following institutions generously provided copies of Murie correspondence: the National Anthropological Archives, Smithsonian Institution; the American Museum of Natural History; and the Field Museum of Natural History. Mr. Fritz Malval, archivist at Hampton Institute, Hampton, Virginia, supplied me with copies of that school's file on Murie, which includes articles written by Murie for the school paper when he was a student, letters which he wrote back to his former teachers, and newspaper clippings reporting on his activities after leaving school.

NOTES

1. In all of his publications on the Pawnee and Arikara, Dorsey listed only himself as author and acknowledged Murie's indispensable aid merely by an introductory sentence or two (cf., prefaces to 1904a, 1904b, 1906d). This was inadequate acknowledgement of Murie's actual role in most of the publications, especially in the case of the volumes of traditions. As Dorsey admits, Murie secured and wrote down nearly all of the material while he simply edited it. Spoehr (1940) is more accurate in listing both Dorsey and Murie as authors of *Notes on Skidi Pawnee Society*. Linton, however, was most guilty of publishing under his own name the work of another. He had never done any field work among the Pawnee, nor did he ever work with Murie. Yet in his Pawnee publications he listed himself as sole author, despite having drawn almost exclusively from Murie's and Dorsey's notes, frequently verbatim. In none of the publications does he acknowledge Murie; although in four of them (1922a, 1922b, 1923a,

1923b) he states that his description is compiled from Dorsey's unpublished notes!

2. There are some 200 cylinders of recorded Pawnee texts and 501 cylinders of both Pawnee and Arikara songs. Most of the song material has been transcribed onto master tapes, but the textual material remains only on the cylinders.

3. The cylinders, of which 96 remain, were transferred from the Bureau of American Ethnology to the Archives of Folk Song of the Library of Congress. The music has been transcribed onto master tapes, but unfortunately the sound quality is so poor as to render the music virtually useless for scholarly purposes.

4. In the early 1930s Gene Weltfish, then a graduate at Columbia University, retranscribed and retranslated the entire set of song texts with the help of Pawnee informants.

LITERATURE CITED

Dorsey, George A.

1902 One of the Sacred Altars of the Pawnee. In International Congress of Americanists, 13th Proceedings. Pp. 67–74. New York.

1903 How the Pawnee Captured the Cheyenne Medicine Arrows. American Anthropologist 5:644–658.

1904a Traditions of the Skidi Pawnee. American Folk-Lore Society, Memoirs, 8. Boston and New York: Houghton, Mifflin.

1904b Traditions of the Arikara. Washington: Carnegie Institution.

1905 A Pawnee Ritual of Instruction. Pp. 350–353. In Boas Anniversary Volume. Berthold Laufer, ed. New York: G. E. Stechert.

1906a Pawnee War Tales. American Anthropologist 8:337–345.

1906b Social organization of the Skidi Pawnee. Pp. 71–77. In International Congress of Americanists, 15th Proceedings. Quebec.

1906c The Pawnee: Mythology. Washington: Carnegie Institution.

1906d The Skidi Rite of Human Sacrifice. Pp. 65–70. In International Congress of Americanists, 15th Proceedings. Quebec.

Fletcher, Alice C.

1899 A Pawnee Ritual Used When Changing a Man's Name. American Anthropologist 1:82–97.

1900 Giving Thanks: a Pawnee Ceremony. Journal of American Folk-Lore 13:261–266.

1902 Star Cult among the Pawnee: A Preliminary Report. American Anthropologist 4:730–736.

1903 Pawnee Star Lore. Journal of American Folk-Lore 16:10–15.

1904 The Hako: A Pawnee Ceremony. 22nd Annual Report of the Bureau of American Ethnology. Washington: Smithsonian Institution.

Hampton Normal and Agricultural Institute
1893 Twenty-two Years' Work of the Hampton Normal and Agricultural Institute. Hampton, Virginia: Hampton Institute.

Harlan, Louis R., ed.
1973 The Booker T. Washington Papers. 2 Vols. Urbana: University of Illinois Press.

Linton, Ralph
1922a The Sacrifice to the Morning Star by the Skidi Pawnee Department of Anthropology, Leaflet 6. Chicago: Field Museum of Natural History.

1922b The Thunder Ceremony of the Pawnee. Department of Anthropology, Leaflet 7. Chicago: Field Museum of Natural History.

1923a Annual Ceremony of the Pawnee Medicine Men. Department of Anthropology, Leaflet 8. Chicago: Field Museum of Natural History.

1923b Purification of the Sacred Bundles: A Ceremony of the Pawnee. Department of Anthropology, Leaflet 7. Chicago: Field Museum of Natural History.

1926 The Origin of the Skidi Pawnee Sacrifice to the Morning Star. American Anthropologist 28:457–466.

Murie, James R.
1902a Pawnee Ethnographic and Linguistic Notes. Unpublished. Box A1-2, Anthropological Archives. Chicago: Field Museum of Natural History.

1902b Arikara Ethnographic Notes. Unpublished. Box A-15, Anthropological Archives. Chicago: Field Museum of Natural History.

1914 Pawnee Indian Societies. Anthropological Papers 11:543–644. New York: American Museum of Natural History.

1921 Ceremonies of the Pawnee. Clark Wissler, ed. Manuscript 2520, National Anthropological Archives, Smithsonian Institution.

1940 Notes on Skidi Pawnee Society. With George A. Dorsey. Alexander Spoehr, ed. Anthropological Series 27:67–119. Chicago: Field Museum of Natural History.

Spoehr, Alexander, ed.

1940 Notes on Skidi Pawnee Society, by George A. Dorsey and James R. Murie. Anthropological Series 27:67–119. Chicago: Field Museum of Natural History.

Wissler, Clark, ed.

1921 Ceremonies of the Pawnee. Manuscript 2520, National Anthropological Archives, Smithsonian Institution.

CHAPTER SEVEN

GEORGE BUSHOTTER THE FIRST LAKOTA ETHNOGRAPHER[1]

Teton Sioux, 1864–1892

RAYMOND J. DeMALLIE

George Bushotter was a Lakota Indian born in 1864 in Dakota Territory, in a camp on the Moreau River at its confluence with the Missouri.[2] He died twenty-eight years later, on February 2, 1892, in Hedgesville, West Virginia. During his lifetime he participated in the traditional Lakota life, traveled east and became a student in the White man's schools, studied to become a minister, worked as a teacher for the Bureau of Indian Affairs, and married a White woman of West Virginia. He also became the first Lakota to write an account of his own people in their own language. This work was done under the guidance of James Owen Dorsey of the Smithsonian's Bureau of Ethnology, and although Bushotter spent less than a year at it, his pioneer efforts in describing the Lakota way of life entitle him to be remembered as the first Lakota ethnographer.

George Bushotter was the son of a Yankton man and his wife Grey Whirlwind, a Minneconjou Lakota. His father had two wives who were jealous of one another. When Bushotter was born the other wife, a Winnebago woman, was furious with jealousy and came to Bushotter's mother's tent with a large knife. Grey Whirlwind hid her baby behind the dew cloth in the tipi, between it and the tipi wall. The Winnebago woman came to the lodge in a furor, slashing the tipi with her knife, cutting it to pieces. As she came to where the baby was hidden, Bushotter's father stepped forward and saved the boy at the last moment. In commemoration of the trouble that women caused for him, the father named his son *Oteri*, meaning "trouble."[3]

Bushotter tells us that the name was meant to symbolize the trouble that he would meet with throughout his life.

This unpropitious beginning marked Bushotter for a special life, one different from those of his brothers and sisters. When he was yet very small, just beginning to walk, Oteri one day counted coup on a bird. The boy was crawling around on the ground and managed to catch a little fledgling. He held it in his hands and made it chirp by squeezing it. His mother took the bird from him just as he was about to put it in his mouth. This was another sign that Oteri was set apart. The people said that he had no respect for anything, and would probably grow up to be a medicine man. As the boy grew, further signs of his special power were seen. He would pull moles out of their holes—a dangerous action since moles were known to be the cause of scrofula—and he had no fear of snakes. Yet his improper behavior towards sacred things brought no supernatural vengeance on him, and the people were more and more convinced that he would become a medicine man.

While Bushotter was still a small boy, his family was traveling down the Missouri to the Yankton country, and his father was killed by White men. His mother swore that she would never follow the ways of Whites. A deep fear of White men impressed itself on Bushotter, but at the same time a kind of curiosity was aroused as well.

Grey Whirlwind remarried, this time a man from Lower Brule reservation named Amos Goodroad. The family spent part of the time at the agency, and part of the time traveling about.

Bushotter was brought up to be a warrior. He wrote, "My whole preoccupation was to be brave" (Bushotter 1887:No. 101). Lectures from his father and his mother both enjoined him to be brave, to be a man. His father believed that there would inevitably be war between the U. S. Army and the Lakota, and he wanted his sons to be ready. Bushotter remarked that he longed to go to war against other Indian groups, but that his father always restrained him and told him to wait until he was older.

Bushotter tells us that when he was a small boy he used to cry easily, undoubtedly another sign that he was different from other boys. One technique that his parents used to stop his crying was to have someone put on a cap with a visor and suddenly poke his head into the tent. Bushotter's parents would cry, "There's a White man; he has come to take you away!" Bushotter wrote that at that time he hoped he would never have to meet up with even a single White man, and that he would shake with fear at the thought of them.

Despite the fear, the curiosity about Whites continued. The boy learned about money from Whites who gave him nickels which his mother used to buy him candy at the agency store. He used to wonder about all the things of the White man, how they were made, and what they were used for. He later wrote "I grew up in dark ignorance" (Bushotter 1887:No. 101).

Some of Bushotter's mother's brothers were among the first Lakota to attend school. They told the family that if the children would dress like Whites, they would fare better later on when the land became full of White people. Bushotter told his father that he might like to adopt White man's dress in order that he might live long and be prosperous. But his father was set against it. Bushotter remembered his father's warning. "White men do nasty things," he would say. "And they eat vile things, and act foolish, and they could suddenly cause your death" (Bushotter 1887:No. 101).

But the desire to emulate his uncles was strong. Whenever Bushotter came across a pair of shoes he would put them on and wear them home, no matter how large, and pretend to be speaking English, much to the merriment of his family. Once he took some newspaper and folded it up many times, cut it down in size, and sewed it together to look like a book. He was proud of it, even though as he later said the type ran in every direction. He kept it a long time, and would pretend to be reading English from it, making a sound like water gurgling in his mouth.

When he was fifteen Bushotter heard that a boat was traveling down the Missouri to take children to school and he wanted to join them. He later told the story to a newspaper man as follows (Document 10):

> As I grew older I began to join in the boyish games and my father pointed me out with no little pride as a youngster destined to be a credit to his race. He wanted me to be like my brother, who is a respectable man among Indians. He has killed thirty men, and has had about as many wives. These constitute the Indian title to respectability. It would not do among white people, would it? I know I regarded my brother with admiration and wanted to be like him, but fate had a better career in store for me. I attracted the attention of some white people, and it was suggested that I should go East and be educated. Such a goodly picture of life among the civilized was painted for me that I longed to try it. My father and mother loved me very dearly and were loath to part with me. . . . After some parleying it was decided that my sister and I should go East. We were warned against the white people. They were pictured to us as an inferior race, made of rags and refuse, while the Indian was the real man. My father told me that they would be cruel to me, give me things out of the water to eat, and do other things calculated to

> cause our death. Well, we came East and went to the school at Hampton. Up to that time, I had dressed as an Indian, painted my face and wore feathers. The only English word I knew was bread. A very useful one, it is true. My sister longed for her home, and soon withered and died. Father and mother both believed that her death was the result of cruelty.

When the boy arrived at Hampton Institute in Virginia his name was recorded as George Bush, Oteri, giving both his English and Lakota Names. However, the names soon became amalgamated by the school officials into Bushotter—hence the unusual name (Hampton Institute 1893:340). He kept it throughout his life, signing his name as George Bushotter, Oteri.

Bushotter entered school at Hampton in 1878 and stayed there until 1881. He was enthusiastic in learning and made good progress. In 1881 he spent a year as an assistant teacher in the boarding school at Lower Brule and was reported to have done well. He got together with a large party of children and brought them to Hampton during the winter of 1882–1883. After one more year at Hampton he returned home for a short visit. He then decided to return east and entered the Theological Seminary of Virginia in the fall of 1885 with the idea of becoming a minister and returning to help his people. Although he seems to have been diligent in his studies, Bushotter's inadequate English made the study of Latin and Greek impossible and in the spring of 1887 he gave up his study of theology at the advice of the faculty (Hampton Institute 1893:340).

During these years the Reverend James Owen Dorsey, the great Siouan scholar, was resident in Washington as a member of the Bureau of Ethnology. Dorsey apparently met Bushotter at Hampton, and since he himself was a graduate of the Theological Seminary of Virginia, it seems likely that it was Dorsey who encouraged him to study there. When Bushotter left the seminary he was financially destitute, and hoping to earn money to continue his education later, he appealed to Dorsey for help. Dorsey had previously brought Indians from the West to Washington to work on linguistic studies and could readily see the potential value of Bushotter to the science of ethnology. Dorsey's own work on the Omaha language had been interrupted by the demand from J. W. Powell that he take over the editing of Stephen Return Riggs' grammar and dictionary of Dakota. Dorsey decided that Bushotter would be valuable in contributing comparative data in the Lakota dialect.

Powell was out of town, so on March 19, 1887, Dorsey wrote to him to propose hiring Bushotter to help in three areas: providing comparative

Teton linguistic forms for Riggs' Dakota dictionary, writing myths and other texts in Lakota, and helping Dorsey prepare the synonomy of Dakota tribal names that was part of the original project which later developed into the *Handbook of American Indians North of Mexico* (Hodge, ed., 1907, 1910). Dorsey proposed that Bushotter be paid $1.50 per day (9 a.m. to 4 p.m.) (Document 2). Powell wired back to J. C. Pilling, his chief clerk, on March 22, "Let Dorsey have the Teton" (Document 3).

Bushotter began work at the Bureau on March 23 and from both his and Dorsey's point of view the work was very successful. Bushotter began by writing a myth in Lakota. He then read it carefully to Dorsey who used red ink to correct and refine the phonetics and to indicate stress. Then using Riggs' dictionary as a reference, they worked out a word-for-word interlinear translation, and a free translation. Bushotter must have felt in a creative mood, for the pages continued to flow from his pen in his large, somewhat irregular, but extremely legible handwriting. Dorsey was able to turn his attention to other projects, and let Bushotter continue writing alone.

As spring advanced toward summer, the heat and humidity of Washington and the windowless room in which Dorsey and Bushotter worked together with other members of the Bureau began to wear on Dorsey's fragile health. His doctor ordered him to leave the city and accordingly Dorsey decided to go with his family to his wife's parents' home at Hedgesville, in the mountains of West Virginia, and to take Bushotter with him. On April 1887, Dorsey wrote to his wife, already at Hedgesville (Document 4):

> Bushotter has finished his 75th story. . . . I wish to know if I could get board for him in Hedgesville after June 1st, and at what rate. Please find out. Here he pays $5 a month for a room and from $12 to $15 for meals. He is very polite and gentlemanly, refined but not fastidious, and would not be troublesome anywhere.

Dorsey wrote to Powell on May 5th asking permission to take Bushotter to Hedgesville after June 1. "There we can work in a room by ourselves (impossible at the office), and I am sure that we can accomplish as much there in one day, as we have been doing here in two." (Document 5)

On June 1 Bushotter and Dorsey left Washington on the 3:15 train to Hedgesville (Document 1). They worked together there throughout the summer, and established excellent rapport. Dorsey wrote to Powell on June 11 and reported that he had been able to convince Bushotter to add material to three of the myths he had written that he had previously omitted as unfit to be made public. He was enthusiastic about Bushotter's scholarship and suggested to Powell that he ought to be retained by the Bureau as an interpreter and even asked if it would not be possible to send him out to the Lakota to collect more myths and other cultural data (Document 6).

While in Hedgesville Bushotter stayed at the boarding house owned by Jacob Hull, an important man in the town and the father of three unmarried daughters. Before Bushotter returned to Washington on October 26 he had become engaged to the eldest daughter, Evalina Hull. She was several years older than he, and the circumstances of the engagement are now unknown. Dorsey himself did not approve of the match, but Bushotter seems to have made himself very popular in the small town, and the local people readily accepted him.

There is no doubt that Bushotter took his work very seriously, and Dorsey wrote that he enjoyed it (Document 6). They continued their collaboration throughout the fall. A newspaper reporter came to interview Bushotter and produced a long article entitled "A Gentlemanly Savage at the Smithsonian." The reporter says of Bushotter (Document 10):

> The civilizing process through which he has gone has taught him to smile at these stories which, when a lad, he learned from his father's lips in awesome silence. He is giving away secrets at a most surprising rate, and is furnishing the data for a work that would net him a handsome amount, if placed in the hands of a private publisher. Bushotter is a very gentlemanly young man, and his intelligence wins for him the admiration of his associates.

The reporter also remarked that Bushotter intended to return to his people to join their secret societies, "for the purpose of telling the world all about them."

Yet after his engagement to Miss Hull it appears that Bushotter was no longer content to stay in Washington. Dorsey noted in his diary on December 22, 1887, "Bushotter 'resigned'" (Document 1). It was suggested that he had so neglected his work that he was discharged (Hampton Institute 1893:341). The facts in the matter are no longer known.

Bushotter's career as an ethnographer came to a close ten months after it began. He had finished writing 258 stories, a total of 3,296 handwritten pages. In the newspaper interview he characterized his writing as follows (Document 10):

> The stories I am writing will for the first time give an authentic statement of my tribes and their foundations. I take up everything from the games of the boys and the girls to the religious beliefs. I think, judging from the profound ignorance of the white people of all matters concerning the Indian, that the work will be both inter-

esting and instructive.

It is unfortunate that Bushotter did not continue to write about his people. Perhaps he did, but if he left any papers they have not been located.

Bushotter's health was never good after coming east to school. His return to Lower Brule in 1881 was due to poor health. While working for Dorsey he wrote at least three letters asking to be excused because of illness. The first of these, dated July 26, 1887, was submitted to Dorsey in Lakota, with an interlinear and free translation, all in Bushotter's hand. Bushotter's translation reads (Document 7):

> My friend: I was not feeling very well last night, and I did not sleep well at all. and now this morning I want to take a knape. Friend my eyes are also troubles me. These are the reasons I ask you to have mercy on me. Bushotter.

The second letter was August 2, informing Dorsey that he had just learned of his elder brother's death, and had been unable to sleep because of it (Document 8). The third letter was December 9, complaining of weakness and dizziness (Document 9).

Bushotter married Evalina Hull on March 8, 1888. He was financially destitute and had on January 7 written asking for a teaching position in one of the government Indian schools (Document 10). On March 17 he wrote to the Commissioner of Indian Affairs again, in reply to a letter offering him a job as a teacher at the Fort Stevenson Indian School in North Dakota. In the letter he says that he moved to the country because he could live there more cheaply than in the city, and does not mention his marriage. His desire to teach Indian children seems to have been very real and very strong, just as his desire to record his people's way of life had been. But the two were diametrically opposed. Bushotter wrote to the Commissioner (Document 11).

> I know this is a great work because the teacher must have a good moral character and a tact in management of the children. And I must do what is right every day before the children as well as the people. I shall obey and do all I can before God and men. I shall teach them nothing but the English language according to your order to the Agents and teachers, in regard to the education of the Indian children which I believe to be the right. This is my idea about teaching the Indian children.

The improvement in Bushotter's writing was doubtless owing to judicious editing by his wife-to-be.

March 27, 1888, Bushotter left Hedgesville and his bride to take the position in North Dakota. But after he began his work at the Fort Stevenson school he got on the wrong side of the school superintendent, George W. Scott. The latter accused Bushotter of taking female students into his room, of being disagreeable to fellow employees, of loafing in the kitchen, of being deficient in scholarship, and being generally a troublemaker. But probably the worst charge was the first one that he levelled against Bushotter (Document 12):

> He is a Sioux Indian, and is constantly talking his language to the pupils, and learning the Arickaree language from them.

In the world from which he had just come such ethnographic efforts were highly laudable; in the Indian school system they were anathema. In February 1889, Bushotter resigned. Later he wrote a statement that Superintendent Scott was cruel; that he on one occasion gave a male student a black eye, knocking him down with his fist and kicking him out of the school room; that he drank to intoxication, was profane and abusive in his language, an infidel without interest in the moral welfare of the students, and dishonest in his use of government property. In the Indian Office the statement was simply marked "File" (Document 15).

In his letter of resignation Bushotter asked that he and his wife be jointly assigned to a school among the Sioux (Document 13). In August 1889, they visited Captain R. H. Pratt, in charge of the Carlisle Indian Training School, to enlist his aid. This time they asked to be sent to the Southwest, probably because of Bushotter's declining health (Document 14). Finally, in November of 1889 the Bushotters were offered a day school on the Rosebud reservation but were forced on account of George's health to refuse (Document 16). He had consumption, and was under the care of a Hedgesville physician. He lived only a little more than two years longer. After his death on February 2, 1892, the pastor of the Episcopal church of Hedgesville said of him (Hampton Institute 1893:341):

> He was devoted to his people, and, although suffering repeatedly from hemorrhage of the lungs, he hoped to live to benefit them. He was industrious and worked at cabinet making, showing great skill and talent in designing and in execution as a carver of wood. A leading trait of character, at least in his last days, was a gratitude and thankfulness for any and every kindness and attention shown him.

Mrs. Bushotter outlived her husband by fifty years, filed her claim for his allotment at Lower Brule, but spent the remainder of her days in

Hedgesville, loyal to Bushotter's memory. In 1968 Bushotter was still remembered in Hedgesville—vague memories persisted of his jogging around the town in the early morning, wearing his beaded moccasins, and of his teaching archery to the local boys. And there were more tangible memories: some of his woodworking still survives.

Bushotter's ethnographic material has suffered a fate not unlike that of Bushotter himself. Dorsey published much of the material in translation or paraphrase, but he never completed editing the manuscripts for publication, for he died prematurely himself in 1895. For many years thereafter Franz Boas was interested in seeing the Bushotter material published. In 1899 he had his student John R. Swanton working on it; he made a field trip to South Dakota to revise the texts (Document 18). During the 1930s Boas had Ella Deloria prepare a new translation, but in 1936 he declared the Bushotter texts "linguistically disappointing" and unworthy of publication (Document 17). Several other scholars worked with the collection since then, and all gave up on publishing it.

The Bushotter texts are a very diffuse body of material, unorganized, with a feeling of incompleteness about them. Yet they are important, not only because they are the first material contributed by a Lakota, but also because they are a first-hand interpretation of Lakota culture. Viewed as rough drafts for a book never completed, they provide a personal view of Sioux culture that is comparable in scope to Ella Deloria's *Speaking of Indians* (1944), Charles Eastman's *The Soul of the Indian* (1911), *Black Elk Speaks* (Neihardt 1932), Luther Standing Bear's *Land of the Spotted Eagle* (1933), and even Amos Bad Heart Bull's *Pictographic History of the Oglala Sioux* (1968).

A rough classification of the subject matter of the Bushotter texts can be made as follows:[4]

Classification	No. of Texts	No. of Pages
Myths and Legends	95	1,046
Games	70	756
Social Customs	36	526
Ceremonies	7	291
Societies and Dances	14	211
Autobiographical	5	186
War Stories	19	163
Ghost Stories	10	91
Material Culture	2	26
Total	258	3,296

In addition, seventeen of the stories are illustrated with a total of 41 drawings and sketches in pencil, colored pencil, and ink.

Bushotter's manuscript pages have at least 30 Lakota words per page, for a total of perhaps 90,000 words.

Most modern anthropologists have found these texts to be of minimal utility. On the whole, the ethnographic details recorded by Bushotter were also recorded later by professional anthropologists, as were his myths, legends, and stories. But the most valuable portion of the collection, its heart, are those texts that I have called social customs and autobiographical, some 700 pages. Edited and integrated in a fashion that neither Bushotter nor Dorsey envisioned, they would form an interpretive ethnography of Lakota social life, an ethnography organized around basic themes that I interpret as those values which Bushotter saw as most distinctive in his traditional culture, setting it apart from White America.

The first question to ask in interpreting this material is the reason for which it was written. Money was certainly one reason, but the amount of profit in it was slight. It had been Bushotter's own idea to write these texts; Dorsey did little by way of encouraging him in his subject matter. This is what makes the collection so valuable. He wrote (Bushotter 1887: No. 225):

> I have done my part, what little I know about my people—as our thought and deeds should be written in books that they may be preserved and known in future.

Bushotter was not trying to preserve his people's culture for purposes of action. Nor was he attempting to put any of his Lakota values into practice in his life as a White man. He repudiated many of the Lakota customs, and expressed disbelief in the traditional religious concepts of the Lakota. His was definitely an assimilationist philosophy. In his autobiography he wrote (Bushotter 1887: No. 101):

> My friends, I grew up in a bad manner, in darkness. . . . The good that your God and my God has done for me, I thank him very much, and I wish that I might live according to his ways. My life has been filled with troubles and suffering, but I believe in him. As the country becomes better, and wise, so too will the Lakota people grow. If the Lakota will, they too can learn to do the things that the white men do. I think that in the future they will live only according to the white man's way.

The record that Bushotter made was an unbiased one, a recording of a quickly passing way of life for the enlightenment of posterity—a purpose that approximates the traditional meaning of the word "ethnography." With encouragement from Dorsey that it was proper to do so, Bushotter even recorded matters of esoteric or sexual nature, thus making a record of all aspects of Lakota life. From Bushotter's point of view, both the good and the bad were fairly recorded.

The major theme around which Bushotter's interpretation centers is the cultural duality of men and women. Bushotter's father put it thus (Bushotter 1887: No. 101): "Only women have weak hearts, but it is proper that men should have hearts like stone!" Over and over again the emphasis is on bravery, the bravery of men which is defined by contrast with women. Again, quoting from Bushotter's autobiography (Bushotter 1887: No. 101):

> My father continually gave us good advice. . . . He made us train wild horses. He taught us to have strong hearts for war. My father made me especially do many difficult things. My father told me to practice with the bow. . . . He told me to think about the things I would do on the warpath. "Son, a man who lives desiring to do difficult things will be very brave. He who is brave becomes famous, but he who is foolish, his name also becomes famous." When I was afraid of something they would say "No, no, my son, you are a man!" And when I hurt myself and cried my father would say, "Why my son is brave! He will pay no attention to his hurt! This is what I used to think, but now I see that my son will be a *winkte* (hermaphrodite)! . . . Come on! If you are unable to flee from the enemy by swimming among cakes of floating ice, or if you are unable to charge the enemy, from that very time you must dress like a woman and live like a foolish woman. . . ."

Bushotter traces this complementary duality of male and female throughout the kinship system, writing of the circumspect behavior between brothers and sisters and between men and their mothers-in-law; telling of women who hanged themselves in shame for the actions of their brothers; of man-crazy women who became harlots; and of adultery and its punishments. Gang rape as a symbol of Lakota men's pent-up hostility towards women is a recurring theme. The avaricious sexual appetite of women is another such theme. In his writing Bushotter neither praises nor condemns the Lakota way that he is interpreting, but presents it as merely the way things are, a philosophical positivism that rivals that of nineteenth century anthropologists.

If bravery in terms of the sexual duality is the major theme, bravery in terms of White men is the minor. Bushotter gives much insight into the

Lakotas' views of Whites. He gives a genuine feeling for the "mysterious" (*wakan*) quality exuded by Whites. He recalls the first time he entered a church and saw people standing around an organ; he interprets the box as the home of a sacred being, the music as its singing, and understands the people to be worshipping it. When he returns he is told that this is the house of God; immediately he starts looking around for him. The people tell him that this house is a place for prayer. The Lakota term is chekiya which has at least three different meanings: to pray, to cry out (beg), or to address someone formally by kinship term (thus honoring them and likely asking for a favor). He interprets the church in the latter sense and assumes that the church service will consist of everyone present shaking hands and calling each other by the terms of their kin relationships. He remembers asking his mother, as a small boy, of what use the White man's houses could be, and how they managed to move them around when they broke camp. He recalls his own fear on his first trip east that whatever was pulling the train along the track would eventually tire, leaving them stranded. He remembers that as a child he could not believe that the strange things of the White man were actually man-made. Remarking on his first trip east he wrote (Bushotter 1887: No. 101): "Whatever I saw for the first time, I could not know, and thought that it was not possible to understand it; all I did was marvel the whole way."

These data of the meeting of two life ways are very scarce in the written record, especially from the Indians' point of view, and Bushotter has preserved some valuable insights into the minds of the late nineteenth-century Lakota.

Bushotter's writings speak for themselves and must be read to be appreciated. They are a treasure house of data, long neglected by anthropologists. They remain as a fitting memorial to a man who made a heroic effort to overcome cultural and racial differences in an age when these presented more difficulty than they do in our own, but whose reward was a fatal disease contracted in the East that ended his career almost before it had begun. The great granite monument erected by his wife in the Hedgesville cemetery that depicts columns draped in mourning, emblazoned with the name BUSHOTTER, is a cold and oddly inappropriate memorial. His real monument is his writing, his enduring contribution to understanding between the Indian and White races.

NOTES

1. This paper grows out of a long interest in Bushotter and his association with J. Owen Dorsey. The writer is collecting material for a biogra-

phy of Dorsey and intends to edit the Bushotter texts for eventual publication. Special thanks are due to Virginia L. Maclean, Dorsey's granddaughter, for generously providing Dorsey's personal papers.

2. Unless otherwise noted, all biographical data on Bushotter are taken from his autobiography (Bushotter 1887: No. 101). Quotations from Bushotter's texts are free translations based on Dorsey's interlinear translation (in Bushotter 1887) and Ella C. Deloria's free translation (Deloria 1936). Information on Bushotter in Hedgesville was obtained by interview there in 1968.

3. *Otehi*, "difficulty" (h = unvoiced velar fricative).

4. A listing of the texts is found in DeMallie 1970.

DOCUMENT LIST

Abbreviations:

	BAE	Bureau of (American) Ethnology
	CIA	Commissioner of Indian Affairs
	LR	Letters Received
	NA	National Archives
	NAA	National Anthropological Archives, Smithsonian Institution
	RG	Record Group
1	1/87–12/87	J. O. Dorsey personal diary. Author's collection.
2	3/19/87	J. O. Dorsey, BAE, to J. W. Powell. NAA, BAE-LR.
3	3/22/87	J. W. Powell to J. O. Dorsey, telegram. NAA, BAE-LR.
4	4/18/87	J. O. Dorsey to V. Dorsey. Author's collection.
5	5/5/87	J. O. Dorsey to J. W. Powell. NAA, BAE-LR.
6	6/11/87	J. O. Dorsey to J. W. Powell. NAA, BAE-LR.
7	7/26/87	G. Bushotter to J. O. Dorsey. NAA, Ms. no. 4800.
8	8/2/87	G. Bushotter to J. O. Dorsey. NAA, Ms. no. 4800.
9	12/9/87	G. Bushotter to J. O. Dorsey. NAA, Ms. no. 4800.
10	1/9/88	H. R. Dawson, Bureau of Education, to CIA, enclosing letter from G. Bushotter, Hedgesville, to Dawson, 1/7/88, with newsclipping "Indian Life. A gentlemanly Savage at the Smithsonian" from *The Capital*, Washington, D.C., n.d. NA, RG 75, CIA-LR, 1888-829.
11	3/17/88	G. Bushotter, Hedgesville, to CIA. NA, RG 75, CIA-LR 1888-7438.
12	1/8/89	G. W. Scott, Superintendent, Fort Stevenson School, to CIA. NA, RG 75, CIA-LR 1889-1725.
13	2/3/89	G. Bushotter, Fort Stevenson, to S. H. Albro. NA, RG 75, CIA-LR 1889-3578.

14	9/13/89	R. H. Pratt, Superintendent, Carlisle Indian School, to CIA, enclosing letters from G. Bushotter, Hedgesville, to Pratt 8/29/89 and L. Bushotter, Hedgesville, to Pratt 8/29/89. NA, RG 75, CIA-LR 1889-25846.
15	10/14/89	G. Bushotter affidavit making charges against G. W. Scott. NA, RG 75, CIA-LR 1889-29359.
16	11/13/89	G. Bushotter, Hedgesville, to CIA. NA, RG 75, CIA-LR 1889-32811.
17	10/30/36	F. Boas, Columbia University, to Matthew W. Stirling, BAE. NAA, BAE-LR.
18	ca. 1950	J. R. Swanton, "Notes Regarding my Adventures in Anthropology and with Anthropologists." NAA, Ms. no. 4651.

LITERATURE CITED

Bad Heart Bull, Amos
1968 A Pictographic History of the Oglala Sioux. Lincoln, Neb.: University of Nebraska Press.

Bushotter, George
1887 (Texts in Lakota). National Anthropological Archives, Smithsonian Institution, Ms. no. 4800.

Deloria, Ella C.
1936 (Translation of the Bushotter Teton Texts). American Philosophical Society, Ms. no. 30(X8a.15).

1944 Speaking of Indians. New York: Friendship Press.

DeMallie, Raymond J.
1970 A Partial Bibliography of Archival Manuscript Material Relating to the Dakota. Pp. 312–343. In Ethel Nurge, ed., The Modern Sioux: Social Systems and Reservation Culture. Lincoln, Neb.: University of Nebraska Press.

Eastman, Charles A.
1911 The Soul of the Indian. Boston and New York: Houghton Mifflin Co.

Hampton Institute
1893 Twenty-two Years' Work of the Hampton Normal and Agricultural Institute at Hampton, Virginia. Hampton, Va.: Normal School Press.

Hodge, Frederick W., ed.
1907–1910 Handbook of American Indians North of Mexico. Bureau of American Ethnology, Bulletin 30.

Neihardt, John G.
1932 Black Elk Speaks: Being the Life Story of A Holy Man of the Oglala Sioux. New York: William Morrow & Co.

Standing Bear, Luther
1933 Land of the Spotted Eagle. Boston and New York: Houghton Mifflin Co.

CHAPTER EIGHT

EMMET STARR: HEROIC HISTORIAN

Cherokee, 1870–1930

RENNARD STRICKLAND AND JACK GREGORY

The historians of culture are the heroic historians. They are the chroniclers of epochs in the William Prescott and Francis Parkman tradition. Such historians are heroic, Professor Bert James Lowenberg argues, not because of qualities of style or even the powers of imagination which cause them to be read; they are heroic historians because "the subjects they . . . treat are heroic." These historians write of "the drama of peoples, the clash of civilizations, the role of great men" (Lowenberg 1972:286). The Cherokee Emmet Starr, writing from a Native American perspective, deserves a place among them.

Emmet Starr, according to tradition, dreamed of becoming the "Herodotus of the Cherokees" (Harper 1930:130–131). Today, Starr's *History of the Cherokee Indians* (1922) is widely acclaimed as the "single most valuable source of authentic material on the personal history and biography of the Cherokee People." Ironically, Starr died in a two room walk-up apartment in St. Louis suffering a self-imposed exile and convinced that he had failed his people in a mission to "perpetuate the facts relative to the Cherokee tribe" (Gregory and Strickland 1967:xii).

Emmet Starr was, in truth, a "Herodotus of the Cherokee." He became, according to historian and bibliographer Carolyn Thomas Foreman, "the greatest native historian of an American Indian tribe" (personal interview, July 3, 1964). Starr's *History of the Cherokee* (1922) is, in its simple way, an eloquent testimony to the people. This is so because the book pictures the Cherokees as a nation. It is impossible to read Starr's

History without developing an understanding and appreciation of the Cherokees as a people.[1] For Starr understood and appreciated both the traditionalists (of the Knight hawk Kee-Too-Wahs) and the acculturationists (of the Ross party).

In many ways Emmet Starr was typical of the citizens of the Cherokee Nation who were born in the period immediately following the American Civil War. The independent political entity which was the Cherokee Nation was coming to an end as young Starr was coming to manhood. The invasion of the railroads and White intruders are dramatic illustrations of the breakup of the Indian empire. By 1907 the Cherokee Nation had become a part of the State of Oklahoma. Students of Cherokee history know of the removal of the tribe over the "Trail of Tears" from their southern mountain homelands. Many do not realize that the treaty following the American Civil War which allowed railroad development was equally disastrous to the ultimate survival of the tribe. Negotiations with the Dawes Commission and the passage of the Curtis Act of 1898 were the fatal blows to the so-called "Five Civilized Tribes" including the Cherokees. In truth, enrollment and allotment were ghostlike operations of a doomed tribal state (Debo 1940; Strickland 1975; Prucha 1975:103–126; and Miner 1976).

Emmet Starr, the eldest son of Walter Adair Starr, was born in the Going Snake District, Cherokee Nation, Indian Territory, on December 12, 1870. Both his parents were "mixed-blood" Cherokees who were well versed in the history and traditions of their distinguished families.[2] Starr was educated in the Cherokee public schools and graduated from the Cherokee National Male Seminary in 1888. He received a degree in medicine from Barnes Medical College at St. Louis in 1891 (Chronicles of Oklahoma 1930; Claremore Progress 1930; Smith 1930; and Gregory and Strickland 1967:vii–xiii).

Starr began gathering materials for his history of the Cherokee about 1891. For five years he practiced the profession of medicine but in 1896 began to devote himself to the full time job of becoming the Cherokee's historian. In 1899 Starr issued a prospectus for his book *Gazetteer of the Cherokee Nation, Indian Territory*. The book never appeared (Starr 1899). Starr also served one term in the Cherokee National Council as a representative of the Cooweescoowee District and as a delegate to the Indian Territory statehood meeting known as the Sequoyah Convention.[3] Active in the movement for a separate Indian state, Starr considered the rejection of the State of Sequoyah and the subsequent union of Indian Territory and Oklahoma Territory as a major blow to the Indian people (Maxwell 1953). The Cherokee Nation, thereafter, ceased to exist. The death of the Nation as a governing body in 1907 marked the end of an era for the Cherokee people. While numbers of Cherokee leaders successfully made the transition from tribal government to statehood, many more did not. Hundreds who might have been leaders in Cherokee district government or prominent in the Cherokee National Council chose not to participate in the transformation. Gradually, the Cherokees began to lose their sense of being a Nation. Today, there are many descendants of distinguished Cherokees who have no idea of the contributions which their Indian ancestors made to the Cherokee tribe.

Nevertheless, even after Oklahoma statehood, Starr continued the preparation of his Cherokee histories. He published four books. *History of the Cherokee Indians* (1922) is without doubt his most significant and valuable contribution. His smaller volume *Early History of the Cherokees* (1917) is concerned primarily with the Arkansas or Western Cherokees. *Cherokees "West"* (1910) is essentially a reprint of the memoirs of Cephas Washburn and a collection of Cherokee laws. A very rare volume among his works is *Encyclopedia of Oklahoma* (1912).[4]

While working on his histories Starr was associated with the Cherokee National Seminaries and the Normal School which became Northeastern State University in Tahlequah, Oklahoma. In 1958, a bronze plaque was placed on the wall of the Northeastern State College Library honoring him as a former college librarian.[5] The plaque, financed by the Cherokee Seminaries Student Association, was inscribed:

Emmet Starr, M.D.
Librarian 1913–1916
Author - History of the Cherokee Indians - Cherokees West

Starr's *History of the Cherokee* was originally published in 1922 by the Warden Company and sold by subscription only in bound or unbound sheets. Slightly more than three hundred copies of this history were printed and sold. The book was poorly bound and broke apart easily. Few copies have survived; even fewer in the original binding; but it has been reprinted a number of times.

In a sense, Starr's *History* (1922) is not a history at all. Its major value is as a source of primary documents and genealogical data on the Cherokee Tribe. Starr does, however, chronicle the story of early colonial wars, Cherokee removal and civil war, the Cherokees in the Texas Revolution, the Indian in the American Civil War, and hundreds of other events of Indian history. Much of this history is comprised of the texts of the laws, constitutions, treaties, and officers of the Cherokee Nation. Many of these had never before been printed. Others are found only in Cherokee Nation publications, often in Sequoyah's Cherokee language syllabary. There may be better interpretive histories of the Cherokee but there is no other work of such unique value to the student.

How did Starr go about his self-appointed task of recording the story of the Cherokee people? Where did he gather his information? How did he amass the intricate and detailed materials which fill more than seven hundred pages of text? Starr began with oral history and tradition, which he supplemented with exhaustive research in primary documents and books. He was both a field and a library researcher, who was determined to expend whatever effort might be required to get his facts. He was particularly fond of piecing together records of the individual Cherokee district governments, including such items as the names of office-holders. One gets an excellent picture of his historical work habits from requests which he made to Joseph Thoburn after the Oklahoma Historical Society had acquired Starr's personal Cherokee library. Two of these inquiries are as follows:

> (1) If you have unpacked the little canvas bound manuscript book that I had filled with manuscript notes I will appreciate if you will look in the back of the one in which I have made notations as to the election of officers of the Cherokee Nation and find on which years Wm. C. Rogers was elected a member of Cherokee Council and Senate. I have lost all of my manuscripts among the lot my lists of Cherokee National and State officers. (Thoburn papers, Feb. 19, 1918)
>
> (2) I am very desirous of obtaining a loan of the set of Cherokee laws that is in the collection that I sold the state so that I may make proper references on my list of officers of the Cherokee Nation from 1839 to 1908 and graduates of the two seminaries. (Thoburn papers, Dec. 17, 1919)

The extent to which the instinct of a compiler dominated Starr's research is shown by the joy with which he reported in 1919 "I have just completed a revision of the territorial state, and county officers from 1890 to date, some eleven thousand names, and my list is full with the exception of less than two hundred names." (Thoburn papers, May 4, 1919)

Starr, as a Cherokee, had access to oral tradition and manuscript material which no White historian could ever have acquired. The full-bloods' confidence in Starr is particularly striking. The materials in his Chapter Twenty (1922), entitled "The Full Blood Cherokee's Progress: Political, Business and Social Activities," includes previously unrecorded Kee-Too-Wah letters and pictures. Perhaps the most striking of these illustrations is of the Kee-Too-Wah Council of 1916 showing the ancient Cherokee Wampum belts.

Starr was frequently an Indian at war with the Oklahoma historical establishment, especially with the land allotment, settlement and statehood historians who wrote from the obvious White bias of Dawes Commission and Oklahoma constitutional forces. On the other hand, he greatly admired the historian Joseph Thoburn and many of the fieldwork and preservation efforts of the Oklahoma Historical Society. In 1929, he wrote Thoburn

> I am exceedingly glad that you are going to author an authoritative history of Oklahoma which will be a monument to your indefatigable and painstaking research in every nook and corner of the state, that (even) the united efforts of Governor Williams, Mrs. Condon, the Two Gun Historians and their bunch can in no way mar. I am especially glad as you are the one person that accurately knows more of Oklahoma history than any and always dares to tell the facts. (Thoburn papers, June 3, 1929)

The "Two Gun Historian" was clearly Starr's Public Enemy Number One. "Enough historical mistakes," he noted, "are being made by each number of the *Chronicles of Oklahoma* to fill the maws of future two gun historians for several decades." Recent critical comments with regard to the preconceived pro-statehood and allotment-of-Indian-land attitudes of former Dawes Commission attorney Grant Foreman are mirrored in Starr's earlier observation. "I have long ago judged Mr. Foreman," Starr wrote, "over opinionated and vacuous." Such historians were, to Starr, "unfortunate impediments who should above all things be carefully discriminative" (Thoburn papers, Oct. 24, 1927).

At a time when much Indian history, especially the history of the Five Civilized Tribes, was being written as a Tory Historical tribute to inevitable "civilized progress," Emmet Starr wrote about the traditionalist Knighthawk Kee-Too-Wah as well as Cherokee achievements in government and education. At a time when Grant Foreman cast Cherokee history as a Republican tribute to acculturation, Emmet Starr dared write of the pernicious influence of Baptist missionary groups who exerted inordinate control over full-bloods. He is quite specific in attacking White missionary power:

> (Reverend) Evans and his son John B. Jones were men of magnetic and sympathetic presence, splendid acquisitive minds and rare executive abilities. . . . They were the real directors of the Cherokee Nation from 1839 to 1867, though the numerically dominant full-

> bloods as a body were always swayed by impulse rather than reason. As ministers of the gospel they were apparently meek and humble but the sentiments that they powerfully and insidiously engendered among the full-bloods were perforce the governmental policies of Chief Ross. (Gregory and Strickland 1967:257–258)

Starr's *History* was in many ways a book of the turn of the century, although it was not published until 1922. It reflects the overwhelming concern with family and geneology that was a part of the enrollment process for the Five Civilized Tribes. What, to many, may seem an unreasonable concern with family was, in fact, the central issue of tribal existence. At this time thousands (perhaps as many as a hundred thousand) illegal intruders were seeking shares of the Indians' landed estate, and family history was crucial to the preservation of tribal integrity. William R. Harper noted the particular time context of the book in his memorial tribute to Starr.

> (Starr's) life work—his "Geneology" had it been published at an opportune time, when the final rolls of the Cherokees were in process of completion would have made his place in history secure . . . ; but this he would not permit until some controverted points upon which the world was ready to accept his conclusions as final, could be verified. By the time this could be done the opportunity had passed, yet so important were his manuscripts to the Dawes Commission and the Cherokee Attorney General that they would pay him, in real money, the first and last that he ever made, for their use. (Harper 1930:130–131; Gregory and Strickland 1967:xii–xiii.)

Undoubtedly, the most popular features of Starr's *History of the Cherokee* were the chapters and charts on "Old Families and Their Geneology" (Gregory and Strickland 1967:303–476). Starr began gathering material for these records as early as the 1890s. Assembling the genealogical data involved visiting the old Cherokee District Court Houses, taking detailed statements from individual family Bibles and tracing family lineage through wills, birth certificates, and property transactions. There are few Cherokee families who do not recall Starr coming for a visit in his old buggy and staying for the night or even for the week. The tribal tradition about "the Doctor" is that he talked and listened and talked and listened. He also wrote as evidenced by the manuscript genealogical notebooks preserved at the Oklahoma Historical Society (Starr n.d.).

Starr's genealogical notes were used as evidence by the Dawes Commission in establishing eligibility for Cherokee settlements and for listing on the official tribal rolls. The precision with which Starr undertook the task of gathering this material is apparent from an examination of his notebooks. According to Indian historian Muriel Wright, "Dr. Starr's fine genealogical records of mixed-blood families were basic to determining the final rolls of the Cherokee Nation when the Dawes Commission was making allotments of land" (Gregory and Strickland 1967:vii–viii).

There is some question concerning family relationship errors in the final text of Starr's *History* (1922). At the time the book was in press a printer's strike involving his publisher, the Warden Company, caused considerable trouble in the final printing and proofreading. Furthermore, the book was set from drafts which Starr had intended to revise. Starr, a most sensitive man, wrote to several subscribers about the errors. The mistakes, however, are essentially typographical and spelling errors. A good many alleged "errors" seem to be "wishful thinking" on the part of would be claimants to Cherokee allotments. Muriel Wright seems most accurate when she notes, "Starr's *History of the Cherokee*, especially the section on Cherokee genealogy, has remained a great work" (Gregory and Strickland 1967:viii).

Starr's *History* was the culmination of his life work. As a young boy he had begun to observe his people. In describing his work, he wrote:

> My father, who has been a soldier in the Confederate Cherokee service, was after I can remember successively deputy sheriff, deputy clerk, and judge of Cooweescoowee District, which comprised about one-third of the Cherokee Nation. My father's home (which was three miles from the District court house) and hospitality was open to his friends and in this way I was afforded at an early age the opportunity of listening to the conversations and reminiscences of many of the most brilliant minds among my own people. I listened as a boy to the Adairs, Bells, Rosses, Mayeses, and many others who were born reconteurs and savants.
>
> I commenced the collection of material for genealogical and historical work on my people in 1891.
>
> As a result of my work along these lines I am attempting to present to you a true and correct history of the Cherokees. (Starr 1917:5–6)

The value of Starr's work in preserving the history and tradition of his people is clearly noted in the 1930 statement of R. H. Fowler, a native Cherokee historian:

> Dr. Starr was the best versed, on Cherokee history and old family genealogical lines in the far back past, that has ever lived. It was his chosen life work from his young days. No one dare dispute or go back on Dr. Starr's records for he was considered the highest recognized authority living at that time. (Gregory and Strickland 1967:viii)

As is often the case, the merit of Starr's achievement was not widely recognized during his lifetime. While he was, in fact, sad and lonely, some considered him eccentric. He was a man who, according to a Claremore friend of thirty-five years, "died as he had lived—misunderstood, and, therefore, disappointed" (Gregory and Strickland 1967:vii). There is poignancy in his letters written from St. Louis; there is a constant sense of the misplaced. Again and again he writes that he hears little of Oklahoma, of the Cherokees. In 1929 he lamented, "I hear and know just as much about Oklahoma now as I do about China" (Thoburn papers, April 3, 1929). And yet, he never stopped thinking or writing or talking about his people and the State of Oklahoma into which their political destiny had been merged. A friend from his last days in St. Louis recalled:

> He liked to talk politics, especially as concerned Oklahoma. . . . He could tell stories concerning territorial and early statehood days in Oklahoma for hours at a time, and nothing seemed to please him more than to have an interested listener to these stories. (Gregory and Strickland 1967:viii–ix)

Why then did Starr leave Oklahoma? Why did he abandon his beloved Claremore in the heart of the old Cherokee Nation? Starr maintained (Gregory and Strickland 1967:viii) "he had come to St. Louis because he felt he could make a better living." Money is too convenient an excuse although, after he abandoned his medical career, he moved from job to job. The Department of the Interior Indian Bureau in Muskogee, the Northeastern Normal School (formerly the Cherokee Seminary) in Tahlequah, the Public Schools of Rogers County, and a Jewish bookseller in St. Louis furnished him with temporary employment (Thoburn papers, May 13, 1913; Feb. 28, 1914; Feb. 8, 1918; May 30, 1927; Sept. 23, 1928). Starr sought other employment with a variety of Oklahoma state agencies but especially with the Oklahoma Historical Society (Thoburn papers, Oct. 1, 1918; Mar. 15, 1919; May 4, 1919; July 3, 1928). The simple truth was that he was a man whose country was gone, destroyed as completely as if it had been bombed from the face of the earth. To Starr, and other Cherokees of his age, the end of the Nation was a catastrophic blow. In his case, it was a blow from which he never recovered. Nonetheless, he left, in his history, a monument to the Cherokee Nation and the glory he could never fully and personally experience. In the grandiose prose of the educated Cherokee, William R. Harper (Gregory and Strickland 1967:xii–xiii) captures what is the most valid explanation for Starr's tragic exile:

> But finding that the parental fortune has disappeared and the education of his younger orphaned brothers and sisters about to be neglected, he magnanimously, forsook his own plans and ambitions and took upon his own shoulders this task. By the time this was completed the old order of things had passed away and the new had passed in. Transformation from tribal government to statehood eliminated his opportunity—there was no more demand for the services he was so able and so anxious to render. So, like the "Last of the Mohicans," he passed out. Finding his occupation gone he wandered "off the reservation" only to be swallowed up in the maelstrom of modern "efficiency" and greed.

Emmet Starr was the Cherokee historian for all times. He performed one of the greatest services possible for the Cherokee people. Sequoyah, it is said, gave his people "talking leaves." Starr gave his people a recorded history. Starr's *History of the Cherokee* is of more significance today than ever before. Those who can remember the greatness of Cherokee tribal government, education, and culture are almost gone. For the new generation, and generations yet to come, Starr's *History of the Cherokee* is a constant reminder of Cherokee achievements. As the Cherokees seek a renewed glory in a National Cultural Center and in a reawakened spirit of the importance of being Cherokee, every member of the tribe and every admirer of this proud people should know their noble heritage as Starr set it forth.

There is an eternal flame of the Cherokees—a fire so carefully guarded that it has continued to burn for them through forceable removal, civil war, and tribal dissolution. Starr brought to the Cherokees a new light—the light of their history. This flame burns even brighter and will burn even longer. Emmet Starr was the heroic Cherokee historian for all time.

NOTES

1. For a detailed Cherokee bibliography see Rennard Strickland, "In search of Cherokee History: A Bibliographical Foreword," In Morris Wardell,

A Political History of the Cherokee Nation, Norman: University of Oklahoma Press, 1977. Second printing.

2. The obituary of Emmet Starr's father Judge Walter Adair Starr is found in the *Claremore Messenger*, January 12, 1906, typescript, "Cherokee papers, 1901–1925," page 294, Indian Archives, Oklahoma Historical Society, Oklahoma City.

3. Unpublished Cherokee Tribal Records, Vol. 302, page 185 and Vol. 313, page 157, Indian Archives, Oklahoma Historical Society. Starr was paid $140.00 for his service to the Cherokee National Council. The Thomas Gilcrease Institute in Tulsa, Oklahoma has a candidate's broadside issued by Starr during his 1901 election campaign.

4. It is believed that there are fewer than half-a-dozen copies of this work extant. In a letter to Joseph Thoburn, Starr explains the process by which he sought publication. "I have the manuscript of my *Encyclopedia of Oklahoma* completed, and as soon as I get two hundred and fifty subscribers, at one dollar each, I can publish it. I have been able to make it much better than I anticipated." (Thoburn papers, July 16, 1912)

5. The College is now known as Northeastern State University. Gilbert Fites, who has also served as librarian at the former seminary, supplied the only known photograph of Starr and other biographical information.

LITERATURE CITED

Chronicles of Oklahoma
1930 Necrology: Death of Dr. Emmet Starr. Vol. 8: 129–130.

Claremore Progress, The
1930 Obituary, Emmet Starr. February 6, 1930.

Debo, Angie
1940 And Still the Waters Run. Princeton, N. J.: Princeton University Press.

Gregory, Jack and Rennard Strickland, eds.
1967 Starr's History of the Cherokee Indians. Fayetteville, Arkansas: Indian Heritage Association.

Harper, William R.
1930 Dr. Emmet Starr— A Tribute. Chronicles of Oklahoma 8:130–131. Reprinted in J. Gregory and R. Strickland, eds. Starr's History of the Cherokee Indians, p. xii. Fayetteville, Arkansas: Indian Heritage Association, 1967.

Lowenberg, Bert James
1972 American History in American Thought. New York: Simon and Schuster.

Maxwell, Amos D.
1953 The Sequoyah Convention. Boston: Meador Publishing Co.

Miner, Craig
1976 The Corporation and the Indian: Tribal Sovereignty, 1865–1907. Columbia, Missouri: University of Missouri Press.

Prucha, Francis Paul, ed.
1975 Documents of United States Indian Policy. Pp. 103, 104, 112, 117, 118, 120, 126. Lincoln: University of Nebraska Press.

Smith Micah Pearce
1930 "The Latter Days of Dr. Emmet Starr." In Chronicles of Oklahoma 8:339–342.

Starr, Emmet
n.d. Unpublished notebooks. Indian Archives, Oklahoma Historical Society.

1899 Prospectus. Gazetteer of the Cherokee Nation, Indian Territory. Tahlequah, Cherokee Nation: Private printing for the author.

1901 To all Cherokee Voters. Claremore, Cherokee Nation: Private printing for the author.

1910 Cherokees "West," 1794–1839. Private printing for the author.

1912 Encyclopedia of Oklahoma: Based on the 1910 Census. Claremore, Oklahoma: Private printing for the author.

1917 Early History of the Cherokees Embracing Aboriginal Customs, Religion, Laws, Folk Lore, and Civilization. Private printing for the author.

1922 History of the Cherokee Indians and Their Legends and Folk Lore. Oklahoma City: The Warden Company.

Strickland, Rennard
1975 Fire and the Spirits: Cherokee Law from Clan to Court. Norman: University of Oklahoma Press.

1977 In Search of Cherokee History: A Bibliographical Foreword. In Morris Wardell, A Political History of the Cherokee

Nation. Norman: University of Oklahoma Press. Second printing.

Thoburn, Joseph
1913–1929 Joseph Thoburn papers, Letters of Emmet Starr. Unpublished. Indian Archives, Oklahoma Historical Society.

Wardell, Morris
1977 A Political History of the Cherokee Nation. Norman: University of Oklahoma Press. Second printing.

CHAPTER NINE

RICHARD SANDERVILLE, BLACKFOOT INDIAN INTERPRETER

Blackfoot, ca. 1873–1951

JOHN C. EWERS

The eastern motorist bound for Glacier National Park must cross the Blackfeet Indian Reservation as he nears his destination. Just east of the little town of Browning—headquarters for both the Tribal Council and the Indian Agency—he will find one of those large and informative roadside signs erected by the Montana Highway Department near localities of historic interest in that state. This one is titled "The Blackfeet Nation," and the last of its four paragraphs reads:

> The Government record of the sign language of all American Indians, started by the late General Hugh L. Scott, was completed by the late Richard Sanderville, who was official interpreter of this reservation.

Richard Sanderville died in the Indian Hospital on the Blackfeet Reservation February 25, 1951, at the end of a long and very active life. His sign language studies alone might qualify him for consideration among twentieth century Indian intellectuals. But those of us who knew Dick Sanderville, as he was known to his many friends, also knew that his skill as a sign-talker was but one of his many accomplishments as a Blackfoot interpreter. We knew, also, that as a true interpreter he conveyed White men's ideas to Indians and Indian ones to Whites.

Like a number of the other Indian intellectuals we are considering in this symposium, Sanderville was not a full-blood Indian. Like others, also, he was not the first member of his family to play a role of some prominence in the history of his tribe. Dick came to his position as a Blackfoot interpreter quite logically—both his father and his father's father were interpreters.

The American Fur Company Papers in the Missouri Historical Society in St. Louis mention that his grandfather, Isidore Leroy Sandoval, was serving that firm in the fur trade of the Upper Missouri as early as the spring of 1829. He helped James Kipp to establish the first American trading post among the Blackfoot Indians in 1831–32, and he married a Piegan Blackfoot woman.

During the late summer of 1833 this man served as interpreter for the German naturalist, Maximilian, Prince of Wied-Neuwied, when the latter visited the Blood and North Blackfoot camps near the American Fur Company's post of Fort McKenzie at the mouth of the Marias River. The Prince referred to Dick's grandfather as "the Spanish hunter." He also learned that "Sandoval and his Indian wife, Doucette, four engages and two Kutenai Indians" were sent from Fort McKenzie on a dangerous mission to try to open trade with the Kutenai Indians west of the Rocky Mountains. That mission failed, because the Blood Indians, who resented the company's efforts to extend its trade to their Kutenai enemies, shot Doucette" (Wied-Neuwied 1906, Vol. 6:132, 136, 153–4).

James Larpenteur, a contemporary of Dick's grandfather, wrote of Isidore Sandoval's murder by the ill-tempered trader, Alexander Harvey, in 1841. He implied that Sandoval had imbibed too heavily before he threatened Harvey's life. Next day, as Sandoval stood behind the counter in the retail store at Fort Union, Harvey shot him through the head (Larpenteur 1933:141–146).

Liquor also shortened the interpreting career and the life of Dick's father, who also bore the name of Isidore Sandoval. He was official interpreter at the old Blackfeet Agency on Badger Creek before May 1883, when he was discharged for drunkenness. Agency records also reveal that he was killed in a drunken brawl on August 31st of that year (Blackfeet Agency Records 1883).

Well aware of the damage alcohol had done to both his father and grandfather, Dick grew up with a strong aversion to the use of liquor. As a boy, his maternal uncle, Red Paint, had a very strong influence upon him. Dick told me he received his first schooling at the Catholic mission to the Flathead and Pend d'Oreille Indians west of the Rocky Mountains. His uncle, Red Paint, accompanied him to that school on long horseback trips over the mountains. On those journeys and on shorter travels nearer home Red Paint took pains to point out to the boy sites where stirring events in tribal history had taken place, recited memorable deeds of tribal chiefs and heroes of the past, and explained Blackfoot customs of earlier times. Surely Red Paint helped to rouse Dick's interest in tribal history and his pride in being a Blackfoot Indian. In his conversations with me Dick credited Red Paint with teaching him a great deal about the history and customs of his Indian people.

Dick transferred to the government school at Old Agency on his own reservation during the late 1880s. Classes were conducted in a log schoolhouse inside the tall stockade that still surrounded the Agency buildings. When that Agency was built in 1879 the Blackfoot Indians still hunted buffalo for subsistence, and enemy war parties from the Crow, Assiniboine and other tribes still raided the camps of the Blackfoot, even when they were pitched near the Agency. Intertribal horse raiding persisted until 1887. Dick appears in a photograph of a school group taken at Old Agency in the next year (1888). Like Dick, many of the other students were of mixed-blood parentage, and were sons or daughters of Agency employees (Ewers 1944:52, Fig. 38).

Dick Sanderville was a member of the first group of Blackfoot Indians to be enrolled at the famed Carlisle Indian School in far-off Carlisle, Pennsylvania during the late winter of 1890. They numbered some 39 boys and girls when they posed for a group photograph on the steps of one of the school buildings (the photograph is preserved in the archives of the Cumberland County Historical Society in Carlisle, Pennsylvania).

The Carlisle Indian School Records in the National Archives indicate that Dick was enrolled at that school on March 26, 1890, as Student No. 1101, as a half-blood Piegan Indian whose mother and father both were dead. His last name was given as Sanderville (no longer the Spanish, Sandoval). His age was stated as 17, height 5'11-3/4", and weight 155 lbs. Although he enrolled for the full five-year course, ill health forced him to leave Carlisle after but two and a half years, on November 8, 1892.

Carlisle School records also inform us that during his student days Dick participated in Carlisle's famous "outing" program for two extended periods. From April 2 to September 9 in both 1891 and 1892 he worked on White-owned farms in fertile Bucks County, Pennsylvania. I often heard Dick speak of those outings—of how efficiently the farms were managed, of their fine crops, of how well the farm families treated him, and how much he learned as a student farmer.

Dick treasured a letter written to him by Captain Richard H. Pratt, the famed founder of Carlisle Indian School who was still administrator during Dick's student days. Dated June 9, 1891, when Dick was about midway through his first "outing" on the farm of Mr. C. Moore of Solebury in Bucks County, this letter reads:

> Dear Richard: I am pleased to have such good reports of you and know you are in a good home. I want you to be particular about attending church and sabbath school, and it is best you go when the family wish you to, in the morning. I learn this is their wish from the reports. I expect you to set the example for the boys in your vicinity.
>
> It is not a good custom to visit other boys, and you must not invite the boys to visit you. It makes too much work on Sundays. Be at home for meals and say to the other boys it is against the rules to have boys come to see you and stay for meals.
>
> I tell you this in warning, not that Mr. Moore has said anything about the meals, for they have not, but I know some of the boys visit too much. Improve your time, when not at work, reading or studying, you can gain much in that way.
>
> Your friend, R. H. Pratt
>
> (Letter in Richard Sanderville student file, Carlisle Indian School. The National Archives.)

Surely this letter confirms other evidence that permissiveness was not a characteristic of Pratt's administration of Carlisle. Even so, Dick did not look back upon the rules and discipline of that school as having been oppressively strict. In a follow-up report on his accomplishments, written two decades after he entered Carlisle, and preserved in his student file, he wrote:

> Ever since I left Carlisle I still obey the rules yet. I never touched the liquor or tobacco . . . I love Carlisle. If the Father Almighty spares our lives I might get the chance to see the dear old school and the kind supt. I used to love Capt. Pratt so much.

Apparently, Sanderville did not know that Pratt had been relieved of all duties at Carlisle Indian School on June 30, 1904, some six years *before* Dick wrote the preceding paragraph.

Dick Sanderville must have recovered his health fairly quickly after he returned to Montana from Carlisle. Through the year 1894 he was enrolled as a student at Fort Shaw Indian School south of the reservation, on Sun River, at the abandoned military post of Fort Shaw. In 1895 he entered government service. Although he served for many years as official interpreter, he was carried on the Agency rolls as either a farmer or carpenter.

As "United States Agency Interpreter" Richard Sanderville signed the land agreement between the United States and the Indians of the Blackfeet Reservation in Montana, dated September 26, 1895. He was one of three interpreters at that rather stormy council in which George Bird Grinnell and two other government commissioners obtained the signatures of a majority of the adult male members of the tribe who agreed to sell the western or mountain portion of their reservation for the sum of one and one-half million dollars (Kappler 1904, 1:604–609).

Dick told me that at the time of that council White Calf and Three Suns were rivals for the head chieftancy of the tribe. While Three Suns sought to hold out for a much larger payment, White Calf secretly signed the agreement. Sanderville, a follower of Three Suns, believed that White Calf sought to curry favor with the government by showing his willingness to sign for a lower amount. Be that as it may, the record indicates that Three Suns also signed the agreement.

During the late years of the 19th century and early years of the 20th century Sanderville aided the Blackfoot Agent in taking the reservation census and compiling official records of family relationships and tribal membership. Some Canadian Indians who lived on the reservation were stricken from the roles. Accurate records of family ties became especially important in the settlement of heirship problems after the Blackfoot lands were allotted between 1907 and 1912.

In mid-1910 Sanderville reported that he was an Assistant Farmer with a salary of $600 a year. He then owned 960 acres of good land, 74 head of cattle, and 18 horses. He and his wife lived in a two-room log cabin, which he described as "made very neat." He also stated, "I am a member of the Indian Council and respected by my people." (Richard Sanderville File, Carlisle School Records, The National Archives.)

Dick was a member of the tribal council that strongly opposed the government's efforts to allot lands of the Blackfeet Reservation to Rocky Boy and his several hundred Chippewa-Cree followers in 1912. These homeless Indians, many of whom had fled to Montana from Canada after the Riel Rebellion in Saskatchewan, later were placed upon a portion of the abandoned Fort Assiniboine Military Reservation, which was named Rocky Boy's Reservation (Ewers 1974:140–142).

By 1921 economic conditions on the Blackfeet Reservation were at a low ebb. Then a new and energetic Agent, Frank C. Campbell, accompanied by the Agency doctor, visited every family on the reservation to learn at first hand of their financial, health, and social problems. In this methodical house-to-house survey Dick Sanderville served as interpreter for the many family heads who could not speak English well. Out of this study developed the Five Year Industrial Program for the Blackfeet Reservation that came to be regarded as a model by the Bureau of Indian Affairs during the middle 1920s. Dick helped to organize the Piegan Farming and Livestock Association, with 29 local chapters in various reservation communities. It was a program that proved especially helpful among the older full-bloods, many of whom became able for the first time to raise enough crops and livestock to feed themselves (Ewers 1958:320–323).

I knew Frank Campbell and recall his expressions of gratitude to Dick Sanderville for helping him to gain the interest and cooperation of the older full-blood Indians in his agricultural program. The Agent could not have done this alone. Dick's basic training in farming on those outings from Carlisle served him well in later years in helping his own people. When I knew Dick he was still an enthusiastic gardener. He advised my wife and me what vegetables to plant in our garden beside the museum in order to gain the best yields in the very short growing season in that locality. The season was too short for corn or tomatoes—but peas, beans, and root crops did well.

Dick Sanderville and General Hugh L. Scott probably first became acquainted when the retired Chief of Staff of the United States Army visited the Blackfeet Reservation as a member of the Board of Indian Commissioners during the 1920s. Scott was greatly impressed by the achievements of Agent Campbell's industrial program. However, it must have been their mutual interest in the Indian sign language that drew Scott and Sanderville together. The General's interest in that subject went back to his early service in the famed 7th Cavalry following his graduation from West Point in 1877. In 1930 Dick Sanderville assisted the General in assembling able sign talkers from 14 different tribes in an Indian Sign Language Council in Browning. There the participants told silent stories to each other and their actions were recorded in motion pictures which have been preserved in the National Archives.

In 1934, after General Scott's death, Matthew W. Stirling, Director of the Bureau of American Ethnology of the Smithsonian Institution, invited Richard Sanderville to Washington to complete Scott's "Dictionary of the Indian Sign Language," which had been deposited in the Bureau's archives. The project received considerable attention in Washington newspapers and national magazines of the time. The *Literary Digest* for July 7, 1934, termed Sanderville "the greatest living authority on the vanishing and almost forgotten universal sign language used by the American Indians." *Science News Letter* for July 14, 1934, announced "The dictionary of the Indian Sign Language is at last finished."

It is impossible to ascertain precisely what contribution Richard Sanderville made to the completion of General Scott's Dictionary of the Indian Sign Language during his sojourn at the Smithsonian Institution in 1934. The Dictionary was compiled in the form of a silent motion picture demonstration of the meaningful gestures employed in the sign language. In the Motion Picture Branch of the National Archives is preserved a 79 minute-long, 35mm film which consists entirely of views of General Scott executing an extensive series of signs for specific rivers, land areas, animals, tribes, individuals, and occupations known to the Plains Indians. Perhaps Sanderville reviewed and verified the printed captions that accompanied the visual presentations of these signs. This Film No. 106.14 was transferred to the National Archives from the Smithsonian Institution.

The only record of Dick Sanderville's own demonstration of signs during the period of his residence in Washington in '34 appears in a much shorter film, some 360 feet in length, identified as Film No. 106.25. It was taken on the grounds of the Smithsonian Institution on July 11, 1934, and pictured Dick demonstrating the sign language by telling an Indian love story, briefly contrasting buffalo hunting practices before and after Indians acquired horses, and describing the ceremonial transfer of a black buffalo painted tipi among the Blackfoot—entirely through hand gestures, very precisely executed. A written text of each gesticulated account was shown on a blackboard immediately before the sign language version was presented.

Sanderville's interest in the sign language had other and quite literally concrete results. When the participants at the Sign Language Council gathered in Browning in September, 1930, he arranged for each of the Indian participants to leave his footprint in a small block of cement as he left the council tipi. He also asked General Scott and the few other White participants to leave their footprints—with their shoes on. In an interview published in *The Washington Star* of July 29, 1934, and titled Unique Memorial to a Vanishing Race, Dick told of his plan to preserve these prints as part of a sign language memorial to be erected at Browning, Montana.

For several years thereafter these footprints in heavy slabs of cement remained in storage at the Agency in Browning. Doubtless, Agency employees tended to think of this project as Dick Sanderville's folly. Meanwhile, the National Park Service developed a proposal for an Indian Museum in nearby Glacier National Park. They justified their project to the Congress and the Department of the Interior received an appropriation to construct the museum from federal funds. At this juncture, so the tradition goes, Richard Sanderville convinced then Secretary of the Interior Harold L. Ickes that a Blackfoot Indian Museum belonged on the Indian Reservation, *not* in nearby Glacier National Park. So the Bureau of Indian Affairs acquired a museum project it had *not* requested, while the National Park Service lost one it *had* successfully justified. Early in the year 1941 I became the first Curator of the new Museum of the Plains Indian on the Blackfeet Reservation. When I arrived in Browning in late March the red brick building was virtually complete as a spacious hollow shell. But there were no cases, no other furnishings, and no specimen collections other than a few pieces Dick Sanderville had collected and squirreled away at the local high school in anticipation of getting a museum one day. Within three months other collections were obtained, cases were built by Indian carpenters, and exhibits were installed. When the museum was formally opened to the public in late June of 1941, both Willard R. Beatty, Director of Indian Education, and Richard Sanderville were speakers.

During the museum's first summer Sanderville's historic collection of footprints, recast in metal, was made part of an outdoor exhibit on the sign language on the museum grounds. The footprints were set in a circle and explained by a large, illustrated label which pictured each of the Indian and white participants in that 1930 Sign Language Council in Browning. At the dedication ceremonies Richard Sanderville and James White Calf, the last living son of the last head chief of the Piegan Indians, White Calf, who died while on a visit to Washington, D.C. in 1903, gave a lively demonstration of the sign language.

Unlike many of the other Indian intellectuals we are considering, Richard Sanderville was not a writer of books or articles about Indian history or tribal customs. He preferred to communicate through those media his grandmother's people had traditionally employed—the spoken word, the language of signs, and picture-writings. One of these picture-writings, preserved in the Museum of the Plains Indian, is built around a small photograph of White Quiver, the most successful of all remembered Piegan Indian horse raiders. Dick employs graphic symbols to enumerate White Quiver's memorable deeds on the warpath—the number of times he raided enemy camps, captured horses from those camps, parties, and served as scout. The information I obtained directly from several older Indians, some of whom had been on war parties with White Quiver, suggests that Dick's claims for White Quiver may have been on the modest side (Ewers 1955:191–193).

In my own investigations of Blackfoot history and culture I found Dick to be a willing and helpful informant, with a very wide range of interests in traditional tribal life—both secular and religious. His understanding of past conditions and events did not always agree with the testimony offered by full-bloods who were somewhat older. Yet he had paid closer attention to some aspects of history and culture than had they. Sanderville readily recognized the value of my efforts to write a history of his people based upon the oral testimony of elderly informants and written records—both published and archival. He never disparaged written records as sources on Indian history.

In the first paragraph of my book, *The Blackfeet, Raiders on the Northwestern Plains*, I quoted Richard Sanderville on the need for providing young members of his tribe a written history of their people:

> When I was a boy, very few members of my tribe could read or write. But now all our young people are in school. They learn a lot about the Pilgrims, George Washington, and Abraham Lincoln. That's fine. But they learn nothing about the history of their own people and their great chiefs. That is American history too. (Ewers 1958:ix)

Dick Sanderville learned much about the customs and the beliefs of White men in church as well as in school. As a boy he was a Catholic, but in later years he became a member of the Board of the Methodist Mission in Browning. Repeatedly he accompanied the minister to summer convocations where he served as a living testimonial to the fine work the Methodists were doing among his people. In reality the very great majority of the Indians on the reservation were Catholics

Dick himself consistently supported the principal of religious freedom and the right of Indians to publicly practice their traditional ceremonies if they wished to do so. He was one of the tribal leaders who, in 1906, persuaded their Agent that Indians should be permitted to revive their tribal Sun Dance, their major annual religious ceremony, which had been prohibited since 1894.

I was in the Sun Dance encampment on land adjoining the museum west of the town of Browning one summer more than thirty years ago when missionaries of a very evangelical Christian denomination, who hoped to convert some Blackfoot Indians, drove into camp with a sound truck playing hymns loudly. It was on the afternoon of the climactic day of the Sun Dance, shortly before the raising of the center pole. Dick calmly walked over to the operators of the intrusive sound truck, explained to them that the Indians were in the midst of a worship service, and asked them to please turn off their music which, under the circumstances, was a distraction. At the same time he invited the missionaries to remain in camp and to observe the Indians' service if they wished to do so.

There can be no doubt that Richard Sanderville took pride in his role as a marginal man—a man who was much at home in two quite different cultures. He used to take pride in his record of having met every President of the United States since the second Harrison. He was especially proud to have conducted the ceremony inducting President Franklin D. Roosevelt into his tribe when that President visited Glacier National Park in 1934. He was proud to have been an American.

Even so, as an enrolled member of an Indian tribe who resided on the reservation established for members of his tribe, Sanderville could not avoid involvement in tribal politics and factional disputes within that tribe. As a young man he was a follower of Three Suns in that chief's rivalry with White Calf for tribal leadership. After Three Suns' death in 1896, Dick belonged to the faction which lived on the southern portion of the reservation, and which vied with the faction north of the Great Northern Railroad crossing of the center of the reservation from east to west. As a mixed-blood he also became involved in the mixed-blood vs. full-blood factionalism which existed on the reservation during the 1930s and 1940s. After his tribe accepted the Indian Reorganization Act of 1934 Dick represented Heart Butte, one of the southern communities on the reservation, in the elected Tribal Council. However, he did not hold a position on the Council consistently.

Sanderville's status as a mixed-blood proved both a help and a handicap to him as an organizer and leader of small groups of Indian entertainers. During the mid-30s he was in charge of a group of Blackfoot Indian dancers and singers which participated in the National Folk Festival in Constitution Hall in Washington, D.C. I saw the performance and I recall that Dick's costume was very much in the mixed-blood tradition. He wore a hat, a fringed and floral-beaded jacket of buckskin which buttoned down the front. The lower portion of his jacket was covered by a wide, woven sash. He also wore a pair of cloth trousers, and shoes.

During the early '40s when Sanderville served as master of ceremonies for the small group of Indians from the nearby reservation who pitched their painted tipis on the lawn of the large hotel at Glacier Park Station and greeted and entertained summer tourists, he appeared under his Indian name of Chief Bull, wore a flowing feather bonnet, whitened buckskin shirt and leggings, breechclout, and moccasins handsomely decorated with geometric beaded designs. The evening performances of these Indians in the spacious lobby of the hotel were very popular attractions for the tourists. Dick told some funny stories, gave a brief demonstration of the sign language, and introduced the other members of the troupe who sang and danced to the beat of an Indian drum. In the concluding act White visitors were invited to join the Indians in a Rabbit Dance.

Dick's popularity with the tourists roused the envy of some of the less outgoing full-bloods who were members of the troupe. They grumbled about "that Mexican," and eventually prevailed upon the hotel management not to invite Dick to work there a following summer because he was not a full-blood Indian.

This action hurt Dick—perhaps more than he would admit to his White friends. But that very summer some of them helped him to obtain a position as instructor of Indian crafts and lore at the summer school of Culver Military Academy in the Midwest. So he continued to keep busy interpreting Indian traditions and customs to new and appreciative groups of non-Indian Americans.

When one compares Richard Sanderville with some of the other Indian intellectuals considered in this symposium one must be impressed by the variety as well as the importance of his accomplishments over a period of more than a half century after he attended Carlisle Indian School. Although he studied there for but two and a half years he learned well the Carlisle teaching that Indian students must serve their own people. Unlike some other Carlisle students who gained recognition as Indian leaders, Dick *did* go back to his reservation. But it could never be said that he "went back to the blanket." He employed his talents and energies in a host of ways to prepare other Indians for the future. At the same time he demonstrated his deep and reasoned concern for preserving knowledge of the Indian past.

In some respects Richard Sanderville shared the concerns of other educated Indians of his generation. In other respects he appears to have been a generation or two ahead of his time. When I hear young Indians today calling for on-reservation museums and tribal history projects to help solve Indian identity problems, I am reminded that Dick Sanderville actively *and* effectively espoused those causes on the Blackfeet Reservation in Montana more than 35 years ago.

LITERATURE CITED

Published Sources

Ewers, John Canfield

1944 The Story of the Blackfeet. Life and Customs Pamphlet No. 6. Lawrence, Kansas: Haskell Institute.

1955 The Horse in Blackfoot Indian Culture. Bureau of American Ethnology. Bulletin 159. Washington, D.C.: Government Printing Office.

1958 The Blackfeet, Raiders on the Northwestern Plains. Norman, Oklahoma: University of Oklahoma Press.

1974 Ethnological Report on the Chippewa-Cree Tribe of the Rocky Boy Reservation and the Little Shell Band of Indians. In Chippewa Indians VI:9–182. New York and London: Garland Publishing Co. Inc.

Kappler, Charles J.
1904 Indian Affairs, Laws and Treaties. Vol. 1. Laws. Washington, D.C.: Government Printing Office.

Larpenteur, Charles
1933 Forty Years a Fur Trader on the Upper Missouri. The Personal Narrative of Charles Larpenteur, 1833–1872. Chicago: R. R. Donnelley and Sons Co.

Richard Sanderville obituary. Great Falls Tribune. Great Falls, Montana. February 27, 1951.

Unique Memorial to a Vanishing Race. The Sunday Star. Washington, D.C. July 29, 1934.

Wied-Neuwied, Maximilian Alexander Philip Prince of
1906 Travels in the Interior of North America. In Early Western Travels. Reuben Gold Thwaites, ed. Vols. 22–24. Cleveland: The Arthur H. Clark Co.

Unpublished Sources

Cumberland County Historical Society, Carlisle, Penna. Carlisle Indian School Photographs.

Missouri Historical Society, St. Louis. American Fur Company Papers.

Museum of the Plains Indian, Browning, Montana. Blackfeet Agency Records.

National Anthropological Archives, Smithsonian Institution, Washington, D.C. Richard Sanderville Correspondence.

The National Archives, Washington, D.C.
Carlisle Indian School Records. Individual student jacket: Richard Sanderville.

Motion Picture Branch. Film No. 106.25, The Indian Sign Language.

CHAPTER TEN

ARTHUR C. PARKER

Seneca, 1881–1955

HAZEL W. HERTZBERG

Arthur C. Parker was one of the most interesting and complex Indian intellectuals of his day. In the first four decades of his life he sought, and finally found, a vocation which suited him reasonably well—one in which he could use his exceptional talents and bring together the varying and often conflicting ideas, interests and forces which he attempted to reconcile. The story of his search is significant for his time and for ours. Parker was unusually sensitive to some of the major intellectual and social trends of his day, both in American life as a whole and in the life of American Indians. He was one of the very few Indians who were social scientists. Because there were so few Indians in Parker's position, the problems which he faced did not have the same widespread urgency or impact of those of more recent Indian intellectuals. Parker lived in a very different historical period and intellectual and social context. He drew on the experience and ways of conceptualizing that experience which were available to him. From these he attempted to fashion a position which would enable him to function productively and in some fashion be true to the multiple worlds of which he was part and to his own commitment, or ambition, to excel in these worlds.

Parker's biographers have faced a common problem; so rich and complex was his life and so varied, numerous and productive were his vocations that brevity becomes both difficult and unfair.[1] I found that when I had discussed Parker's life largely through an analysis of his major writings, the resulting manuscript was far too long for this symposium. The concluding section turned out to be just about the required length but depended on evidence earlier set forth. My solution to this quandary is to present here the minimal biographical information and interpretation needed to provide a context in which to discuss some of his ideas, to outline the bare bones of his search for a vocation, and then to offer the concluding section. The analysis and evidence on which the conclusions are based will, I hope, be published elsewhere. In sketching here Parker's biography, I have given more emphasis to his childhood than to his later life for two reasons: first, because his childhood on the reservation by no means conforms to the picture often held today about reservation life, and second, because it was at that time and place that his fundamental loyalties were formed. I have ended the account when Parker himself had effectively abandoned the two vocations which most personally and passionately engaged him—ethnology and Pan-Indianism—and finally committed himself primarily to museology, in which he spent the remainder of a long and productive professional life.

Parker was born in 1881 on the Cattaraugus Seneca Indian Reservation in western New York. His Seneca father, Frederick Parker, was an accountant with the New York Central Railroad and a graduate of Fredonia State Normal School. His White mother, Geneva Griswold Parker, of Scottish and English extraction, had been a teacher at the Cattaraugus and Allegany Reservations.

The Parkers were a leading family in reservation and Iroquois affairs, "progressives" who mingled distinguished Iroquois and distinguished White New England ancestry. They believed that "the world is large but I will catch it." (W. N. Fenton to author, personal communication.) Parker's Iroquois progenitors, so it was said, could be counted back to the founding of the Confederacy, and included Handsome Lake, Old Smoke, Red Jacket, and Cornplanter. Among his New England relatives, his lively and beloved missionary grandmother, Martha Parker, was the niece of the Reverend Asher and Laura Sheldon Wright whom Parker called those "sainted missionaries who gave their very lives to the Senecas," (Parker 1919:199). His paternal grandfather, Nicholson Parker, a farmer who had attended the State Normal School at Albany, served for years as chief clerk of the Seneca Nation. Parker's great-uncle, General Ely S. Parker, was Lewis Henry Morgan's collaborator, a Life Chief at Tonawanda, an aide to General U.S. Grant, and President Grant's Indian Commissioner under whom the Peace Policy of ca. 1865–1880 was initiated. His great-aunt, Carrie Parker Mountpleasant, was the wife of a Tuscorora chief. This "grandfather generation," as Parker called them, linked him with deep Seneca, Iroquois, and American patriotism, with the beginnings of anthropology as a science, with varieties of religious reform, and with the long struggle for Indian rights in which both his Indian and White forebears had participated.

Arthur grew up in the busy and cheerful household of his Seneca grandparents. Between grandfather and grandson there existed a special bond which Parker honored throughout his life. Grandfather Nicholson Parker was Arthur's teacher and exemplar, a bearer of two cultures. It was his grandfather who read to him from Milton, Shakespeare and the Scriptures and who recreated for him the glories and tragedies of the Iroquois and the Seneca, and of the American past with which these were intertwined. Parker later wrote of Nicholson,

> Like his other brother Ely, he could never completely accept civilization's teachings or wholly neglect the philosophy of his fathers. Seeing true virtue in each, according to his mood he argued for each. Many Indians have this same characteristic and often appear vacillatory and uncertain in judgment when in reality the quality is merely the involuntary mental struggle between hereditary impressions and proclivities and those acquired. Until civilization crushes out all of the old instincts, or wisdom brings with it a strongly balanced judgment, Indians will ever be at moral odds, for character, point of view, methods and philosophy, like religion, may be historical and ethnic. (Parker 1919:198)

Such a characterization, aside from Parker's now discredited views on inheriting culture through the genes, could as well describe the grandson as the grandfather. But unlike his grandfather, Parker was not born a Seneca. The Seneca count descent through the mother's line and Parker's mother was White. Like his father, he later became a Seneca by adoption into a clan. Despite or perhaps because of this ambiguity in his relationship to the Seneca, which haunted him both personally and professionally, Parker throughout his life returned in person and in spirit to Cattaraugus and to the multiple loyalties he had there acquired, extending them to the Senecas in the back country who practiced the ancient religion and who looked with suspicion on progressives like himself. By birth, upbringing, and choice Parker was thus inevitably involved in conflicts of loyalty and status, most of which he well recognized. By the same token, his heritage as he experienced it so richly at Cattaraugus enabled him to enter sympathetically into the life and thought of the diverse groups from which he came and by extension, into those of similar groups in the wider American society in which he participated.

When Parker was eleven or twelve years old, his father's work took the family to White Plains in suburban New York. The move seems to have been permanent although visits to the reservation were frequent. At about the same time Grandfather Nicholson died. Parker graduated from the public high school, and attended briefly Dickinson Seminary near Carlisle in preparation for the ministry—a vocation he soon abandoned. He also participated in Frederick W. Putnam's informal tutorials at the American Museum of Natural History, and in Harriet Maxwell Converse's salon in New York, where Indians and friends of Indians gathered; he considered but ultimately rejected Franz Boas' suggestion of becoming an anthropologist through the academic route at Columbia College and Boas' seminar; and became a field archeologist with Mark R. Harrington, his first important dig being at Cattaraugus. An offer of a job as ethnologist to collect materials for the New York State Library and Museum came in 1904. It was temporary and involved a risk but Parker seized the opportunity. The following year he took the Civil Service examination for archeologist in the New York State Museum and won the post. He had now irrevocably cut himself off from an academic career in anthropology just at the moment when the balance was decisively shifting from the field to the academy, a choice which invested his anthropological career with an ambiguity from which it never fully recovered. Nevertheless, between 1904 and 1910 Parker's fieldwork was exceedingly productive, resulting in a series of major articles and monographs on various aspects of Iroquoia: medicine societies, material culture, the Code of Handsome Lake and what he called the "constitution" of the Five Nations. He also published important works in Iroquois folklore and archeology (1908, 1909, 1910, 1913, and 1922a). Between 1911 and 1918, Parker was the chief intellectual influence in the first national Pan-Indian reform movement, the Society of American Indians. As the Indian wing of progressive reform, the Society included most of the leading educated Indians of the period. Its common ground was the idea of a nonvanishing Indian race, an Indian version of the melting pot. Parker served as the founder and editor of the Society's journal, as its secretary-treasurer and eventually as its president.[2] His vocations thus included prospective minister, archeologist, folklorist, ethnologist, editor, writer, Pan-Indian reformer, and museologist. In 1924 he left the New York State Museum to become director of the struggling Rochester Museum, which he built into a major institution and where he remained for the rest of his professional life. He died in 1955.

Of the vocations which Parker tested, museology offered him the most congenial home, a place where he could fruitfully combine and reconcile his multiple interests. But it was in ethnology and Pan-Indian reform that he sought most insistently an intellectual grounding for his life situation. Both were close to the core of his being. In both he experienced triumph and pain and from both he eventually retreated. To each he left a continuing legacy. Over half a century later Parker's ethnology continues to be drawn on by anthropologists. The patterns of Pan-Indian reform which he created still influence members of the modern Pan-Indian movement even though they may know little of his work.

Arthur Parker's search for a vocation reflects his time and place as well as his individual experience. But in it there are also continuing themes with which many Indian intellectuals are preoccupied today. In fact, so rich is Parker's search for meanings today that it is impossible within the scope of the present paper to discuss them all. Two, which are central, will be mentioned briefly: Parker's relationship to anthropology; and his attempt to place American Indians within a larger framework of American nationality.

Parker's selection of vocations had a consistent theme. In each he was an interpreter of one way of life to another. In his own person he combined these and he also sought to interpret these varying ways of life to himself and to give them coherence. The circumstances of his birth and upbringing made this role both necessary and useful and offered him unusual—in his generation virtually unique—opportunities to do so.

Of the three branches of anthropology in which he sought a vocation, archeology and folklore were relatively simple. In both—certainly in folklore—being Indian was an advantage. Both were fields in which the distinction between academic and self-acquired training was blurred and relatively unimportant. In these Parker could discover and publish information acceptable to Indians and non-Indians and welcomed by both. Neither had a theoretical super-structure which interfered with or inhibited what he wished to do. The work of interpretation could be performed in a manner which enhanced Parker's reputation. But ethnology was another, and much more complex, matter.

On the one hand, ethnology offered much to Parker. It was in his family tradition and therefore congenial. It provided him with relationships to the Senecas and the Iroquois which it is highly doubtful he could otherwise have obtained. As an ethnologist, he was able to participate in and report upon ceremonials from which he would normally have been barred. Ethnology gave him ways of finding out and organizing new information about the Senecas and the Iroquois which was valuable to social science and so recognized, and at the same time of exploring dimensions in his own background which he did not know existed, or which had been inadequately studied. Thus he could, through ethnology, celebrate the Senecas and the Iroquois, at once presenting 1) to the larger society, their achievements; 2) to them, a record of what they had been and done; and 3) to himself, a richer definition of being a Seneca and an Iroquois.

But there were problems in ethnology for Parker also. He was alone among Indian ethnologists in belonging to the generation in which the shift from the field to the academy took place. J. N. B. Hewitt and Francis La Flesche, the only other Indian ethnologists of repute, were from the old, or self-taught school; had already established their reputations; and were part of an important institution—the Bureau of American Ethnology. Because Parker rejected the academic route which his contemporaries took, his credentials were bound to be considered not quite right. He felt this keenly and compensated for it by claiming some which he had not earned, but for which he invented equivalents.

But probably more important were some of the prevailing trends in anthropological thought. One of these was the Boasian rejection of Lewis Henry Morgan's evolutionary views. Not only was Parker predisposed to these because of his familial connections with Morgan and because of Morgan's towering importance to Iroquois studies, but an evolutionary conception permitted him to sort out the various strands in his own background and life and to place them in meaningful relationship to each other. Morgan, it will be recalled, wrote sympathetically and respectfully of the old life but considered it doomed in man's struggle upward on "the evolutionary ladder." Of this "upward movement," Parker was himself a product with roots which also reached back to the old life. Change, in the evolutionary view, was in general for the better, although painful. Parker believed that Morgan could be improved upon—he tried, after all, to "out-Morgan Morgan" (Arthur C. Parker to John M. Clarke, April 16, 1909, cited in Fenton 1968:25) but he does not seem to have questioned the framework within which Morgan thought, and in fact he used it consistently.

Boasian anthropology, with its focus on salvaging as much information on the old life as possible, tended to downgrade or denigrate the changes which had taken place in Indian life as a result of White contact. The closer persons or groups were to aboriginal life, the more genuinely Indian they were believed to be. By the same token, the more they departed from aboriginal characteristics, the less Indian they were. The process of acculturation tended to be seen as a fall from aboriginal grace and its products not the genuine article. There was little room in this conception for a man like

Parker, who attempted to assert the validity of his own situation and experience as also genuinely Indian but as Indian in a new environment to which, from his viewpoint, one had to adapt or die.

The intensity of this conflict does not seem to have been a serious problem for Parker as anthropologist until he moved into a national stage as a Pan-Indian leader faced with the problem of defining "Indian" in a broader fashion. In his work on Seneca secret societies, on material culture, on agriculture, and on the code of Handsome Lake, he was on relatively safe and acceptable ground in recapturing aboriginal culture or practices and viewpoints sufficiently close to aboriginal life. But when with his Constitution of the Five Nations (1916a) he moved into a contemporary area in which acculturation was a major issue, he became involved in bitter conflicts of fact and interpretation with other Iroquoianists both Indian and White. Whatever the merits of this controversy, at bottom it seems to have stemmed from attitudes towards acculturation (cf. reviews of Parker 1916 in Goldenweiser 1916 and Hewitt 1917, as well as Parker's 1918 rebuttal).

Thus ethnology offered much to Parker but in the end its current premises were insufficient and eventually antagonistic to his personal situation. Had there been a substantial number of ethnologists who were Indians of Parker's experience, or had ethnology at the time been less preoccupied with salvage ethnography, or had ethnologists been more interested in acculturation as a positive rather than negative process, or had ethnology then even focused on acculturation as worthy of sustained analysis, Parker's role would have been different. It is sometimes implied today that somehow Parker failed ethnology. There is justice in this view if one accepts as entirely valid the viewpoints then dominant in ethnology. But a very strong case can be made conversely that the ethnology of his day failed Parker, not only as an individual but as a representative of an Indian experience and viewpoint to which most ethnologists were either indifferent or hostile. It did not seem to occur to them that in their efforts to be objective and scientific, they were advancing an interpretation in addition to "the facts," that their selection and interpretation of the phenomena to be studied reflected points of view, or that they were part of rather than outside of an historical process and context.

Parker was unable to derive from ethnology a satisfactory conceptual framework for defining the relationship of contemporary Indian life to the dominant society. Especially as a Pan-Indian leader, he needed such a framework in order to define his own position as a participant in multiple worlds, and to explain the diversity of Indian relationships to American life. The dominant view then held and upon which he drew was the conception of the melting pot (Hertzberg 1971:22 ff.). This had the great advantage, from his perspective, of explaining and validating the diversity not only of Indian life but of American life as a whole. It was strongly process-oriented. Within it, one could celebrate an Indian past and foresee an Indian future which would be different but yet Indian. Even when Indians eventually disappeared, enough Indian characteristics would have been contributed to the wider society to ensure some kind of Indian continuity and recognition. Within this framework, which was essentially evolutionary and not unlike Morgan's, Parker attempted to place European immigrants, Blacks, and Indians into a democratic society to which all would be committed and to define their problems and their eventual assimilation (by which he seems not necessarily to have meant amalgamation) (Parker 1916b:285–304).[3] The concept of an Indian race fell comfortably within this definition. A further advantage to the melting pot concept, from Parker's viewpoint, was that it corresponded to a process which he could observe taking place, albeit imperfectly, and it offered both a rationale for and hopeful outcome of this process. It also happily defined as most legitimate those who, like Parker, most fully accepted the procedures and viewpoints of a democratic society. In addition, the melting pot view did not imply that American life was above criticism. Many advocates of the melting pot concept by no means accepted contemporary American life as ideal, but rather sought to reform it to make it more true to what was regarded as its essential promise. About the realization of this promise in the future they tended to be exceedingly sanguine in the long if not the short-run, and this was the case also with Parker.

But the melting pot concept also presented problems. Its advocates, many of whom were immigrants or the children of immigrants, believed that readily recognizable groups based on ethnicity or country of origin, would eventually fade away. They thus placed a relatively low present value on ethnic groups, except as a passing or rather unimportant phenomenon, or as one contributing to the evolving future American. The melting pot conception did not take account of the possibility that such groups might persist long into the future, or might take a different view of the necessity or inevitability of their eventual disappearance. Nor was the process of "melting" very closely analyzed. In the case of American Indians, aboriginal life was seen primarily as a reflection of past glories, as a contributor of desirable characteristics, or as a representation of cultures which would disappear. The efforts of Indians and friends of Indians who held these views were directed toward encouraging those conditions which made the process as equitable as possible, while at the same time hastening its outcome. Thus most melting pot advocates concerned with Indian affairs sought to end "the tyranny of the tribe," and favored those persons and groups most committed to acculturation or who showed the most evidence of it. While fond of pointing to the general difficulties encountered in the "race of life," they often were insufficiently aware of the difficulties of those persons and groups involved in the process. In addition, the melting pot tended to focus on the individual rather than the group, and was thus closer to a nineteenth than to a twentieth century conception of American life (Hertzberg 1971:306–309).

These were serious difficulties which Parker encountered in the melting pot idea. He sought to counter them by casting the process of eventual assimilation in comparative terms; by emphasizing the problems which persons from very different cultural backgrounds encountered in fully entering American life; and by defining the process as one which would go on for a long time. He placed considerable emphasis on society's obligation to understand and to aid sympathetically in the process. In truth, Parker did not want the Seneca, the Iroquois, or American Indians to disappear, although he feared that this was inevitable. He resolutely opposed those Indians and Whites who considered instant assimilation either possible or desirable.

The elements of the major alternative view of American nationality, cultural pluralism, were present, but the idea was not yet named in the first decades of this century. Kallen's persuasive essay which set forth the pluralist position first appeared in *The Nation* in 1915 although it is not known whether Parker read it (Kallen 1924). In any case, the failure of the Society of American Indians was to Parker also the failure of the melting pot itself (Hertzberg 1971:199 ff.). His rejection of melting pot ideology in the early twenties appears to reflect not only this but also the polarization among intellectuals at the time in which many persons, including social scientists, eschewed the melting pot for a variety of Anglo-Americanization on the one hand or cultural pluralism on the other. For a time, at any rate, Parker so lost confidence in the promise of American life and in the possibility and efficacy of the melting pot process, that he rejected it (Parker 1922b).

Today many American Indian intellectuals face dilemmas similar to Parker's, although this historical context has changed. They, too, have multiple loyalties and for them, also, available conceptual tools are inadequate. In the past half-century anthropologists have studied acculturation rather extensively, but the terms in which it is described tend to be negative ones. Persons in transit—or thought of as being in transit—between what are defined as "two cultures" are often described as "marginal men." The implicit assumption seems to be either that what has been lost in the process is more valuable than what is being gained, or that both cultures are substantially lost to the individual or group which thus exist in a kind of limbo. In anthropology, the focus tends to be on studying those who have had most difficulty, rather than those whose adjustment has been easier. The model of "two cultures," i.e. an Indian tribal culture which is most valid where it is most aboriginal, and a larger American culture which is assumed to homogenize everyone, has tended to persist. Thus an Indian intellectual whose roots are as diverse as Parker's, tends to find that as yet anthropology does not offer a sufficiently complex or sophisticated set of conceptual tools to analyze the realities of his own situation or to assign them validity.

The larger conception of American nationality now more prevalent, cultural pluralism, presents similar difficulties. It has the advantage of validating distinct ethnic groups, including tribal groups, as well as a more generalized category of "Indian." It does little, however, to clarify the relationships among them, to explain the wide divergences in Indian life, or to mediate conflicts. In this conception, America is a nation of nations, sometimes thought of as a society without a culture, the role of culture-bearing being assigned to ethnic groups. One who is not easily categorized as belonging to one of the nations which are assumed to comprise American nation thereby becomes a kind of unperson, while ethnic groups tend to be thought of as static entities which are most valid when they most closely exhibit what are believed to be their original characteristics. Little attention is given to the problem of relationships among groups except as they define a common enemy. In the cultural pluralist viewpoint, Indian intellectuals tend to be cast as either/or: they are assumed to represent either their respective tribes or some overall Indian entity, with considerable confusion between the two. They are often representative of neither, even granting the difficulty of defining "representative." In fact, Indian intellectuals are in most cases the product of an extensive interplay between Indian and non-Indian life, and the tribe or tribes from which they derive have likewise gone through a complex history of acculturation and/or amalgamation. Somewhat like the situation of Parker and the melting pot, the ideology of cultural pluralism tends to place contemporary Indian intellectuals in a position at best drastically oversimplified and at worst false. The response of some has been an assertion of a nostalgic and romantic revivalism of their identity with what is presumed to be aboriginal and therefore valid, and from others a cry of pain that they are expected to be what they are not.

Is it not now time to stand back and ask what is needed and what we may contribute to classification and analysis? Parker's search for a vocation raises some of the unanswered questions. To begin to answer them, I would suggest that in anthropology much more attention be given to the study of the processes of acculturation and that at least some attempt be made to define and view them in more positive terms, or at least to shed implicit negative biases. As to theories of American nationality, we need, I believe, a new definition which is more in tune with what seems to be the reality: namely, that an enormous amount of both cultural and biological mixing of our population has indeed taken place and that at the same time distinct groups flourish although they have changed much more than they may imagine.

There seems to be a consanguinity between Morgan's evolutionary theory and the melting pot on the one hand, and Boas' view of culture and cultural pluralism on the other. I would therefore suspect that a new definition of American nationality, if it emerges, will similarly bear a relationship to the development of new ways of thought in anthropology. But only the future can answer this speculation.

NOTES

1. Biographical information on Parker is drawn extensively from Parker 1919, as well as from Fenton 1968, Hertzberg 1971, and Thomas 1955.

2. For a discussion of the Society of American Indians and Parker's roles in Pan-Indianism, see Hertzberg 1971:1–284.

3. Parker's 1916 article "Problems of Race Assimilation in America, with Special Reference to the American Indian" was one of the few extended analyses in the period of the comparative situation of European immigrants, Blacks and American Indians. It may have been the only one.

LITERATURE CITED

Fenton, William N.

1968 Parker on the Iroquois. Syracuse, New York: Syracuse University Press.

Goldenweiser, Alexander A.

1916 Review, The Constitution of the Five Nations, By Arthur C. Parker. American Anthropologist 18:431–36.

Hertzberg, Hazel W.
1971 The Search for an American Indian Identity: Modern Pan-Indian Movements. Syracuse, New York: Syracuse University Press.

Hewitt, J. N. B.
1917 Review, The Constitution of the Five Nations, By Arthur C. Parker. American Anthropologist 19:429–38.

Kallen, Horace M.
1924 Democracy Versus the Melting Pot. In Horace M. Kallen, ed., Democracy in the United States: Studies in the Group Psychology of the American Peoples. New York: Boni and Liveright.

Parker, Arthur Caswell
1908 (Editor) Myths and Legends of the New York State Iroquois, by Harriet Maxwell Converse. Albany, New York: New York State Museum Bulletin 125.

1909 Secret Medicine Societies of the Seneca. American Anthropologist 11:161–185.

1910 Iroquois Uses of Maize and Other Food Plants. Albany, New York: New York State Museum Bulletin 144:3–119. Reprinted in Fenton 1968: same pagination.

1913 The Code of Handsome Lake, The Seneca Prophet. Albany, New York: New York State Museum Bulletin 163:5-148. Reprinted in Fenton 1968: same pagination.

1916a The Constitution of the Five Nations. Albany, New York: New York State Museum Bulletin 184:7–155. Reprinted in Fenton 1968: same pagination.

1916b Problems of Race Assimilation in America, With Special Reference to the American Indian. American Indian Magazine 4:285–304.

1918 The Constitution of the Five Nations: A Reply. American Anthropologist 20:120–124.

1919 The Life of General Ely S. Parker. Buffalo, New York: Buffalo Historical Society.

1922a The Archeological History of New York. Albany, New York: State University of New York. Two Volumes.

1922b America The Melting Pot of Nationalities. Typed manuscript dated January 18, 1922, Parker Papers, New York State Museum, Albany, New York.

Thomas, W. Stephen

1955 Arthur Caswell Parker: Leader and Prophet of the Museum World. Pp. 18–25 In Museum Service (Bulletin of the Rochester Museum) 28(2).

CHAPTER ELEVEN

WILLIAM BEYNON, ETHNOGRAPHER

Tsimshian, 1888–1958

MARJORIE MYERS HALPIN

William Beynon, Tsimshian, did ethnography for White anthropologists for over 40 years (1915–1956). Yet he is known to anthropology, and identified in its literature, as an "informant and interpreter." There is an injustice here, which this paper seeks to redress. In so doing, the paper itself becomes evidence of the change that is taking place between anthropologists and the people they study.

Beynon did not call himself an ethnographer, at least insofar as I can determine from his manuscripts and correspondence. How, then, can it be stated that he was one? There are many definitions of "ethnography" and "ethnographer," most of them inadequate insofar as they attempt to specify the content of what are to be considered ethnographic data. An adequate definition of this sort must include a statement of the dialectical relationship of such data to, and their determination by, the more inclusive ends of anthropology, as has been well argued by Kenelm Burridge (1973). Without this dialectic "anthropology would be a haphazard and entirely ethnocentric collection of curiosa: at best trivial, at worst an unpardonable trespass on the integrity and patience of those being studied" (Burridge, 1973:60). I am not yet sufficiently clear in my own mind concerning the nature of the central dialectic of the anthropological enterprise to attempt a definition of ethnography that would meet this criterion.

Fortunately, there is another and simpler way to define an ethnographer. Miles Richardson (1975:520) says it most clearly: "In the field the relationship most critical to the ethnographer, the one that actually changes him from tourist to ethnographer, is the relationship with his informant." Further, Richardson located the present moral crisis in anthropology in terms of that same relationship. His argument is pertinent:

> Because the informant is so central to the ethnographer's reason for being, any change in the informant or in his relationship to the ethnographer, and any change in his society's relationship to the ethnographer's, will create anxiety in the ethnographer, and through him stress in ethnology, and ultimately conflict in anthropology. This is what has happened, and this is why anthropology's self-criticism is at its present strident pitch (Richardson, 1975:521).

For the purposes of this paper, then, I will define an *ethnographer* as one who solicits cultural information from an informant, and *ethnography* as the data resulting from that solicitation, i.e., produced during the course of the informant/ethnographer relationship.

It is thus significant that William Beynon was working independently with Tsimshian-speaking "informants" (so labeled by him) as early as 1916, when he wrote in his field notes of the difficulties he encountered at Kitkatla in persuading "informants" to work with him (Beynon field entry for January 31, 1916; Kitkatla Field Notes, Vol. III, Canadian Centre for Folk Culture Studies, hereinafter CCFCS). From the beginning, Beynon's relationships with informants had a financial aspect, one which he managed to maintain throughout his career, albeit with some difficulty. For example, in 1953 when Philip Drucker paid him $1.25 an hour (the then current informant's fee) for producing ethnographic materials, Beynon simply billed Drucker for his own hours plus those of his informants, even though the latter costs had not been specified in their agreement. The following year Beynon complained to Marius Barbeau in a letter dated July 26 (CCGCS) that "my informants are very demanding, and these have been spoiled by various anthropologists who come through here, paying as high as $1.50 for informants. . . ." If Richardson's definition of an ethnographer as one defined by his or her relationship to an informant is accepted (and I will provide additional evidence of Beynon's ethnographer/informant relationships below), there can be no doubt that William Beynon was an ethnographer. The remainder of this paper constitutes the first attempt to outline his career.

***

William Beynon was born in Victoria, British Columbia, in 1888, the first child of Captain and Mrs. William Beynon. His father was Welsh, his mother Tsimshian. Captain Beynon was for many years in command of steamers sealing and trading along the North Pacific Coast (Wright 1895:298). Mrs. Beynon was a member of the Laxkibu ("wolf") clan of the Gitlan group of the Tsimshian; her mother was a Niska from Gitlaxdamiks on the Nass River; her father was Clah (Arthur Wellington), the man who taught the missionary William Duncan to speak Tsimshian in 1857, and is credited by Arctander (1909:133–134) with saving Duncan's life by holding a gun on Legaic, the highest-ranking chief of the Fort Simpson Tsimshian. It is interesting to note, in the light of Beynon's own reputation among Whites, that Clah is described by Arctander (*loc. cit.*) as a man "who had impressed everyone (at Fort Simpson) with his apparently greater intellectuality than the common, ordinary Indian." Beynon's mother's only surviving brother, Albert Wellington, held the high-ranking Niska Laxkibu name, Gusgain, which Beynon himself was later to assume. His sister, Martha, was the second wife of Captain William Henry McNeill, Master of the Steamboat "Beaver" from 1837, and an important figure in the history of Fort Simpson (Pethick, 1970:49).

Beynon was raised in Victoria and attended high school, although he did not graduate. He was the only one of the six Beynon brothers to learn to speak Tsimshian from their mother. While still a young man, he worked for the Canadian Pacific Railroad and the Department of Public Works. He spent most of his later adult life, when not in the employ of anthropologists, working in the fishing and canning industries. He went to Port Simpson in 1913 for the funeral of his uncle, Albert Wellington, and stayed in order to begin a new life among his mother's people.

William Beynon made his first appearance in the anthropological record in Marius Barbeau's notes from his first field trip among the Tsimshian in an entry dated December 29, 1914 (Barbeau field notes, CCFCS). Barbeau refers to him as follows in a letter to Edward Sapir (his superior at the Geological Survey, later the National Museum of Canada), dated January 9, 1915 (Barbeau/Sapir correspondence, CCFCS): "(Beynon) I use simply as an interpreter, he is not versed in Indian matters, being young and having lived away from here most of the time; his mother was a Tsimshian."[1] On January 23, 1915, less than a month after Beynon was first introduced to the ethnographic enterprise, Barbeau wrote to Sapir about him again (Barbeau/Sapir correspondence, CCFCS):

> I am very fortunate in having gotten the services of Wm. Beynon, a very intelligent young half-breed Tsimshian, who proves more useful still in working directly with informants for me. He records myths quite successfully and with good speed. He has them recited

> in Tsimshian and writes them down in English at once, sentence by sentence. *The work could not be done any better if I were working with them.* Meanwhile I work with other informants, with another interpreter (emphasis added).

Sapir's reply (letter to Barbeau, February 1, 1915, CCFCS) is instructive:

> I am very glad to see that you have found it possible to get your best interpreter to work independently, somewhat in the manner in which Alex Thomas has been working for me among the Nootka. I am sure that this is an excellent method with a really intelligent interpreter. There is, after all, no absolute reason why every bit of material that one utilizes in his work should have been personally obtained. . . . In other words, one should by no means underestimate the usefulness of an intelligent native or half-breed in recording materials.

Sapir advised Barbeau to teach Beynon to write Tsimshian phonetically, so that he might send him by mail "texts of songs, speeches of all sorts, personal experiences of ethnological interest, war stories, accounts of shamanistic performances, and many other types of texts that might easily occur to you" (*loc. cit.*). Barbeau took the advice and taught Beynon to write Tsimshian using the phonetic system he had learned from Sapir.

Wilson Duff (1964:65) has written about that first 1914–15 field partnership of Barbeau and Beynon: "Judging from the field notes and publications which resulted (Barbeau, 1917a, 1917b), that must have been one of the most productive field seasons in the history of American anthropology." On his return to Ottawa, Barbeau made arrangements for funds with which to pay Beynon to do additional, and unsupervised, field work at Kitkatla. He agreed to pay 50 cents per page or $25.00 for each 50-page notebook Beynon sent him (the notebooks were Canadian government field notebooks; Beynon was to use them for many years).

Beynon was thus an employed and experienced ethnographer, in fact although not in title, when he went alone into the field in January, 1916. The trip was a field worker's nightmare. In a chartered boat on his way to Dolphin Island, the site of the Kitkatla Village, Beynon ran into Chief Seks and his party in a disabled boat. As he was towing them a storm broke, and the motor of his own boat became swamped. They drifted all night in zero-degree cold and piled up on Stephens Island, where they stayed for ten days. Although there was no loss of life, Beynon lost all of his money and personal effects. Later during the trip he was quarantined for a month with measles and was late reporting to his job at B. C. Packers (from copies of Beynon letters to Barbeau, January 28 and February 6, 1916, Wilson Duff Tsimshian File).

The Kitkatlas were more conservative than the people in Port Simpson, and Beynon ran into some difficulty at the beginning of his work. His informants made him get permission from Chief Seks before they would work with him, and he reports that at least one of them "handed all the money over to the chief and took only what the chief allowed him for telling me what I wanted" (Beynon, 1916: Vol. III, CCFCS). He paid his informants 60 cents an hour. Barbeau's instructions had been to duplicate the work they had done together in Port Simpson the previous year—to secure a census of the Houses in the village and their present and former territories, lists of names and crests and their related myths, data on the origins of the Houses and lists of their foreign relatives, and, if time permitted, to gather information on potlatches, secret societies, and first fruits ceremonies. Such data, and more, are indeed included in the six notebooks Beynon sent to Ottawa.

Beynon was ill during the summer of 1916 and in 1917 and returned for a time to Victoria. He obviously lost none of his enthusiasm for his new vocation, however, and in 1918 he sent Barbeau some new material. He had by this time acquired a typewriter which he used to work for the people at Port Simpson in order to gain their confidence.

> I have been able to get the full confidence of the people by rendering them what assistance I can as a sort of secretary . . . for if you do not have their confidence at the start, you cannot get all the information wanted. . . . Mr. Henry Tate . . . did not have the full confidence of all his informants . . . nor money to pay them. In spite of that he seems to have done well (Beynon letter to Barbeau, March 19, 1918, Wilson Duff Tsimshian File).

In the same letter, Beynon asked Barbeau to send him any of Steffanson's books on the Eskimos, for "I am trying to read all the reports on native works I can lay my hands on."

Beynon's comparison between himself and Henry Tate quoted above is worth developing further. Henry Tate sent texts of Tsimshian narratives to Franz Boas between ca. 1904 and 1914 (they form the bulk of Boas, 1916). Boas paid him 15 cents and then 20 cents a page. There are no indications in the Boas/Tate correspondence (Library of the American Philosophical Society, hereinafter APS) that the two men had ever met, nor did Boas train Tate in phonetic transcription (Tate wrote Tsimshian in the alphabet devised by Bishop Ridley of Metlakatla for translating the Gospels; before Boas published six of Tate's texts in Tsimshian in 1912, he had them read to him by another Tsimshian speaker, Archie Dundas of New Metlakatla, then a student of Carlisle Indian School in Pennsylvania).

Unlike Beynon, who asked questions and collected ethnographic information as well as texts, Tate collected only narratives. Furthermore, Tate not only did not pay his informants, he apparently worked in secret. Barbeau (1917b:561) wrote of him as follows:

> While in Port Simpson, we have learned that Tate was not in the habit of taking down the stories under dictation. He was loath to divulge to other natives that he was really writing them down at all. Our assistant Beynon knew only of his "keeping a little book at home for these things." The fact that he had made such a large collection was practically unknown in Port Simpson.

Not only was Tate "loath" to let other Indians know what he was doing, which must have affected the accuracy of his work, he was also reluctant to record material that might be considered objectionable. Boas was aware of this (see also Boas, 1916:31), and his letter to Tate on the point is quite revealing of the relationship between the two men:

> I was very much interested in reading what you have written, but you must allow me to say one thing. You write in your letter that you have omitted some of the stories which to you seem very improper; but if we want to preserve for future times a truthful picture of what the people were before they advanced to their present condition, we ought not to leave out anything that shows their ways of thinking, even though it should be quite distasteful to you.
>
> It is just the same as with some of the horrid customs of olden times, like dog eating and man-eating. You have no reason to be ashamed of what the people did in olden times, before they knew better: but if we want to give a truthful account of what there was, we ought not to be ashamed or afraid to write it down. I hope, therefore, that you may be willing to overcome your reluctance to write nasty things, since they belonged to the tales that were told by your old people. For our purpose it is all-essential that whatever we write should be true, and that we should not conceal anything (Boas letter to Tate, March 28, 1907, APS).

In 1954 Beynon wrote to Philip Drucker, then at the Smithsonian Institution, and offered to correct the narratives collected by Tate and published by Boas (1916). "I treasure this volume of work very much, but Tait (sic) mostly from religious scruples, omitted some very important parts and also whole narratives which involved sex and sexual references" (Beynon letter to Drucker, March 8, 1954, National Anthropological Archives, hereinafter NAA). Beynon himself collected references to sexual matters as early as his 1916 field trip to Kitkatla.

In comparison with Henry Tate, then, William Beynon's attitudes and conduct were, from the beginning of his association with Barbeau, much more those of a professional ethnographer. This was probably a function at least in part of the relative degree of acculturation of the two men. There is no question but that Tate was by far the more "Indian" (although he, too, may have had a White parent: Boas (1912:67) wrote that he was a "full-blood Indian of Port Simpson;" while Barbeau (1917b:561), who is likely to have had the better information, wrote that he was a "half-breed Tsimshian"). The fact that Tate was reluctant to record texts openly is indicative of his close involvement with the Indian community. Tate's command of English was also considerably poorer than Beynon's. Beynon was certainly much better educated in the European tradition.

Returning to Beynon's ethnographic career, he was employed in 1918 by Sir Henry Wellcome to collect museum specimens for the Wellcome Historical Medical Museum in London. Wellcome was an executor of the William Duncan Estate, and Beynon also acted as his local representative in New Metlakatla, Alaska, spending two years there between 1918 and 1924 (Beynon, 1941:83 ff.). He wrote to Barbeau in 1922 and told him that he had assembled a large and valuable collection from Chilkat to Bella Bella (Beynon letter to Barbeau, March 19, 1918, Duff Tsimshian File). This was apparently the collection of some nine cartons shipped to London from Montreal in 1924 (Wells, 1968, 1974); 14 items of which are now in the UCLA Museum of Cultural History. The whereabouts of the other specimens is unknown. Also lost are any notes Beynon might have made to accompany the collection; all that has been preserved are the village proveniences of the pieces.

Barbeau made a second field trip in the winter of 1920–21 to work in the Gitksan villages of the Upper Skeena River. Although the Gitksan are closely related, in both language and culture, to the Tsimshian, he apparently and inexplicably made no attempt to enlist Beynon's services before going. The initiative was Beynon's and, when he learned from the Prince Rupert newspaper that Barbeau was in Hazelton, he wrote to him. Barbeau hired him in November and, as before, wrote enthusiastically of Beynon's work to Sapir: "Everything is going extremely well here, especially since Beynon has joined me; his work is far better, as interpreter, than that of those I have had previously. Since he arrived a month ago, he has had his first day off today (Sunday), and he seems to be as enthusiastic as when he arrived, if not more" (Barbeau letter to Sapir, December 13, 1921, CCFCS).

In 1924 Barbeau went to Terrace and studied the Kitselas, Kitsumgalum, and Kitwanga, with Beynon again engaged as interpreter. They also went to Kitwancool, but were rebuffed by the people who refused to work with them. In 1926 Barbeau established his field headquarters at Usk on the Skeena and engaged Beynon again. In 1927 the team worked the Nass River. In 1929 they spent their second field season on the Nass. During this trip Beynon negotiated for the totem poles which Barbeau acquired for several museums and the two of them made a large ethnographic collection for the Royal Ontario Museum. They worked together again in coastal villages in 1939. I have not yet found any evidence that Beynon worked with Barbeau during the 1923 field season, nor any direct confirmation of Duff's statement (1964–65) that Beynon worked in the field with Barbeau in 1947.

In 1929 Beynon again began sending field notebooks to Barbeau in Ottawa. Between then and 1956, when illness forced him to stop (he died in 1958), he sent Barbeau approximately 54 volumes of field notes (Vols. AA–XX, 1929 to ca. 1950; Vols. I–XI, 1952; Vols. I–VI, 1953; Vols. I–X, 1954; Vol. I, 1956, CCFCS). By 1948, Barbeau had raised the price per notebook to $35.00. The materials in the notebooks are primarily texts of the Tsimshian, Niska, and Kitkatla, but also included are texts of the Haida, Gitksan, Kitkaita, and Kitasoo. Interspersed among the narratives are ethnographic observations, by far the most important of which is Beynon's 4-volume (200 pages) participant observer's account of eight days of potlatches and masked dramatizations held at Kitsegukla in 1945 (of which more below).

Barbeau put the Beynon materials along with his own in one large Tsimshian File, which is still preserved as he arranged it in a "Salle Barbeau" at the CCFCS in Ottawa. Regrettably for those interested in Beynon's work, Barbeau cut up most of the Beynon notebooks in order to extract narratives for typewriter copying and publication. It should be possible, however, to reconstruct the whole series of 54 Beynon notebooks (the earlier six notebooks from the 1916 Kitkatla fieldwork are intact), since it seems unlikely that any of the material has actually been lost or destroyed. Until such time as this is done and a detailed inventory has been prepared for the File, I strongly urge that any general bibliographic or other reference to it be cited as the "Marius Barbeau and William Beynon Field Notes." Specific materials should, of course, be cited according to their recorder, where this is known (Barbeau was quite consistent in his publication of the Beynon materials in indicating which were "recorded by William Beynon"). Wilson Duff has worked more with the File than I have and is undoubtedly correct when he says that the "greater part of the Tsimshian file is the result of Dr. Barbeau's own field work" (Duff, 1964:65), but we have also seen that Barbeau's field work was greatly expedited by Beynon's contribution as interpreter and co-ethnographer.

In 1918 Edward Sapir asked Beynon to send him Tsimshian kin terms corresponding to Niska kin terms he had previously received from a Niska chief who had visited Ottawa. Beynon went further than requested and sent him not only the Tsimshian kin terms but a new set of Niska terms which he obtained from a Nass River woman who was visiting Port Simpson. In his covering letter he asked Sapir if there was any additional work for him to do (Beynon letter to Sapir, October 31, 1918, Canadian Ethnology Service, hereinafter CES). In a published article Sapir (1920:269) hypothesized that the Niska kin term *hadi•´ᵓˡ* ("father"), which was used by female children only, was borrowed from the corresponding Haida term *ha•da•´i*. Beynon, who obviously was reading the *American Anthropologist*, then wrote to Sapir about the term:

> Your theory, I am sure, is correct. I was struck by this term being used only by the female children of Haida parents, three of maternal descent and one paternal. These have been adopted into the Tsimshian tribes. *ha'ᵊt* and *hädi* are the terms used by these female children to their fathers. On making inquiries among them as to the reason the term was not general among all the Tsimshian I learned that it was not a true Tsimshian word but was a term introduced by those of Haida origin. There are only four such families here, but strong enough to show or bear out your theory on this (Beynon letter to Sapir, November 16, 1920, CES).

In other words, the kin term in question was still felt as intrusive by the Tsimshian, but had become established among the Niska (Sapir, 1921:234). Sapir published Beynon's comments in the next volume of the *American Anthropologist* with the statement that it "turns the hypothesis into a practical certainty" (Sapir, 1921:234).

In 1932 Beynon began sending materials to Franz Boas at Columbia University (see their letters preserved in the Boas Professional Correspondence at the APS). There is no evidence in the extant correspondence of how the two men came to be in contact with each other. The relationship could well have been initiated by Beynon himself, who remained consistently eager for ethnographic work and wrote a number of anthropologists offering his services. He had a copy of Boas' *Tsimshian Mythology* (1916) and certainly knew of the errors and omissions in it, most assuredly he was aware of what was perhaps Boas' greatest error—his belief that it contained "the bulk of the important traditions of the Tsimshian" (Boas, 1916:31). Now, it happens that there are two kinds of Tsimshian narratives or tales: those general and aetiological tales, such as in the Raven cycle, that are known to and told by anyone, and those others which are owned by a House and should properly be told only by members of that House. The tales collected by Tate and published by Boas were almost exclusively of the first type, while Beynon and Barbeau had collected many dozens of the second type.

In any event, Beynon sent Boas some 252 narratives and ethnographic reports between 1932 and 1939. Ninety-nine of these have been typed and edited for obvious publication in a manuscript entitled "Ethnographic and Folkloristic Texts of the Tsimshian" (Boas Collection, Number 33, 544 pages, APS). Unfortunately, the APS Library does not have the other 153 narratives known from the letters to have existed, and I cannot find any mention of their being elsewhere. Also, although I have not located a manuscript and do not know if the work was actually completed, there is evidence from several letters that Beynon rewrote the materials Henry Tate had earlier sent Boas and which had formed the bulk of *Tsimshian Mythology*. For example, Boas wrote to Viola Garfield (June 8, 1934, APS) that "during this winter I have had Mr. Beynon rewrite for me the whole Tate materials which was written in such bad phonetics that I could not use it."

Beynon charged Boas 50 cents an hour for his own services in recording, translating, and rewriting his material, and 35 cents an hour for informants' fees. He kept his services to about $50.00 per month at Boas' request. His letters to Boas convey very clearly his sensitivity when working with informants. For example, in 1936 when he was working on a series of narratives concerning Txemsem and Lagabula (at Boas' request), he wrote as follows: "I am not for the time being making a direct probe for Lagabula, but would rather that he should come out in the picture without any effort on my part. When I have exhausted all then I will make a direct inquiry for Lagabula, in full" (Beynon letter to Boas, July 29, 1936, APS).

Boas' instructions were brief to the point that it would be misleading to conclude that he "trained" Beynon in any way. For example, on February 21, 1939, he wrote to Beynon as follows:

> I asked you some time ago to send me information in regards to the customs of medicine men: the methods of burial of medicine men, the way in which they allow their hair to grow and become matted, and whatever else you know or can find out. You have never answered that question so far. (APS)

Beynon sent the requested information on June 2 of the same year. It is one of the missing narratives. On September 22, 1939, Boas asked for some examples of what Beynon had earlier referred to as "underground speech." Beynon replied on November 1:

> As you instructed I took a number of conversations at random as you will see. I trust that these will be of value to you. . . . I put this out to show a number of veiled remarks with hidden meanings, which is termed literally by the Tsimshians as *underground talking*, a method of speech often resorted to by the olden speakers to hide their direct meanings. (APS)

This information is also missing.

Other of the missing narratives would be of considerable ethnological interest should they be found. Missing narrative Number 217 is entitled "Rewriting of Asti-wal" (11 pages, 1938). Another entitled "The Dances Given by the Gitksan in Honor of the Kitkatla" (Number 233) describes a series of four *halait* rituals held at Kitwanga and Kitsegukla in 1938 at which "many nax-noxa were revived and dramatized" (Beynon letter to Boas, November 25, 1939, APS). Still other missing narratives include Number 240, "The Third Exogamous Group of the Tlingit," and Number 248, "The Origin of Totem Poles."

It seems fairly clear to me that Boas employed Beynon to send him material to comprise a second monumental publication on the Tsimshian (i.e., the 544 page manuscript mentioned above). One of the pieces in this edited collection (Number 109) was a *haldaogit* ("witchcraft") narrative which Beynon specifically asked Boas to "keep . . . away from public publication for some time in any event and when publishing it to change the names concerned. It really happened" (Beynon letter to Boas, October 7, 1935, APS). I regret to say that this narrative, under the name of the informant who had given it to Beynon, is included in the manuscript prepared for publication. With this exception, or perhaps with the narrative changed as Beynon requested, it seems to me that the manuscript in the APS should be published as Boas obviously intended it to be. (It should also be mentioned that Barbeau left in the CCFCS a massive four-volume manuscript of Tsimshian narratives, many of them collected by Beynon, that he had been unable to get published.)

In 1939, Boas wrote to Beynon that "You have such great difficulty in getting a consistent way of writing Tsimshian that I think the only way to solve this difficulty is to send somebody out to work with you some time in order to see to all the doubtful points" (Boas letter to Beynon, February 16, 1939, APS). Accordingly, Boas' student Amelia Susman went to Port Simpson in the winter of 1939 to work with Beynon on standardizing his orthography. The two of them rewrote Boas' 1910 Tsimshian grammar and a number of the narratives in an improved orthography and she returned to New York in April, 1940, well-satisfied with Beynon's work. There then follow a series of letters in the Boas Professional Correspondence between Boas and Beynon and Boas and Susman concerning plans for Beynon to come to New York to continue the work. He was obviously eager to go: "It is my ambition to be able to get to New York this coming fall and if possible continue studying" (Beynon letter to Boas, April 24, 1940, APS). Susman was equally eager to have him come:

> I have been doing a lot of thinking about the whole matter, and I have no doubt in taking this particular step. If, despite the complications and difficulties, it works out as I hope and intend it should, we will try to convince you that from every angle there are excellent reasons for, and no positive reasons against. (Susman letter to Boas, August 10, 1940, APS)

Boas, however, seemed to be against it, and the proposed trip never materialized. Neither Boas nor Susman ever worked with Beynon again.

Beynon also began a new role in his ethnographic career in 1932 with Viola Garfield—that of informant. She notes in the publication resulting from her Port Simpson field work that Beynon was used as "interpreter as well as an informant. . . . He is conversant with all aspects of pre-White native culture. His unflagging interest in all matters pertaining to native cultural background and his tireless energy are worthy of special mention" (Garfield 1939:169). In other words, the young man who had been raised in Victoria and who had not even had an Indian name when he first worked with Barbeau in 1914 had become, by 1932, an expert on traditional Tsimshian culture and, as such, an anthropologist's informant. Indeed, the Tsimshian potlatch described by Garfield under the heading "Gɨt-laˊn Chief's Potlatch" was the occasion at which Beynon assumed both the name Gusgain and the chieftainship of the Gitlan (Garfield 1939:

204–206).[2] Unfortunately, she does not give a date for the potlatch in her account of it, so that we cannot tell precisely when in Beynon's career it occurred. She does mention in another context (quoted below) that he had held the chief's position for "about twenty years," suggesting that the potlatch was given ca. 1919 (Garfield 1939:190).

Garfield's description of the Gitlan chief (Beynon) is significant in what it reveals of his use of both modern political and economic interests and traditional clan solidarities to achieve his position:

> The Git-la'n chieftainship is now held by a man who belongs to a high ranking Wolf House on the Nass River, but not to the traditional lineage from which Niəs-langanu•'s, the chief of this tribe, should come. The true chief's lineage has been extinct in Port Simpson for over thirty years and the incumbent has been in office for about twenty years. He succeeded to another name and position, that of his mother's brother, Gusgai' in, and he immediately began to build up a following for himself in the village by taking an active part in all village activities. He speaks English well and has acted as interpreter and conciliator between the natives and the Indian agent and the law officers. He has held office in the Native Brotherhood for several years, and has been active on behalf of the native interests in fishing, hunting and land ownership controversies. Since there are only twenty-five members of the Git-la'n tribe in the village of Port Simpson, he could not exert much influence, political or social through so small a group. He belongs to the coast branch of the Wolf clan which traces its origin mythologically from the Nass River and ultimately from the Tahltans. The members of this branch traditionally aid each other in potlatching, funeral contributions, etc. Gusgai' in has activated this loyalty and organized all the Wolf clan members in this branch in other tribes as well as his own. He is now the recognized spokesman for this group and receives financial support from it as well as from his tribe. (Garfield, 1939:190)

The events leading up to the potlatch are also of interest, in that they reveal Beynon's sensitivity to traditional pressures and insults (Garfield, 1939:205). Soon after arriving in Port Simpson, he was addressed in a potlatch by his deceased uncle's name, Gusgain. Since Beynon had not yet formally assumed the name at a potlatch of his own, this was perceived by him and his Laxkibu ("wolf") clansmen as an insult. Because neither Beynon nor his small group of kinsmen was in a financial position to give a potlatch at the time, nothing was done. Later, however, a second insult was made that they could not ignore. Beynon and a clansman were caught between the piles of a bridge in a boat while the tide went out. The remark was made by others that "We saw a wolf hanging up under the bridge" (*loc. cit.*) Beynon and his kinsmen were then obliged to give a feast at which he could assume the name Gusgain and the insult of the bridge incident could be wiped away. According to Garfield (1939:206), he became the new chief of the Gitlan at the same time.

Garfield's use of Beynon as one of her chief informants raises a number of questions. Paramount among these is the question of his acceptability as an expert on traditional Tsimshian culture. He had not been raised in that culture, except insofar as his mother might have passed parts of it on to him in Victoria, and we have Barbeau's 1915 statement, quoted above, that "he is not versed in Indian matters." In point of fact, of course, Beynon *did* become an expert on Tsimshian culture, and he became so in the same way that anthropologists become experts—by doing ethnography. Regardless of our esteem for one another's knowledge, however, none of us would accept a non-native ethnographer as an informant. On the other hand, Beynon was, as an Indian, in a position to put his expert knowledge to a test that no non-native ethnographer has ever passed: he was able to use the cultural rules he had learned in "real" cultural situations, such as becoming chief of the Gitlan. Does this validate his knowledge in a way that our own is never validated?

The final chapter in William Beynon's ethnographic career opened in 1953, when he acted as informant for Philip Drucker, then of the Bureau of American Ethnology of the Smithsonian Institution, who was studying the Indian Brotherhood of British Columbia, of which Beynon had been a founding member (Drucker 1958:105). The two men corresponded after Drucker returned to Washington and, in his usual fashion, Beynon began sending the anthropologist materials he had been collecting on the Tsimshian. Quite obviously impressed with him, Drucker wrote to H. L. Shapiro at the American Museum of Natural History in New York and requested funds with which to support Beynon's work. His description of Beynon to Shapiro raises echoes of Arctander's description of his maternal grandfather, Clah, quoted above: "Beynon is very far from being an ordinary Northwest Coast Indian. Unfortunately, he is about the only one I know who is both literate and pretty well informed" (Drucker letter to Shapiro, December 14, 1954, NAA: 4516:50). Shapiro produced two grants of $500 each for the project, out of which Beynon was paid $1.25 per hour of work, which was the current informant's fee on the Northwest Coast.

As the material came in, Drucker and Shapiro began to write to each other about publishing it as a monograph. Drucker wrote to Beynon that he was going to "try to get the job published—under your name of course" (Drucker letter to Beynon, December 21, 1954, NAA: 4516:50). Beynon replied in his final letter to Drucker (February 1, 1955, NAA: 4516:50): "I must thank you for your work on my behalf which I certainly appreciate and I will do all I can to justify your confidence in me." By then, however, he had suffered a heart attack and he had no time left for his plans to go on and write for Drucker about the Kitkatla, Hartley Bay (the Kitkiata), Klemtu (the Kitasoo), and, finally, the Nass.

The material he did produce, however, should be published. It is no less than a synthesis of the *adaox* or traditional histories of the Houses of a number of Tsimshian groups. Drucker had asked for an ethnogeography, and Beynon included some geography and place names in his account, but he had been working for forty years on the *adaox* collecting them for himself and for Barbeau and Boas, and he knew better than Drucker what he could do. As one who had read through dozens of the *adaox* of Tsimshing-speaking peoples, I can appreciate the attempt at synthesis Beynon was making, and believe that it should be made available. It is contained in six volumes of handwritten notebooks Beynon sent to Drucker at the Bureau of American Ethnology, and subsequently sent by Drucker to the Department of Anthropology at the American Museum of Natural History. Drucker had three of the volumes and part of a fourth type copied (133 pages) and this manuscript is in the National Anthropological Archives (4516:49).

Of even more urgency, however, is the need to publish Beynon's four volumes of notes on the Kitsegukla potlatches and naxnox dramatizations in 1945 (now in the CCFCS).[3] There is no comparable record of northern Northwest Coast potlatching in existence and scholarship of that complex institution will remain seriously retarded until Beynon's account is made available. I have had occasion to read large portions of the Beynon account to Mrs. Olive Mulwain, of the House of Hanamux, Kitsegukla, who was a participant in 1945, and they accord well with her memory, except for an occasional mistake made by Beynon in recording the names of participants. Beynon not only recorded these potlatches and dances, he participated in them as a Laxkibu chief. His account is, therefore, something that no White ethnographer could have produced, and it seems only fitting that his particular role in the development of Northwest Coast ethnology should be commemorated with its publication under his name.

***

I keep wondering why Beynon did it for all those years. He certainly was not well paid, nor did he achieve what I would consider adequate recognition for his work. Perhaps the only answer is to be found somewhere close to that of Alfonso Ortiz (1972:7): "Let me begin by stating flatly that I initially went into anthropology because it was the one field in which I could read about and deal with Indians, all of the time and still make a living. It was just that simple."

Finally, I will conclude by questioning the utility of the concept of "marginality" for describing the cultural position of men and women like William Beynon. It leads all too readily to the idea of someone, somehow, being somewhere in between two cultures—wherever that is. In its place, I suggest another formulation of Kenelm Burridge (1973) from his book on the history of anthropology in Australia. The doing of anthropology, he writes,

> entails a movement of the mind between the Aborigines themselves and their cultures, and the investigators and their cultures: a quadratic relationship whose intricacies the mind has to hold and map. (Burridge, 1973:1)

White anthropologists must receive two of the terms of that quadratic relationship; William Beynon embodied or contained all four. That is surely a more remarkable intellectual accomplishment than is accorded in the concept of cultural marginality.

ACKNOWLEDGMENTS

Archival visits upon which this paper is based were supported by a Canada Council Research Grant. I am grateful to the Canadian Centre for Folk Culture Studies and the Canadian Ethnology Service of the National Museum of Man, the National Anthropological Archives of the Smithsonian Institution, the University Records Center of the University of Washington, and the Library of the American Philosophical Society for making materials available to me. I am also grateful to Philip Drucker, Viola Garfield, Amelia Susman Schultz, Robin Wells, Richard Inglis, Stanley Freed, Jay Miller, Harry B. Hawthorn, and especially, Wilson Duff, who gave me additional information. An earlier version of this paper was read at the Annual Meeting of the Canadian Sociology and Anthropology Association, Toronto, 1974.

NOTES

1. Both Viola Garfield and Amelia Susman Schultz disagreed with this statement when we discussed it in August 1976. They both recalled that Beynon had learned a great deal about the culture from his mother, and believed that his primary identification was Tsimshian rather than White, for which reason he returned to Port Simpson when his maternal uncle died to assume his place as successor. I believe that Barbeau's assessment still has validity, however, insofar as (1) he met Beynon some twenty years before either Garfield or Schultz, and (2) however much Beynon might have learned from his mother, he was in fact raised in an alien community. Tsimshian cultural rules must have been traditionally transmitted in a great many situational and contextual ways denied to Beynon during his socialization. Also, of course, he did not know other members of Tsimshian society until adulthood.

2. Nowhere in *Tsimshian Clan and Society* (1939) does Garfield indicate that her informant, William Beynon, and the Gitlan chief, Gusgain, are one and the same person. There is no doubt, however, of the identification.

3. Beynon sent a manuscript based on these notes to Harry B. Hawthorn at the University of British Columbia about 1948. It is misleadingly entitled "Totem Poles" and contains some information not included in the field notes proper. This information should probably be incorporated, at least in the form of footnotes, in any published version of the field notes.

LITERATURE CITED

Published Sources

Arctander, John W.

1909 The Apostle of Alaska: The Story of William Duncan of Metlakahtla. New York: Fleming H. Revell Company.

Barbeau, Marius

1917a "Growth and Federation in the Tsimshian Phratries," Proceedings of the 19th International Congress of Americanists, 1915, pp. 402–408. Washington, D.C.

1917b "Review of Franz Boas, Tsimshian Mythology," American Anthropologist 19:548–563.

Beynon, William

1941 "The Tsimshians of Metlakatla, Alaska," American Anthropologist 43:83–88.

Boas, Franz
1910 "Tsimshian, an Illustrative Sketch," Handbook of American Indian Languages, pp. 287–422. Bulletin 40, Part 1, Bureau of American Ethnology. Washington, D.C.: Smithsonian Institution.

1912 Tsimshian Texts (New Series). Publications of the American Ethnological Society, III:65–284.

1916 Tsimshian Mythology, based on texts recorded by Henry W. Tate. 31st Annual Report of the Bureau of American Ethnology 1909–1910, pp. 27–1037. Washington, D.C.; Smithsonian Institution.

Burridge, Kenelm
1973 Encountering Aborigines: A Case Study: Anthropology and the Australian Aboriginal. Pergamon Frontiers of Anthropology Series. Elmsford, N.Y.: Pergamon Press Inc.

Drucker, Philip
1958 The Native Brotherhoods: Modern Intertribal Organizations on the Northwest Coast. Bureau of American Ethnology Bulletin 168. Washington, D.C.: Smithsonian Institution.

Duff, Wilson
1964 "Contributions of Marius Barbeau to West Coast Ethnology," Anthropologica VI:63–69.

Garfield, Viola
1939 Tsimshian Clan and Society. University of Washington Publications in Anthropology 7:167–340. Seattle: University of Washington Press.

Ortiz, Alfonso
1972 "An Indian Anthropologist's Perspective on Anthropology," The American Indian Reader: Anthropology, pp. 6–12. San Francisco: The Indian Historian Press, Inc.

Pethick, Derek
1970 S. S. Beaver. Vancouver: Mitchell Press Ltd.

Richardson, Miles
1975 "Anthropologist-The Myth Teller," American Ethnologist 2(3):517–533.

Sapir, Edward
1920 "Nass River Terms of Relationship," American Anthropologist 22:261–271.

1921 "A Haida Kinship Term Among the Tsimshian," American Anthropologist 23:233–234.

Wright, E. W., ed.
1895 Lewis and Dryden's Marine History of the Pacific Northwest. Portland, Oregon: Lewis and Dryden.

Unpublished Sources

Barbeau, Marius and William Beynon
1914–1956 The Marius Barbeau and William Beynon Field Notes. Canadian Centre for Folk Culture Studies, National Museum of Man, Ottawa.

Beynon, William
1916 Kitkatla Field Notes, Vols. I–VI. Canadian Centre for Folk Culture Studies, National Museum of Man, Ottawa.

1939 Ethnographic and Folkloristic Texts of the Tsimshian. Typed ms., 544 pp. Included in Boas Collection, Number 33, Library of the American Philosophical Society, Philadelphia.

1945 Kitsegukla (Skeena Crossing) Field Notes. Vols. I–IV. Canadian Center for Folk Culture Studies, National Museum of Man, Ottawa.

1948? Totem Poles (based on Beynon, 1945). Typed ms., 24 pp. (single spaced). In the possession of Harry B. Hawthorn.

1955 Ethnical and Geographical Study of the Tsəmisyaen Nation. Included in Philip Drucker Papers, Manuscript 4516(49), National Anthropological Archives. Washington, D.C.: Smithsonian Institution.

Boas, Franz
n.d. Boas Professional Correspondence (with William Beynon, Henry Tate, Viola Garfield, Amelia Susman). Library of the American Philosophical Society, Philadelphia.

Canadian Centre for Folk Culture Studies, National Museum of Man, Ottawa
n.d. Marius Barbeau-William Beynon Correspondence.
n.d. Marius Barbeau-Edward Sapir Correspondence.

Canadian Ethnology Service
National Museum of Man, Ottawa
n.d. Edward Sapir Marius Barbeau Correspondence.
n.d. Edward Sapir-William Beynon Correspondence.

Drucker, Philip

n.d. Philip Drucker-William Beynon Correspondence. Philip Drucker Papers, Manuscript 4516:50. National Anthropological Archives. Washington, D.C.: Smithsonian Institution.

Duff, Wilson

n.d. Tsimshian File (Notes on Marius Barbeau, and William Beynon, and notes on correspondence between Beynon and Barbeau based on originals in the National Museum of Man). University of British Columbia.

Wells, Robin F.

1968 Ningum Nemo and Some Northwest Coast Materials in the Wellcome Collection of the Museum of Ethnic Arts. Manuscript in the Museum of Cultural History. Los Angeles: University of California, Los Angeles (UCLA).

1974 Letter to M. Halpin dated September 26.

CHAPTER TWELVE

ALEXANDER GENERAL, "DESKAHE"

Cayuga-Oneida, 1889–1965

ANNEMARIE SHIMONY

Alexander General, to whom I shall refer henceforth by his chief's name, Deskahe, bestowed upon him later in life, was born in 1889, the youngest of eight children. His mother, Lydia, was of Oneida matrilineal extraction, and his father, William General, was Cayuga, although it is risky and uncertain to designate tribal affiliation too specifically. One reason is that most of the residents at Six Nations Reserve (near Hamilton, Ontario) are only partly Iroquois and to a great extent have European ancestors, who in Deskahe's case were Scotch-Irish; and another reason is that the official Canadian band rolls assign individuals patrilineally, whereas the Iroquois themselves still follow matrilineal descent. Particularly, the conservative and traditional population to which Deskahe belonged insisted upon the matrilineal designation. However, as one recedes in time, it becomes increasingly difficult to establish a consistent tribal identity, for the people themselves confuse traditional and legal designations. Yet it should be stressed at the outset that just this question of tribal affiliation played a significant part in the Weltanschauung of Deskahe, for he was well aware that it is the understanding of the community rather than Canadian legality which matters to the people. Deskahe, therefore, felt rather deeply throughout his life that he was essentially an Oneida in a Cayuga environment. Interestingly enough, when he was asked by Speck to list his tribal heritage (Speck 1949:185), he listed Cayuga-Oneida for both his parents, in that order, and I see that listing as a notable assertion of the validity of his status.

He was publicly known as the foremost Upper Cayuga Longhouse ritualist, and as the Four Brothers' principal Cayuga speaker, and his primary language was Cayuga. Yet all his life he had to combat a certain undercurrent of feeling in his neighborhood that the Oneida (who had originally come from the Thames River Reserve) were taking over, and also that his mother's lineage did not have the right to install him as the last Cayuga chief, known as Deskahe, in the Roll Call of the Iroquois chiefs. Deskahe was given his Indian name, Shaŏ•hyowa, meaning Great Sky, by his maternal aunt. This was the correct Iroquois procedure, for a child must receive the name of a like-sexed individual, who is deceased, and belonged to his matri-lineage, which in Deskahe's case was that of the Oneida Suckling Bear.

Deskahe's early childhood was spent with his parents in what must have been the normal circumstances of a marginal subsistence farmer who had to work out during harvest seasons in order to make ends meet. Thus, Deskahe's parents worked seasonally on a White man's farm at nearby Grimsby Beach, Ontario, during the summers. What the young child remembered most vividly from these trips were the horse-drawn trams he took and lantern slide picture shows he saw in Hamilton. And then some seasons later they gave way to steam trains and silent movies, and finally to talking movies, and he was impressed. Living in what must have been miserable camps (they were still such when I first did field work in the early '50s, and in fact, the squatters' and pickers' quarters were so unsightly that the Hamilton police felt called upon to burn some of them one of those years), Deskahe, a rather frail child, at first helped little but watched his parents work. During the winters back at the Reserve, he attended school fitfully (due to numerous absences on account of earaches), and remembered that whereas he was eager for learning, his first teacher was an aged White man, who was not very eager to teach the youngsters. Consequently, Deskahe learned little. He stopped at the "second book," or what would be called second grade.

It was at this time, when Deskahe was about 10 years old, that one of the formative and tragic events of his life occurred. To indicate accurately the way Deskahe remembered the event and the subsequent interpretation which he put upon its consequences, I shall state the nature of the situation under which he disclosed it. Deskahe had taped a short account of his life, but this particular incident was not on it. Soon thereafter, while we were talking late one night, Deskahe must have felt that the absence of this incident would leave the record incomplete, and yet recording this experience would have been too crass, whereas telling it to a friend in an honest and forthright manner would be emotionally more supportable. Even so, he was much moved by the confession, and, although unbeknown to Deskahe I had heard of the incident from a cousin of his, I, too, was so moved by the dignified manner of disclosure and by being privy to such a deep display of emotion, that I did not write down the statement till shortly afterwards, feeling that it would be inappropriate to record it at that moment. Thus, the wording is my memory of the speech, rather than the exact speech itself, yet, I believe, it reproduces quite accurately the syntax and thought pattern of Deskahe.

> There are some sad things too. A really tragedy. My father's death that was a tragedy. It was an accident. When I was a little boy, my father used to go hunting, and come home and clean out his gun. And he used to put the gun in the bedroom, and we played with it. One day, and it was a Sunday too, my father came home and was going to go out, and I was sitting on his lap, too, playing. I got up and ran into the bedroom to get the gun while my father was going out. It was his own responsibility, he had not unloaded the gun. I ran to the window, and the gun went off and grazed my father at the top of his head. That was the end. I'll never forget it. It was an accident. I didn't know; I didn't do it on purpose, and yet. people say I deliberately shot and killed my father. But I didn't, it was an accident. I guess people who don't like me and who don't like the way I do things say that. I'll never forget it. It was a pitiful.

Thereupon, Deskahe wept bitterly.

To deviate, then, from the chronological recounting of Deskahe's life, let me comment briefly on the significance of this revelation. It struck me at the time, as it did subsequently, that Deskahe had emphasized the accidental nature of the incident much more than was necessary. Iroquois cultural patterns can be described as Apolloniant and Deskahe, being a chief, was doubly aware of the ideal of calm deportment. His skin is supposed to be seven spans thick, and indeed, at a hundred occasions when sorrow overcame some member of his congregation, he was the lone, strong, dry-eyed officiator. Never at a funeral at Sour Springs (where he was invariably the orator), nor at public or personal misfortune had I seen him display this degree of emotion. Why should he attempt to impress on me, then, that he was innocent of a criminal act, when he knew that I held him in the highest respect and obviously would not attribute a murder to a child? Why had he wept so bitterly? The answer, I think, is that he wept not at the tragedy of over 60 years ago, but at the injustice I would deliver. I sensed also that he was trying to overcome a guilt he felt he should not have had to bear, and perhaps he reflected on the fact that he was a chief despite the prescription that a chief must never have killed anyone.

In any case, the trauma had changed his life, not only psychologically, but physically as well. Deskahe's family, without a head of house, could not maintain its farm and had to rent it out for a meager pittance against the winter poverty. Much of the rest of the year, Deskahe's mother now worked out amongst the Whites, and Deskahe went with her. As Deskahe grew up he lived with his mother, as he put it, "here and there, random place every year, and we had to go out fruit season to make our living." During the winters, now a teenager, Deskahe went back to school at Ohsweken, and under an excellent teacher learned a lot. But he did not stay long (he never went beyond grade 4 or 5) because he was big enough to work out and had to help support his mother, to whom, by his own and all other accounts, he was exceedingly attached. He had been nursed publicly at the Longhouse till well beyond the age of 5, which even by local standards was considered abnormal, and he never seemed to have contemplated marriage till after the death of his mother. From a psychoanalytic perspective, one might easily see many of the strands of an Oedipal situation. But Freud aside, Deskahe was acutely aware of a particular relationship to his mother, to which I shall return later, when I discuss the legitimacy of his chieftainship.

Deskahe felt that he had learned English not so much during his schooling as by experience during life, particularly as he continued to work out, in the city, on the railroads, and, during World War I, in a foundry. It was from the foundry that he was recalled by his mother, who was lying sick on her deathbed. He then worked for various farmers, at either $12 per month, or at a $1 per day, while paying his own board. Nevertheless, he was able to save enough to go into farming for himself with his brother, Timothy. They were successful, bought "plenty of stock," and added more land to their property. At the death of his mother, Deskahe inherited the family homestead, and he became a comparatively "big farmer" by Reserve standards. Although it was my impression that Timothy and his family (with some boys) farmed more successfully, Deskahe had a surplus of wheat to sell, as well as milk and cream. In any case, both had good land and achieved high status engaging in the occupation which carried high prestige in the community during the first half of the 20th century.

Having gone to the Longhouse all his life, and being acutely aware of the fact that his mother's lineage had been "borrowed" during his grandmother's time as a repository of the Deskahe title, the young man began to pay attention to the ritual speeches at the Longhouse. From the age of 18 or 20, he memorized them in secret, practicing alone at the house at sunrise, as was the custom at Sour Springs and at the Longhouses in general, and he did not begin to speak until coaxed and forced to it by a lack of suitable candidates in evidence at the ceremonial occasions. He remembered, and said he "finds it interesting" to tell me about the teaching of the older chiefs. He was somewhat "backwards," he said, since he had never yet done any speaking in the Longhouse, but he was told that the only way to learn is by doing, whether it is done properly or not. "To fulfill, you will have to practice to learn." Deskahe was told by the principal speaker at Sour Springs that he purposely came late to the ceremonials so that Deskahe would have to take over, for the speaker could not "wait forever" for him to carry on the ceremony. "And from that to today, it appears to be that the people depend on me for many things to carry on the ceremonies." Deskahe especially admonished me that "someone may hear it, or read about my life, and they should know how I began with the speaking before the public. I speak in my own tongue." Then Deskahe went on to explain that in English his language was flawed with failures for which one should excuse him, but that in Cayuga (went the implication), this was not the case. As is well known, Deskahe became the major Sour Springs speaker and ritualist, and it is for this expertise that he was so celebrated among ethnologists. Frank Speck's work, *The Midwinter Rites of the Cayuga Long House*, (1949), is written in collaboration with Alexander General, and this appears on the title page. Speck, as I understand it, pitched a tent at the Generals' homestead and systematically worked over the events he witnessed, reenacting them with Deskahe, with whom he evidently had very good rapport. Speck had begun work at Ohsweken as early as 1924 and 1925, but he repeatedly visited during the winters of 1932–36, and also made subsequent trips between 1938 and 1947. Unfortunately, he died in 1950, so that his work with Deskahe and mine never overlapped. Deskahe remembered Speck with affection, and he specifically stated that "many people have come to me for information in regard to the religion of the Longhouse. Many friends I have got among the anthropologists and ethnologists to take notes on what I have learned in my study as to the ceremonials." These friends are more numerous than I can name, but besides Speck there were W. N. Fenton, C. M. Barbeau, J. A. Noon, M. Rioux, J. Witthoft, F. Lounsbury, M. C. H. Randle, F. Voget, E. Dodge, M. Myers, G. Kurath, S. Weaver, and, of course, myself. Not only did Deskahe talk to us, but he also recorded the ritual music and songs and cooperated in a film of the Longhouse ritual for the Canadian Film Board. Speck gives tribute to the "untiring efforts and patience and to the systematic ceremonial mind" of Deskahe, as well as to his genial and willing cooperation, shown to the anthropologist in the same thoughtful manner in which he served as chief and leader to his own peoples (Speck 1949:7). All of this is true. Deskahe was a thoughtful, reflective, and also articulate interpreter of Iroquois ceremonialism. He was remarkable in being particularly open to sharing his ceremonial expertise with Indian and non-Indian alike, *and* in an attempt to minimize the distinctions between the Good Message and Christianity. Sour Springs always allowed respectful visitors from the outside, and as Speck already noted, there was a certain incorporation of Christian ideas at Sour Springs. Notable examples are the identification of Christ with the Fatherless Boy or the Fourth Angel in the vision of Handsome Lake (Speck 1949:31, 127–129) and Deskahe's reference to Christ in his own essay quoted below.

Why did Deskahe harbor these ecumenical concepts, when as I shall point out in a moment, he was so very uncompromising concerning political ideology? I think that one answer to this question antedates his conscious reflection concerning religious acculturative influences, which must have been discussed with Speck. Namely, some years after his mother's death, Deskahe became affianced to a young Christian woman. Deskahe recounted the event with great emotion (in the presence of his own wife, Ida) in the following way: "She was a Christian faith, but that did not mean that we would be divided. We agreed that we would have nothing to do with our different belief." Unfortunately, the influenza epidemic of 1918, which Deskahe identified as having come "from the Europeans" onto the Reserve, infected both Deskahe and his fiancee, Mary. But, whereas Deskahe luckily was saved by the intervention of an Indian doctor and Indian herbal medicine, his fiancee died. I gained the clear impression that this particular experience, more than the intellectualized discussion with anthropologists, accounted for Deskahe's tolerance. That Deskahe's tolerance was very sophisticated and also sophistical, I think is proven by the following speech which he composed alone and typed out to give to me. Much of the wording and sentiment is remarkably similar to that found in *The Midwinter Rites of the Cayuga Long House*, a work compiled almost 30 years earlier. Obviously this speech is designed for a White audience, which is to be persuaded of religious co-existence.

> While this opportunity lasts, I would like to point out to you people some planks in the platform, objectively, by a mere scan of which the Longhouse religious leaders might wish, were they ever so moved, to present our case as a reason for our inclusion within the wide circle of Christian fellowship.

While we are designated "Pagan" by outsiders in general, we prefer to call ourselves "Deists." Our religious worship centers around our Church, the Longhouse, a large communal structure within which our devotion are paid to the Creator, and where our annual rituals and ceremonial religious cycle is performed.

Now, from a broad social, religious viewpoint, it would be well to reexamine native creed for clearer understanding of our fundamental principles—not categorically as heathenish incantation—but as development of thought evolved from an age-long experience in spiritual emotion and in ethical teaching as well.

As we believe in and worship a Supreme Being: The Creator of the natural universe and man, we believe that the Creator loves all people and provides for our welfare and expects us to live in gratitude to him, and to live in harmony to each other, and to observe his teaching as revealed in our traditions, and to express ourselves through obedience and voiced thankfulness which form a major part in our recurrent rituals.

We believe in the continuation of existence; the immortal soul after death, conditioned by the deportment of the individual during life. We believe in the forgiveness of social sins through confession directly to the Creator.

At every ceremonial service, sections of teaching of the revealer Handsome Lake are recited and made the subject of exposition and preaching. We are to abide by the "Code" of the revealer who left us a body of teaching comprising about 130 Commandments, admonition, warning and examples, many of which are expressed in parable form.

We believe in four minor spiritual agencies appointed by the Creator to guide us, which we called four beings "Angels." And one of these agencies, mysteriously called "Fatherless Boy," is in some way identifiable with Jesus.

We believe in the power of producing effects to the Creator and his lesser agencies, the nature forces, through prayer, song and dance—which are all the same in essence. We believe in the power of producing effects of images—representing various forces, spiritual and actual, active in the world. We do not worship these images but through them, employing them in ritual, as visible icons of such agencies.

> We believe profoundly in the healing power—"spiritual, mental, physical"—of our ritual beliefs and ceremonies, when administered by these in harmony with the Creator and his spiritual agencies, through purity of purpose, good living, and adherence to faith.
>
> Therefore, we say, the old faith of our forefathers is as good for them as the old of your fathers is good for the whites. And yet these same Iroquois "Pagans" of the Longhouse have voluntarily incorporated a belief in the divinity of Christ into our own ritual and teaching. Then, why should we be pressed to become Christians, when others are tolerated, if not admitted as Christian confreres.
>
> In conclusion we denounce ridicule and adverse criticism of others' beliefs and expect that the same consideration be given to ours.

I think one must agree that Speck's comments concerning the Sour Springs community should now be amended, namely, "that it is still free of influence of European social artifice, commercialism, and Christian sophistries. The Cayuga possess that quality which we know as the Indian heart. A delightful unsophistication redolent of an age-old atmosphere of dignified myth and 'superstition' prevails, unfolding a cooperative health preserving ideal framed in thanksgiving and rejoicing" (Speck 1949:4). Certainly Speck's comment cannot be taken at face value concerning Deskahe. Deskahe had learned too much from Speck!

I should like to touch briefly also on Deskahe's belief in the many curing societies. Allusion has been made to the miraculous cure for him during the influenza epidemic. After the failure of a little bottle of pills prescribed by a doctor (which Deskahe adjudged to be "whiskey or something"), and after which he felt worse, with his legs getting cold, the native practitioner prescribed a cupful of steeped herbs. When Deskahe drank it all at once, he had a high fever, and was almost delirious, but as he felt the fluid go down it started to ease off the fever. He gradually improved, though was feeble for several weeks. (The description is almost verbatim from Deskahe.) Prior to 1918, he had also been inducted into the False Face Society, at a time when he was very sick, "was laid up for a week or so," and could not move. This time he had dreamed repeatedly about False Faces, and of course his mother and uncle, when told, had him immediately feasted by the Society. Similarly, he later participated in almost every society active on the Reserve, though I am not certain which of these societies he himself utilized as a medicine of some sort, and which he participated in for the sake of his very fearfully ailing wife and ill children.

Native medical cures effected by the traditional Societies are the normal expectation of the entire traditional community, and Deskahe was acting within his cultural milieu. Clinton Rickard, of Lewistown, recalled independently (Graymont 1973:56–68) how Deskahe's brother, Levi, came from the Rochester Homeopathic Hospital (where according to Deskahe he was confined with pneumonia) to the Rickard home in 1925, after "nine doctors who worked on him were unable to cure him," in such a weakened condition that his doctor said he needed to be nursed and waited on until he regained his strength. But, on Levi's petition, Rickard got two medicine men from the Six Nations Reserve, who stayed in Levi's room for a week treating him, and when they emerged Levi emerged with them. He could walk and work again normally. Later another medicine man was fetched for Levi, and Rickard says that in all he made three trips on Levi's behalf. But after six weeks with Rickard, "in good spirits and . . . recovering his strength after his cure by the medicine men," Levi was handed a letter while eating, presumably indicating that due to the difficulty of border crossing, his medicine men could not come to see him any longer. At least that is the impression which Rickard would like to disseminate. He reports further that Levi left the table without finishing his meal, lay on his bed, and never got up again. Several days later, after some chills, he died, for "nothing, not even the White doctor, could save him." The attending physician listed the cause of death as pulmonary hemorrhage. Interestingly enough, Rickard implies that due to the border crossing difficulties, Levi's family was unable to visit him during his last illness, but Deskahe reported that by lying to the border officials he did manage to visit his brother. However, it is true that there were difficulties and also that some people were turned back at the border. Because the death of Levi was part of the motivation for the founding of the Indian Defense League, and also because his bad treatment by the White governments was a primary inducement for allegiance of the Six Nations population to the Defense League, these details are of interest.

There is no doubt that during a period of his middle life, Deskahe believed in Indian cures so firmly that during the final illness of his nineteen-year-old elder daughter, he repeatedly took her temperature, saw it climb to dangerous heights, and forbade the intervention of "White" medicine or doctors. It is said the girl died of tuberculosis, and this also was one of the great tragedies of his life. I believe his younger daughter had a brush with tuberculosis, as did he and his wife, Ida, both of whom spent a considerable amount of time in the Brantford Sanatorium (Deskahe about 18 months in the middle '50s), which showed some relaxation of his earlier antagonism toward "White" medicine. Whereas I was constantly aware of ceremonials being done for Mrs. General during his illnesses, I do not believe that Deskahe was the recipient at that time of many rituals. He did, whenever possible, officiate and sing for others, not only for Longhouse people, but significantly also for Christian Indians who were desperate or frightened at having deserted their native heritage and beliefs. Deskahe never upbraided these apostates and never refused his free services (as many other practitioners did), but rather instructed them with great care, hoping, no doubt, to bring them back to the Longhouse by good example, helpfulness, and loving faith. He also saw his solicitude as the fulfillment of his duty as both ritual leader and chief, especially since "helping one another," is a cardinal value among the Six Nations Iroquois.

Deskahe's behavior so far described was well within the expected Iroquoian norms. Deskahe was an admirable role model for his people, an interpreter of the religion and the ideal ethic, though more intellectual and more articulate than the ordinary man.

One must now turn to the most outstanding and controversial, and innovative aspect of Deskahe's life, namely his political activity. I think of all the ethnographers working with him, it was perhaps only Fenton who realized fully this side of Deskahe, and perhaps I can add some of the peculiarly Iroquoian gossip to this understanding. As alluded to before, the Cayuga Snipe title of "Deskahe" had been transferred to the Oneida Suckling Bear clan during the lifetime of Deskahe's grandmother. (Incidentally, this is a transfer of title from one moiety to the other at the Cayuga Longhouse, and thus a little irregular.) The rightful lineage had no eligible male heir, and so the matron, Tha•thẽndes, Shaking a String of Corn, gave the validating strings of wampum to Deskahe's mother's mother, and she borrowed Deskahe's maternal uncle, Benjamin Carpenter, as the chief. Tradition has it (and I think the symbolism is rather remarkable, no matter what the truth of the story) that when Carpenter was to be installed and the festal ox was hung on a tree to cool for the Installation Ceremony, an eagle came and got at the meat. Obviously, it is this event which made the elevation of Carpenter memorable. The wampum then passed to Lydia General, who, on the death of Carpenter installed a maternal relative, Dave Jamieson, as the chief, and her son, Dave General, as the deputy chief. But she became dissatisfied with both, took out both (had them dehorned), and passed the wampum to her half sister (same mother), Louise Miller. Lydia General died, and on her death-bed supposedly decreed that she wished no further sons of hers to be installed as chiefs. Perhaps she remembered the injunction against elevating to chieftainship anyone who had killed a person, and therefore she wished to disqualify Alexander. But why she would have wished to disqualify his other brothers is not known. (Dave, the oldest, presumably was dehorned over land squabbles, but I am not clear why Sam, Timothy, and Levi should have been disqualified). Levi later became the focus for the most serious factional split at Six Nations Reserve, and so with hindsight Lydia's qualms were justified, but at the time of her death there must have been other reasons, if, indeed, the tale is true. (I assume it is true, for it helps to explain much of Deskahe's later behavior, and the incident was also attested to by several of his relatives.)

In 1917 Louise Miller installed Levi General as the new Deskahe, and Alexander was made the deputy (the runner, who sits on the chief's roots). Immediately, Alexander learned more avidly than ever the chiefly ritual speeches, the condolence chants for the Installation of New Chiefs, and he became the principal speaker henceforth until his death for the Upper Cayuga Turtle moiety.

At this time the hereditary chiefs were still the governing councillors for the entire band and Alexander took an interest in attending the council regularly. He became vitally involved in 1922 in the discussions of the Compulsory Enfranchisement and Soldier Settlement Acts, the consequences of which he felt would have been the alienation of Reserve lands and the dissolution of the Iroquois peoples as such. (For a similar opinion by Levi General, see Graymont 1973:59 ff.). As the hereditary chiefs perceived it, one Indian Department official, the Honorable Charles Steward, represented the Canadian Government as having the desire to arbitrate the council's reluctance to accede to the proposed legislation. This proposal was discussed and accepted by the chiefs, and their acceptance was communicated to the Indian Department. But to this conciliatory response they allegedly received a reply from a deputy superintendent, Duncan Campbell Scott, that there had never been any governmental intention of arbitration, and rather that the matter would be referred to a Royal Commission composed of Supreme Court judges of Ontario. This the chiefs rejected outright, for they felt they would lose. In 1924 Colonel Thompson was appointed Commissioner, and he came to the Reserve to hold hearings concerning indigenous sentiment. From the chiefs' point of view, they had already voiced the legitimate feelings of the Reserve, and they felt that an independent investigation was extra-legal and also designed to undercut their authority. They therefore refused to have any dealings with the Commissioner. Again from the chiefs' point of view, the Commissioner listened only to those people who had been deposed by the Council, or in other words, to those people who had some cause for dissatisfaction with the hereditary chiefs. To represent for a moment the other side of the controversy, it must be said that the governing institution of appointed hereditary chiefs, who tended to be conservative, was not very responsive to some of the needs of the changing society, especially of the returned veterans, and there were also some legitimate allegations of corruption on the part of some of the chiefs. Finally, a poll to decide whether the hereditary council should be replaced by elected council was unilaterally decided upon (unilaterally meaning by the Commissioner and the dissidents), and was held. Although only a handful voted, the dissidents won, because the chiefs had been advised and had advised their adherents to boycott the negotiations and the voting. It seems to have been primarily on the advice of Levi General, the then Deskahe, that this strategy had been adopted, and when it failed, it was he who was blamed for his unwise advice. The failure was disastrous for the chiefs, for the Indian Agent, Colonel Morgan, representing the Canadian Government and attended by the Royal Canadian Mounted Police, read to the Chiefs the proclamation, by Order in Council, of the abolition of the hereditary council in favor of an elected council. Alexander General states flatly, "So that is one of the most outrageous acts ever committed by the Canadian Government against the Six Nations." The chiefs felt betrayed, cheated, and forced out by military might. They commissioned Levi General to travel to the League of Nations (on a passport written out by the chiefs—"good anywhere in the world"), but he was unsuccessful again. Some under-secretary told him it was the best passport he'd ever seen, but as for his cause, it was a matter for the Canadian Government. Levi returned to Rochester, made a radio speech airing his grievances and failures, and promptly became ill with pneumonia, as alluded to above. It was then that he was taken to the Rochester Homeopathic Hospital, and after 6 weeks went to live with Clinton Rickards on the Tuscarora Reserve, where (as described above) he died in June of 1925.

Now from the point of view of Levi's numerous detractors and enemies (mainly acquired as a result of the above described politics and his technique of collecting money to implement his actions on behalf of the hereditary chiefs), Levi was a troublemaker, he was dishonest, he was a poor leader, he was a *persona non grata* to the Canadian Government, which illegally (contrary to the Jay Treaty) kept him out of the country, and he was punished by the Creator in that he was made to die in an alien land, which proved his guilt. That Alexander General was aware of these sentiments and both agreed and disagreed with them seems very reasonable to me, and it explains his behavior then and later. At the time, he made desperate efforts to effect many border crossings and to be with his ailing brother as much as possible. From the difficulties with the border crossings began the Indian Defense League, one of the first of the nationalist organizations to dramatize the abridgment of the Indians' legal rights (here the free border crossing). Deskahe was active in this organization all his life. In fact, he was one of the guiding leaders, and to this day I can see him, while ill and feeble, making the supreme effort of crossing the Peace Bridge in the colorful August "free crossing" demonstrations that became an annual event. For him it was a visible declaration of his *personal* loyalty to his brother, Levi, and of his *public* loyalty to a sovereign Iroquois nation. It is fair to say that Clinton Rickard, together with the members of the Indian Defense League and the allied Mohawk Workers, which were formed at Six Nations to support Indian sovereignty, were among the fore-runners of the more recently formed activist groups.

In December 1925, Alexander General was elevated to his deceased brother's chieftainship, and became the official Deskahe. Psychologically and behaviorally, I think one must see him henceforth as dedicated to Levi's visions—namely a sovereign Indian Nation ruled by a hereditary council of chiefs.

What means could he have seen himself to have to gain these ends? He was the inheritor of the chiefly title in a borrowed lineage, and the recipient of the title under controversial auspices—for aside from his mother's alleged disinclination to install him as a chief, his brother, who had just preceded him in the position, was actually discredited by a large part of the community, and some of that discredit fell upon Alexander General, too. Furthermore, he had the poor luck to ascend to the chieftainship just at the time that this position was robbed of efficacy and legitimacy. And, finally, the community was seriously factionalized between the loyalists of "dehorners" (Indians in favor of the Canadian Government and opposed to the hereditary chiefs) and the confederates (the contingent which adhered to the customarily appointed hereditary chiefs).

Deskahe's first major effort was a trip in 1930 to England to persuade the monarchy that Canada had no jurisdiction over the Iroquois, and that they should be granted sovereignty. But Great Britain insisted, as had the League of Nations when Levi visited, that the matter of Iroquois governance was legally under Canadian jurisdiction. Thus, after two months, the delegation admitted defeat, was penniless, and allowed itself to be sent back home by the Salvation Army.

And then came the period of Deskahe's life, between 1932 and 1959, in which he most noticeably practiced his ceremonial skills and collaborated with anthropologists. It is my thesis that part of Deskahe's motivation for his activity was to use this very ceremonialism as the means for resurrecting the confederate chieftainships and the confederate council. In the eyes of his own people he was the leading ceremonial authority, due to his vast knowledge, expertise, and willingness to perform at every occasion. But the Upper Cayuga community members (who were Deskahe's ceremonial constituents) knew, and Deskahe knew, that he was using his authority as their acknowledged leader to change some of their institutions. They realized, and Deskahe reiterated, that chiefs were now being declared essential to the Longhouse religion, and more than that, Deskahe made every effort actually to integrate the chiefs into the Upper Cayuga ceremonial center. He declared the center non-functional without them, he always referred to them first in his hierarchical speeches; and he gave the chiefs as many roles in the Longhouse as he could, assigning many of them to himself. As might be expected there was resentment among some of the constituents at Deskahe's ubiquitous ceremonial appearances as well as at his attempts at innovation. Foster (1974:34–5) noted independently that "there is a lingering feeling at Sour Springs that he (Deskahe) may have had too much authority in religious affairs, that he tended to run a 'one-man show.'" But Deskahe was too valuable and too effective a person to lose—and so he stayed on. (For a more detailed explanation of the conflict of chiefs and religious functionaries, see Shimony 1969:95 ff., 195.)

In the eyes of the anthropologists, who fortuitously came into Deskahe's life just at this point, he was one of the most able interpreters of Iroquois ceremonial and ideology. Speck realized that some of Deskahe's interpretations differed from those in the literature, but he says that the variations were due partly to local diversity and partly to the changing nature of "the uncanonized religious life of a native people" (Speck 1949:6). What I think Speck did not realize fully enough was that Deskahe had a very personal conviction concerning the interrelationship of chiefs and religious ceremonial statuses and roles, which he wished to impart to Speck or any other outsider who wanted to report on Iroquoian cultural prescriptions. Consequently, I think that Deskahe cooperated with the anthropologists for several motives: not simply, as Speck thought, out of kindness and consideration (though I agree that Deskahe was an extraordinarily helpful person, who also felt dutybound to instruct the public in Iroquois culture), but also because he saw his cooperation with anthropologists as a means of establishing his version of the legitimacy and indispensability of the Iroquoian confederacy. In other words, he utilized the anthropologists in part to establish himself as the definitive spokesman and in part to increase his efficacy, and thereby to promote his interpretation of the interrelation of the political chiefs to the religious arena. His motives were in his eyes pure, because the end justified the means. If the anthropologists thought that ceremonialism was Deskahe's exclusive interest (and he may have led them to believe that, perhaps because that is what the anthropologists said they were interested in), fine for them—why explain?

But simultaneously with Deskahe's prodigious ceremonial and religious efforts he carried on much political activity, and this, it seems to me, was always uppermost in his mind. Concomitantly with his work with anthropologists he carried on negotiations with various lawyers and Indian sympathizers and activists to further his political aims; and he was turning more and more to newsmen and lawyers in his last years. I think that for various reasons he did not find anthropologists either trustworthy, or effective, or appropriate intermediaries for the dissemination of his political ideas directly, but rather he tried to convince them by a two-step indirect process. That he had just such an attitude to anthropologists as I have described is indicated by a dream which he recounted in a letter to me, concerning my political discussions with him. There had never been any ambiguity about our mutual ceremonial understandings, but I had argued that despite my agreement concerning the propriety of the retention of the hereditary council, I had some doubts about the means adopted by the chiefs in 1924. I felt that some accommodation would have been better tactics than complete isolation, for I felt that with a small degree of cooperation the erstwhile chiefs could have had some input, and thus some leverage, in a political situation. But Deskahe felt that even the slightest concession toward an admission that the Canadian government had a legitimate claim on the Iroquois would have set a precedent for future claims of jurisdiction, which he of course denied. Thus, an "all or nothing" situation had to be set up: one either approved of Levi's tactics, or one was a traitor. In politics Deskahe was a purist, which one again might point out is singular, given his liberal and incorporative attitudes towards Christians and Longhouse people and even Christian chiefs. (Most orthodox hereditary chiefs are not in favor of bestowing the horns of office on non-Longhouse adherents.) Here is the relevant part of Deskahe's letter:

> I dreamed about you, it appears it may mean a bad omen. A dream was something like this. I went across the road from home. When I got in the house I found a few people in a house-most of them were traitors to us Indians, and you was in the midst. Another White lady, she was talking to these people telling them that they are going to get what they are asking for to become as Whiteman, and

> you in turn smile, look somewhat pleased about it, and you spoke. You said, "I know it's coming to that sooner or later." Believe me, I got so disgusted with you that I walk out without saying a word. I come away mad. It seems I went a different direction. I walk through the field and between two bush and it was just about dusk as I went toward sunset and the grass was kind (of) wet and then freezing somewhat icy. When I was part way in the field, I hear you calling me to come back, but I didn't turn to look. I was so mad at you to know that you are a traitor to us. "I kept going," come to another house where I found my folks are living. When I got in the house I told my folks, I am going up stairs to bed, and I told them if anybody come looking for me, tell them I am gone away. That's the dream I had shortly after you went away from here. Now is that a bad or good omen?
>
> Well what more I can say in writing? Well I just thought I would write to tell you about my dream in order to fill the space of my letter, dreams don't always mean anything . . . (from a letter written in the Brant Sanatorium, July 29, 1955).

In summary, then, in this analysis I see Deskahe in three distinct ways. First, I see him as an individual at a specific point in time and space. There is no doubt that the fortuitous events and accidents of his life had important consequences for his ideology and behavior. Being born into a traditional Longhouse matrilineage which was establishing itself at a new locality, having a strong sense of family loyalty, being personally sensitive, intellectual, able, and even charismatic, being imbued with the traditional Iroquoian concept of reciprocal obligations and helpfulness—all contributed to his personality. The convictions of his brother, Levi, and the recollection of Levi's struggle for his people (no matter how it was mythologized afterwards) motivated Deskahe very strongly. His life after 1925 was inextricably tied to his attempt to gain justice for the Six Nations Iroquois, where justice meant to him the restoration of their traditional form of government. Given his particular personal situation and interest, we are not surprised that Deskahe felt so strongly about the retention of the hereditary system, but he also had historical tradition to prompt him. It is unrealistic to believe that a person would champion an idea without any personal motivation, but that there is personal motivation should not be taken as a detraction in any way. Deskahe was convinced of his public position, and he worked for it as constructively and honestly as he knew how. His life overlapped a period of time which was one of great social change (as he himself realized), yet he felt that earlier traditional society should not be swallowed up by a dominant Canadian culture.

Secondly, inextricably intertwined with Deskahe's personal circumstances was his career as a ritualist. He was by profession a farmer, but this aspect of his life was secondary to him when compared to his functions as a ritualist. As such he was the foremost preacher and functionary at the Sour Springs Longhouse, and many an uninformed Christian simply equated him as the Longhouse's minister. Through his participation and knowledge, as well as through his ability to interpret to the outside world, he was *primus inter pares*, despite the fact that strictly speaking he was merely one of the Turtle moiety speakers and singers, and from the standpoint of many of the Sour Springs members he was (or should have been) simply an active participant with no special status. Prior to being a chief he had been a "hondrí'hõnt" (translated either as "deacon" or "faith-keeper"), which meant he was one of the male officiaries at the Longhouse who performs in the capacity of ceremonial leader and assistant, but upon becoming a chief, that duty should have been "taken off" him. (A ritual speech divesting the chief of such duties should have been performed, but I do not know whether this was done.) Aside from Deskahe's very substantial role in the Longhouse ceremonials, he also was the most frequent speaker for the Four Brothers' side in mourning councils, chiefs' installations, etc. These were political and religious ceremonies, and to the extent that they carried ceremonial duties and expertise, Deskahe was usually involved. On the individual level as well, when a person needed a "doing," of almost any type, Deskahe was an obvious choice as performer, not only of the Sour Springs community, but also of many of the "down below" peoples (Iroquois living at the other end of the Reserve, and not necessarily members of the Sour Springs Longhouse). Deskahe's unusual versatility and prominence as a ritualist made him the natural informant for the anthropologists as well as for the many visitors to the Reserve.

There was nothing very controversial about Deskahe's ritual and ceremonial religious duties. He helped all the people just in the manner in which he himself exhorted the congregation to help. Handsome Lake and the Great Creator decreed such behavior, and Deskahe followed in the best of the Iroquoian tradition. He truly set an example by his action, ever helpful and never charging the recipients. Furthermore, as far as the anthropologists were concerned, Deskahe had the ability to describe the ceremonials in an intellectual manner, abstracting from the particular occasion and seeking for the underlying patterns, and he realized that he was a valuable informant. In his autobiographical sketch he sums up his life with:

> But I would also say that being a chief I have many duties to fulfill. As chiefs are much like the priests to officiate the ceremonials of the Longhouse, and that is my duty. Many people have come to me for help. Which I have done to the best of my ability. And there are many people who have come to me for information in regard to the religion of the Longhouse. Many friends I have got among the anthropologists and ethnologists to take notes on what I have learned in my study as to the ceremonials. So that is my work, of my life.

Noteworthy here, of course, is that he says that his religious duties derive from his position as chief, which of course is his *own* interpretation.

Thirdly, and most importantly to Deskahe, as implied by the sentiment stated immediately above, Deskahe was a political activist. More than anything else, he believed in the sovereignty of his people, and he felt that this sovereignty could be guaranteed only through the retention of the hereditary council. He therefore dedicated himself to the task of not only reestablishing the chiefs to their traditional spheres of political action, but also widening their powers into every possible institution. In fact, I believe that his life and his actions were consistently motivated by a desire to prove that his brother, Levi, had the correct conception about the confederate council and had used the correct tactics, and that Levi's presumptive failures must be redressed by himself. As a chief himself, Deskahe would be a living example of his convictions, and he would participate in every imaginable Iroquoian activity. The people would see him, the anthropologists would see him, the Canadian Government would see him, and he would explain to them all how his people had been robbed of their birthright. To this end he helped organize and run the Indian Defense League and the Mohawk Workers. To this end he instructed the ethnologists, to this end he talked to the community, wrote to the news-media, and testified in the courts. He was a chief driven by a noble purpose, and he molded a life of service to his aims. As far as the anthropologists were concerned he was both kind and sophisticated, for though he helped them, he also hoped that they would help him, not by any active measures (which, as I mentioned above, he probably realized they could not or would not do), but by writing Iroquois history and culture from his point of view.

LITERATURE CITED

Boyle, David

1905 The Making of a Cayuga Chief. In Annual Archaeological Report, Minister of Education, Ontario. Toronto: pp. 56–59.

Chadwick, Edward M.
1897 The People of the Longhouse. Toronto: Church of England Publishing Company Limited.

Cusick, David
1848 Sketches of Ancient History of the Six Nations. Lockport, New York: Turner and McCollum, Printers.

Deardorff, Merle H.
1951 The Religion of Handsome Lake: Its Origin and Development. In Symposium on Local Diversity in Iroquois Culture, W. N. Fenton, ed. Pp. 79–107. Bureau of American Ethnology Bulletin 149. Washington: Government Printing Office.

Dodge, Ernest S.
1945 Notes from the Six Nations of the Hunting and Trapping of Wild Turkeys and Passenger Pigeons. Journal of the Washington Academy of Sciences 35:342–343. Menasha.

Fenton, William N.
1946 An Iroquois Condolence Council for Installing Cayuga Chiefs in 1945. Journal of the Washington Academy of Sciences 36:110–129. Menasha.

1949 Seth Newhouse's Traditional History and Constitution of the Iroquois Confederacy. Proceedings of the American Philosophical Society 93: 141–158. Philadelphia.

1949 Collecting Material for a Political History of the Six Nations. Proceedings of the American Philosophical Society 93:233–238. Philadelphia.

1950 The Roll Call of the Iroquois Chiefs: A Study of a Mnemonic Cane from the Six Nations Reserve. Smithsonian Miscellaneous Collection, vol. 111, no. 15. Washington.

1951 The Concept of Locality and the Program of Iroquois Research. In Symposium on Local Diversity in Iroquois Culture, W. N. Fenton, ed. Pp. 1–12. Bureau of American Ethnology Bulletin 149. Washington: Government Printing Office.

1953 The Iroquois Eagle Dance: An Offshoot of the Calumet Dance. Bureau of American Ethnology Bulletin 149. Washington: Government Printing Office.

1961 Symposium on Cherokee and Iroquois Culture; ed. Bureau of American Ethnology Bulletin 180. Washington: Government Printing Office.

Foster, Michael K.
1974 From the Earth to Beyond the Sky: An Ethnographic Approach to Four Longhouse Iroquois Speech Events. Canadian Ethnology Service Paper 20. Ottawa: National Museum of Man Mercury Series.

Goldenweiser, A . A.
1913 The Clan and Maternal Family of the Iroquois League. American Anthropologist 15:696–697.

Graymont, Barbara, ed.
1973 Fighting Tuscarora, The Autobiography of Chief Clinton Rickard. Syracuse: Syracuse University Press.

Hale, Horatio
1895 An Iroquois Condoling Council. Proceedings and Transactions of the Royal Society of Canada, series 2, 1:45–65. Ottawa.

Hewitt, J. N. B.
1944 The Requickening Address of the Iroquois Condolence Council. Journal of the Washington Academy of Sciences 34:65–85. Menasha.

Hewitt, J. N. B. and William N. Fenton
1945 Some Mnemonic Pictographs Relating to the Iroquois Condolence Council. Journal of the Washington Academy of Sciences 35:301–315. Menasha.

Kurath, Gertrude P.
1951 Local Diversity in Iroquois Music and Dance. In Symposium on Local Diversity in Iroquois Culture, W. N. Fenton, ed. Pp. 35–54. Bureau of American Ethnology Bulletin 149. Washington; Government Printing Office.

1953 An Analysis of the Iroquois Eagle Dance and Songs. Bureau of American Ethnology Bulletin 156:223–306. Washington: Government Printing Office.

1953 The Tutelo Harvest Rites: A Musical and Choreographical Analysis. The Scientific Monthly 76:153–162. Lancaster.

Morgan, Lewis Henry
1901 League of the Ho-De-No-Sau-Nee or Iroquois. H. M. Lloyd, ed. 2 vols. New York: reprint, Behavior Science Reprints. New Haven: Human Relations Area Files, 1954.

Noon, J. A.
1949 Law and Government of the Grand River Iroquois. New York: The Viking Fund, Inc.

Parker, A. A.
1916 The Constitution of the Five Nations. New York State Museum Bulletin 184. Albany.

Randle, Martha Champion
1951 Iroquois Women, Then and Now. In Symposium on Local Diversity in Iroquois Culture. W. N. Fenton, ed. Pp. 167–180. Bureau of American Ethnology Bulletin 149. Washington: Government Printing Office.

Rioux, M.
1951 Medicine and Magic Among the Iroquois. Journal of the Washington Academy of Sciences 41:152–158. Menasha.

1952 Relations between Religion and Government Among the Longhouse Iroquois of Grand River, Ontario. Annual Report of the National Museum of Canada, Bulletin 126:94–98. Ottawa.

Shimony, Annemarie A.
1961 Conservatism Among the Iroquois at the Six Nations Reserve. Yale University Publications in Anthropology 65. New Haven: Department of Anthropology, Yale University.

1961 The Iroquois Fortunetellers and Their Conservative Influence. In Symposium on Cherokee and Iroquois Culture, W. N. Fenton, ed. Pp. 205–211. Bureau of American Ethnology Bulletin 180. Washington: Government Printing Office.

1970 Iroquois Witchcraft at Six Nations. In Systems of North American Witchcraft and Sorcery. Deward E. Walker, Jr., ed. Pp. 239–265. Anthropological Monographs of the University of Idaho no. 1. Moscow.

Speck, Frank G.
1942 The Tutelo Spirit Adoption Ceremony, Reclothing the Living in the Name of the Dead. Publications of the Pennsylvania Historical Commission. Philadelphia.

1945 The Iroquois, A Study on Cultural Evolution. Bulletin of the Cranbrook Institute of Science 23. Bloomfield Hills, Michigan.

1949 Midwinter Rites at the Cayuga Long House. Philadelphia: University of Pennsylvania Press.

Witthoft, John

1946 Cayuga Midwinter Festival. New York Folklore Quarterly 2:24–39. Ithaca.

Witthoft, John and W. S. Hadlock

1946 Cherokee-Iroquois Little People. Journal of American Folklore 59:13–422. Boston and New York.

CHAPTER THIRTEEN

"ABORIGINALLY YOURS" JESSE J. CORNPLANTER, HAH-YONH-WONH-ISH, THE SNIPE*

Seneca, 1889–1957

WILLIAM N. FENTON
Howã?ńeyao, the Hawk (1908–)

INTRODUCTION: "AT THE WOODSEDGE"

I met and commenced serious ethnological work with Jesse Cornplanter in September of 1933, when at the end of my first season at Coldspring Longhouse I was asked to drive the "Guardians of the Good Message," and the preacher of the Handsome Lake Code, to the great fire at Tonawanda where the delegates of longhouses in New York and Canada would meet to renew their faith in the prophet's message. The Coldspring delegation—John "Twenty" Jacobs, Hiram "Wadi:dji" Watt, and Henry "Djiwah" Redye—were greeted at the Tonawanda Longhouse by the local committee and assigned to the residences of their kinsmen. "Twenty," our spokesman, told them that their driver yet had no name, but "he is learning to talk, he sings, and he dances; and he thinks our ways are worthwhile." My party then called on Jesse Cornplanter whose residence stood close to the longhouse, for Jesse had formerly lived among them at Quaker Bridge, and knowing that he spoke excellent English, they asked his wife Yowehǫsonh to let me stop for the night. That privileged introduction to the Cornplanter menage was to launch us on a long association—at times friendly, often productive, always stimulating, sometimes leveling, if not abusive, when Jesse's "condition" got the better of him, when he would

**American Indian Intellectuals*, 1976 Proceedings of the American Ethnological Society. © Copyright 1978, William N. Fenton.

lecture me in person or by letter, on some gaucherie committed or some lapse on my part, for I was after all only a "pale face" with Longhouse privileges, and despite my formal education, I could never approach him in experience, certainly not as an Iroquois authority,—that was to endure until his passing and throughout much of my professional career. Jesse assumed with me an avuncular role, and, apart from systematic ethnological statements on particular topics within his competence which interested me, he wrote me some two hundred letters which are remarkable human documents. Indeed he was a prolific letter writer, and I was not his only correspondent.

The Cornplanter correspondence covers his life span from the turn of the century to his death. Early on he learned that writing letters was a way of manipulating White people. Iroquois buffs would send money for letters illustrated with drawings by the "best Seneca boy artist." In writing he found the path to literacy which extended beyond the district school at Newtown. Like many Indians I have known he wrote a beautiful hand, and later he took up the typewriter. It occurred to me after his passing to collect these letters from his many friends, and they fill two manuscript boxes, which together with his writings and publicity comprise the materials for a biography. To my knowledge no one has ever done the life and times of an Indian from literary materials. This sketch may prove the start.

I have tabulated the Cornplanter literary remains that I know to be extant. Beginning with the letters of his father, Edward Cornplanter to Arthur C. Parker, 1897–1912, and to Joseph Keppler of New York, by far the richest of Jesse's early efforts are in the Keppler Papers in the Museum of the American Indian-Heye Foundation, which span the years 1899–1951. Some additional material came from M. R. Harrington, a contemporary of Parker and Keppler, who was early active in Iroquois field collecting for several museums. Keppler, Heye, Harrington and Parker were frequent visitors at Newtown Longhouse on the Cattaraugus Reservation of the Seneca Nation where Jesse grew up. From 1934 to 1937, we have both sides of an ethnological correspondence with J. N. B. Hewitt of the Smithsonian Institution. I do not have his letters to Carl Carmer, to whom I introduced him, in connection with *Listen for a Lonesome Drum* (1936), for which we both supplied original material. Jesse's collection of folktales, in the form of letters to Sah-nee-weh (Mrs. Walter A. Henricks) are in print (1938). Jesse and I called on Clark Wissler at the American Museum in 1936, during one of Jesse's radio appearances to promote Carl Carmer's book and his own, after which Jesse appealed to my old mentor concerning rates of pay for a soon famous author. Meanwhile, I had left Tonawanda to teach briefly at St. Lawrence University where I had reviewed Jesse's book (Fenton 1938), and then took up Hewitt's post at the Bureau of American Ethnology, for which I later learned Jesse had advanced my candidacy (M. W. Stirling, p.c.), and roundly congratulated me on our success. We had several solid sessions and good exchanges of letters before I was caught up in the swirl of "intelligence" activities that engulfed many anthropologists after 1941.

Jesse next received another of Clark Wissler's boys—Harold Conklin, then a student, afterward a soldier, and now a distinguished scholar. Their correspondence, 1942–1953, contains some of the best ethnology on the Iroquois and reveals a rapport between generations of men who served in two wars.

Jesse's claim to Veteran's compensation became, as we shall see, a career in itself. His letters to Charles E. Congdon, Attorney of Salamanca, and historian of the "*Allegany Oxbow*" (1967), during 1942–1957 resolve his "case" and speak to ethnological topics. The other gentleman to whom I introduced Cornplanter was M. H. Deardorff of Warren, Pa., who was as prolific a correspondent as Jesse himself and unexcelled at eliciting information from Senecas by letter, 1942–1952.[1]

Philippa Pollenz, student of the dance, provided Jesse with a wartime diversion.

He met Frank G. Speck, either at Coldspring Longhouse, or on a trip to Philadelphia in 1944, when he addressed Speck's class at the University of Pennsylvania. (American Philosophical Society Ms. No. 3247, 1944–1951.) The distinguished historian, Paul A. W. Wallace, father of the anthropologist, addressed inquiries relating to the League, 1952–1955.

As a lifelong showman Jesse took great pride in his Indian dress, which he referred to as "my custom." He was also a consummate craftsman. One whole box of the correspondence is with hobbyists, collectors, and promoters of dance groups: Ray Fadden, 1949; Red Thunder Cloud 1947–1950; Ken Mynter of Claverack, N.Y., 1947–1954; Robert Gabor of Syracuse, 1949–1956; and David Batholomew of Hudson, N.Y., 1951–1953. Jesse found these men sympathetic, and perhaps less demanding than scientists, and the exchange is rich indeed for our purposes. The end of the chapter is written in letters to Charles Bartlett, D.D.S. of Castile, N.Y. who saw him through a painful period.

Besides these letters, in the author's possession, the Library of the American Philosophical Society holds several Cornplanter manuscripts. In 1933, Jesse obtained through Arthur C. Parker of the Rochester Museum, the loan of the original two manuscript volumes of his father's version of

Gaiwi:yo (the Code of Handsome Lake) from the New York State Museum which Jesse copied and annotated in his own "system" for writing Seneca. To my knowledge Jesse never recorded these 102 pages. He also wrote out the tag lines of the many songs he sang in Seneca (APS 3246), and of several long rituals numbering over 100 songs, he did manage to record three reels of Deswadenyon in 1952 under the supervision of A. F. C. Wallace (APS 3245). On earlier occasions and in better health, he recorded samples of many songs on discs for Martha Huot and myself in 1936 (Indiana University Folksong Archives), and on other visits in 1949 on tape for me. (Fenton Collection)

Jesse illustrated many of his letters with pen and ink sketches of clan symbols, longhouse scenes, artifacts, directions for crafts, masks and other supernaturals. From boyhood he did these on commission for Frederick Starr (1903), for Keppler, Converse, and M. R. Harrington; and his drawings are best known from the works of Arthur C. Parker (Parker and Converse 1908; Parker 1909, 1910, 1913, 1916, 1923, 1968), and from his own book (1938).[2] The New York State Library has 45 originals of those that appeared in the Parker State Museum Bulletins.

During his lifetime Jesse enjoyed publicity, and he was the subject of feature articles in newspapers and magazines. Of these many now lost clippings, he liked best the autobiography he wrote for the Rochester Democrat and Chronicle (1936). And he proudly sent me a feature article in the St. Bonaventure University Alumni Magazine (1941). I have now only the write-ups of his funeral, which, unfortunately, I was unable to attend.

There is no dearth of photographs of the man from boyhood to old age. His favorites were the portrait by Delancey Gill made during a visit to the Smithsonian in 1928, and my own 1941 photograph of him in restoration Seneca dress, herein reproduced. There were doubtless others of which I am ignorant. As a late teenager, before he left Newtown, he put on his best dark suit and laced up his high black shoes to sit for a studio portrait by some village photographer.

From this sketch of his literary remains we now return to Newtown of his youth.

I

"Kanonhsoske hendwe:, Let us go to the Longhouse."

In the words of the old Women's Dance song, let us consider the formative years of his youth at Newtown Longhouse, near Lawtons, on Cattaraugus Reservation of the Seneca Nation. In this so-called "Pagan" community of the embittered conservatives who had come there as refugees from Buffalo Creek in 1842, Jesse grew up, learned Seneca as his first language, played lacrosse and snowsnake with Richard Kettle and their agemates, imbibed the social songs with his corn soup, and was cradled to sleep by the songs of the medicine societies. From the time he could walk he danced in the longhouse, moving up from the end of the line to the front rank, and then to the singer's bench of the Great Feather Dance and the Drum Dance. "The Four Sacred Ceremonies" of the Handsome Lake Religion provided the themes to which he orchestrated his life. With these went the moral preachments of his father, Edward Cornplanter, Sosondo:wah, "deep night," of the Wolf Clan who recited the Good Message of Handsome Lake and was the principal ritual holder of Newtown Longhouse. Jesse would carry the status burden of his father to his own grave, which seems a contradiction of terms in a strongly matrilineal society.

Jesse's mother, Nancy Jack, was of the Snipe Clan of Tonawanda, a lineage that derived from Little Beard's Town on the Genesee River and included Chief Infant, possibly the Infant painted by Trumbull in 1792 in Philadelphia (Jaffe 1975:309). Her Tonawanda kinsmen provided Jesse with a set of relatives after he settled there; but although she as a little girl was adopted at Newtown and lost her heritage at Tonawanda under the old law, Jesse never felt at home there for twenty-seven years. Ganénˀdoa:ˀ, "next to a big hill," whose name as a girl was Gaˀnáˀis, "it strikes the arrow," reached into the bag of Snipe Clan names for her children. Two daughters and a son preceded Jesse, and two more sons and four daughters followed him. Excepting his next elder sister Carrie, nicknamed "dédon," who grew up to have children, and a sister Anna who married at Onondaga, his other siblings died in childhood, one living but seven days; for communicable diseases took a terrible toll of Seneca children until quite recently. Jesse she named first Ganondayéonˀ, "deserted village," and after puberty they changed his name to Hayónwanˀi:s, "he strikes the rushes," and "someone who gathers the canoes together at the shore." This second name at Newtown carries responsibilities at the longhouse as a hodi´ont, or "Keeper of the Faith." The old people sensed that Jesse was destined to fulfill the roles of his father, and throughout his life he felt a responsibility to return to Newtown for the ceremonies, where his "prestige" lay.

Edward Cornplanter, the father, must have been a dominant personality. The Wolf Clan was then strong at Newtown, and Jesse used to say "The Wolf Clan are gluttons," for their vigorous participation. Moses Cornplanter, the father's father, and Jim Cornplanter, his brother, I am told by others, were not lineal descendants of Kayenthwaˀken, "the planter," the great Cornplanter of the Federal Period; that the real family name in English was "Joe," that Jesse's paternal forebears had taken the name Cornplanter because it was good for "show" purposes, much to the dismay of the true descendants by other names of the old chief.[3] Jesse's middle initial "J.", then, was an artifact of the true family line. It should also be apparent that the Longhouse Seneca practice double descent: lineage and clan names descend in the maternal line, as do succession to office, and property; assumed English surnames, and those that are translations into English of Indian personal names—"Burning, Steeprock, Sundown, Cornplanter, Hot Bread, and Sky"—descend in the paternal line and are used for enrollment; while given names, often of Biblical origin, are a later distinction. A parallel train that is disconcerting to anthropologists who have tagged the Iroquois as matrilineal, and have learned to think that way, is the tendency to borrow and loan offices, names and obligations, and duties from the paternal line. This in part explains Jesse's lifelong father fixation.

The image of his father and his father's peers is a recurring theme in his letters to ethnologists. On the eve of a visit to him in June of 1941, he wrote to me:

> I am glad that you realize the fact that I am what I am. That I am rated the best as we have them now [a] days. Why should I be otherwise? Dad was the sole authority: he knew every bit of songs and ceremonies, not only one group or kind, all of them. His versions were of the old Cattaraugus Village variety and not imported (from) elsewhere. He (would) write his songs and speeches, thereby he knew (them) as he was taught and never changed one bit. Then he knew all the histories of every song or groups of them. He taught them to me. He used to say, "Don't let me take them as I pass away. You are my son, try to revive as much of it as you can remember." He sang Dark Dance, Yaie-ond-da-tah (yéiˀondathaˀ), Yaie-dose (ˀi:ˀdo:s) and all its songs, Oh-kee-weh (ˀohki:we:), Bear, Buffalo, and Eagle, and all of the social dances. Then he was the best in Feather Dance songs. I learned all of mine as I sat and listened, when I was not dancing. My songs date back to nearly a hundred years, that is to the songs of Old Truman Halftown, his son James, Dad, James Crow, Lewis Crow, Young M. Lay, Kelly Lay; then Anderson Charles of this place (Tonawanda); Old Hiram Jacobs of Coldspring and David Key of Grand River. All of these [singers] were considered the very cream of this sort of singing. I retain their songs today. Most of them probably will never be used. Now a

> days they only dance about a half hour. In my days they used to dance for two solid hours, and it was the real old-fashioned type, which they knew how to do. Then Religion was as it is supposed to be. It was a big day when the Great Feather Dance took place. I have been a hodiont for many years. We cook the feast and dance our (own Feather Dance).

This authentication of his own versions of ritual songs was to remind me that he merited an increase in informant fees, as suggested by my old teacher, Clark Wissler, with whom he was now in correspondence, and consonant with my new post at the Smithsonian. Grants were not generous then. Indeed during my first years at the Bureau of American Ethnology, I regularly paid all of my field expenses out of a modest per diem for subsistence. I always paid the prevailing hourly rate, although one notable ethnologist paid no informant fees at all, but got by giving presents to his Indian collaborators. At the time, working for a government agency, I thought my way better.

Besides his roles as a longhouse leader, Edward Cornplanter also ran the Seneca Lacrosse Club, for Newtown has always had a reputation for strong teams. This meant that he was frequently away from home playing the "Royal Reds" in Canada or the "Crescents" of Brooklyn. Moreover he was a showman and a musician, beating the snare drum for one of the popular Seneca brass bands. He raised the price of a new instrument in 1899 by collecting False Faces (masks) at two to three dollars each and sending them to Mrs. Harriet M. Converse in New York City, an activity which soon involved his whole family in stripping the community of its oldest ceremonial gear to fill up the empty cases of new museums in New York, and later Albany. Jesse would afterward protest at the finest ethnological art being locked in museums under glass and irretrievable once it got in public hands.

The Cornplanters and their neighbors must have lived a hand-to-mouth existence. Notice of a ceremony to a museum ethnologist might bring a few dollars; a particularly fine mask over one hundred years old from the Genesee country was priced at four dollars; rattles were fifty cents each; silver brooches several dollars; but after buying the snare drum the Cornplanters were very poor. There were no funds for the necessities, particularly when Edward was on tour. On 7 January 1902, Nancy addressed her "dear Husband:" she had received the "3 dollar" he sent, "but I am sorry it wont take us . . . till two weeks. You know that we need money to buy stove pipe—its all torn. I am afraid to have a big fire. It will burn our house. . . ." And then she goes on to enumerate their debts to local storekeepers. Meanwhile, young Jesse was out cutting wood for hire. (Nancy Jack Cornplanter to Edward Cornplanter. Arthur C. Parker Papers, WNF). Later in the month, son Jesse wrote to his father on tour remonstrating with him for not sending money as promised, that they have been to the Post Office daily and no funds, since the three dollars is long since gone and now his mother is turning to friends (Whites) in Lawtons for food; ". . . and we aint got wood for we don't got no money. If we have money we won't beg for something. And it is quite cold this time. . . ." The other news concerns Delos Kittle. "Delos's wife she beat him with an iron poker and throw him to the floor, her son Richard. And when Delos's mother came in his wife hit her with an Iron." And to top it off, Stewart Jones and Willie Crow fell down an elevator shaft in a North Collins factory (Jesse Cornplanter to Edward Cornplanter, 24 January 1903).

Although he thought in Seneca, Jesse had the need to communicate in English to assist the family, and this was the incentive to attend district school. He went as far as the fifth grade, after which he was largely self-taught. At age eleven in 1900 he was writing Joseph Keppler, editor of *Puck*, and prominent member of Mrs. Harriet M. Converse's New York circle of Iroquois buffs, thanking him for presents from the Sunshine Club, which he thought he would like to join, asking for the *New York Sunday World* carrying an illustrated article by Mrs. Converse, and reporting on the upcoming Indian New Year ceremonies. He lacked stamps. Frequently he enclosed drawings. In return Keppler sent the children books—a second-grade reader, "Jack the Giant Killer," a favorite of Jesse's—crayons, paints, and other supplies. Jesse joyfully went to work. One result was a series of drawings for Frederick Starr, dated 1903, which Starr copyrighted. Within a few years he was taking over the family correspondence, reporting on various events, marking the ceremonies, inquiring about "Kansas money," and arranging to greet visitors and to travel.

Not to be outdone by his showman father, or perhaps in his image, in the summer of 1901, Jesse, then twelve, reports that he and his friend Joseph Hemlock were playing in their own show, doing jig dances and singing funny songs (JJC to Keppler, 8/20/01. Fol. C 8.4, No. 5). They were earning up to six dollars per show. Three years later, he was on the road with his father, here and abroad. Years afterward he wrote:

> My father also traveled extensively with theatrical troupes. Once he went with me, when I was a boy of 15, to Europe, visiting England, Holland and Germany. . . . I studied the ways of the white

> people as I traveled and learned much that proved of great help to me as years went on. Such was my education, gained from life and experience, and not from any higher institutions of learning. . . . (Cornplanter 1936)

On their safe return to Newtown, Jesse wrote to Keppler, sending him a drawing of an Onondaga chief, on the stationery of the Holland American Line, T.S.S. Statendam. Perhaps no other Indian at Newtown had been able to go so far.

The following year the name of the famous Chief Cornplanter (Kayenthwaʔkeh) had been conferred upon Keppler whom Jesse thereafter regarded and addressed as "White Father" and signed himself "son." Whether this was a ceremonial relationship I am uncertain, but after the death of Sosondo:wa (Edward), his true father, in 1917, Jesse transferred rights, affection and expected obligations to the surrogate. He frequently mentioned this to me.

One further bit of show business that he frequently recalled was the famous Hiawatha show which toured the southern states. In 1936 he wrote:

> In 1912 I went out with a troupe of show people as a head man or chief, and leading man. This was the dramatization of Longfellow's Song of Hiawatha, an outdoor play. We played week stands in the South, at Birmingham, Ala., Augusta and Atlanta, Ga., Knoxville, Tenn., Baltimore, and York Village, Me. In 1913 we went to Baltimore for the summer. Again in 1915 we were in Ohio. . . .

The following year they ended up in Toledo where he went to work in an automobile plant, which puts us ahead of our story (Cornplanter 1936).

As suggested earlier, the one person before me who derived the most from his long association with the Cornplanter family was Arthur C. Parker, himself part Seneca through his own father of a distinguished Cattaraugus Seneca family. Edward Cornplanter was Parker's chief informant on Seneca rituals and on the Code of Handsome Lake (1913), and the whole family was involved in rounding up other informants and collecting relics for the museums with which Parker was affiliated. This began in 1897, became increasingly active while Parker was understudying with F. W. Putnam who sent Parker and M. R. Harrington to the field during the summers of 1903 and 1904, and intensified after Parker went to the State Museum in Albany the following winter (Fenton 1968:8–12). Jesse was writing to Gawasowaneh (Big Snowsnake) in 1904, asking him to bring a buckskin, "enough for our family for moccasins," which he illustrates; "We like a pair for each of us." And they are going to need one big lot of corn husk to make all the articles that Parker had specified. The back of this letter of November 14, 1904 is decorated with pen and ink sketches of deer, husk dolls in costume, a husk masker, two False Face doorkeepers and a beggar. Jesse was executing commissions for drawings from Parker at the State Museum for the next decade; Parker regularly sent the names of subjects he wanted illustrated. The fees were small, but Parker was without budget for the purpose as he was relying on the generosity of a good friend (ACP to JC 6/3/09; 10/7/08).

Jesse had one great love, for Elsina Billy, Yoweh´sonh, the Little Beaver of Tonawanda, with whom he lived four months in the summer of 1909, and to whom he returned in 1930. A real beauty, she was visiting Newtown during Parker's fieldwork on the medicine societies (Parker to JC 6/3/09; Parker 1913: Plate 21, left to right, No. 1). According to Beaver Clan sources at Allegany, he next lived with Lavina Crouse, daughter of Jonas Crouse, a prominent Seneca Nation leader, who afterward "had a lot of husbands." From 1912 to about 1916, it was Lucinda Lay, Yáhsin, by whom he had one daughter Beatrice who was living in 1957 with children of her own. After returning from the Great War, Jesse bummed around, a disillusioned veteran, and unhappy at Newtown where his parents had both died during his absence. In 1920 he settled at Quaker Bridge at Allegany with Effie Killbuck who persuaded him to get married legally, which he later spent much effort undoing, and whom he left in June of 1925. It was then that he began to hear Yoweh´sonh, once more calling him,

> She stands there on the rim of the earth;
> She calls him there. . . . (Yéiondatha-Déswadenyon)

They lived first in Buffalo, and then went home to Tonawanda where they remained.

II THE WAR YEARS

Jesse's brittle monogamy cannot be said to foretell an unstable personality because it was a pattern typical of the longhouse people then and now. Nor were his periodic binges; like many of his people he simply could not drink to moderation. He blamed it on the war and that is as good an excuse as any.

Jesse has recited his war record repeatedly in many places and to all of his correspondents. He summarized it in his autobiography; the details are in the correspondence with Charles E. Congdon, his attorney, who arranged his divorce from Effie and satisfied the Veteran's Bureau that the Little Beaver was entitled to his benefits.

On tour in 1916 he chanced on an opportunity to work in the Willys-Overland automotive plant in Toledo. At the end of the show season having come home, he returned to Toledo and threw in his lot with the Whites. They put him on the assembly line. Things were going nicely for him when the United States joined the Allies in the Great War. In a patriotic moment he registered for the draft, sent his card back to Buffalo, and then worried. His work suffered. To resolve the conflict, he stopped by the armory and signed up. "This was June 4, 1917." He passed the physical without difficulty, was issued a uniform, and wangled a pass to visit his parents.

> My father was surprised to see me a soldier and told me I made a great mistake by joining; that my place was to help him as he was growing older. I disagreed but I felt bad to displease him. . . . I told him that I would return and that I also . . . would send my pay to help him. Still that did not satisfy him. . . . When my four days [of leave] were up, I went back to Toledo and started my new career. (Cornplanter 1936)

After a month of guard duty, Jesse who seems to have enjoyed the favor of his officers, was promoted rapidly to private first-class, acting corporal, and then full corporal.

> I felt the responsibility keenly. I did not do any handshaking or shoulder-patting. I felt that it was my military bearing and my obedience to orders together with the lack of officer personnel and the fact that I was an Indian. . . . It was no joke, but just one big headache after another. I tried to keep up my end, even studied in spare time all the manuals that could help me. My officers were kind . . . even encouraged me, but somehow I felt that the responsibility was more than I could stand. Still the chevrons stuck to my sleeve, in spite of all that I did to get rid of them.

Enlisted now in a machine company of the Sixth Ohio Infantry, which was about to go south for training, his captain sent him home on a four day pass. "He told me to bid my folks good-bye—and it was that, as you will see."

> This time I came home as a non-commissioned officer. To my surprise my father was at the depot when I got off at Lawton, and instead of rejoicing, he felt grieved. Let me tell you, it all but took

> the heart out of me to see the way he regarded my patriotism. He told me it was no longer my country, that my ancestors had lost their lives trying to retain it. No doubt he was right . . . he was a man of wise judgement. I never dared argue with or contradict him, such was my respect for my father.
>
> He was only a shadow of his former self . . . very much run down, I judged from worry . . . despondent over my going. When I finally bid him goodbye, he told me I might come home, but I would not see him again, as he would be dead by then. And it was a fact. (ibid.)

Within ten months of training, Jesse's company was shipped overseas as the 147th U.S. Infantry, 37th Division. Just before leaving Camp Lee, he received a telegram from his mother that his father indeed was dying. It was the eve of embarcation and no leave was forthcoming. He died June 16. Jesse embarked "with a heavy heart." His sole consolation was his living mother and sisters. He had meanwhile, at his own request, been reduced to the rank of Private First-Class. In a later letter to Harold Conklin he states that he turned down the rank of Sergeant about four times, both here and overseas (JC to HC 6/22/43). He just did not want the responsibility.

In September, his division went to the relief of the British, and finally into the Meuse-Argonne offensive, "our first big push," when he was knocked out by gas, sent to the rear, and spent 24 days in a field hospital near Souilly. This action was the basis of his lifelong claim for veteran's compensation, and the later award of the Purple Heart. Temporarily recovered, he caught up with the outfit in Belgium in time to get into another drive before the Armistice. His was one of the two American divisions selected to escort King Albert back to Brussels.

In the first mail to reach him December 4, 1918, was a letter of mourning from his younger sister. His mother had died October 31 of the influenza, which also took another sister and a brother-in-law.

III

Jesse's long delayed plan and his dream of returning home ended.

> My home was empty. Nothing but sorrow awaited my return. It was a dreadful experience that faced me. I came back to what had once been my happy home. One year was all I could endure. I traded my home and went to Allegany Reservation, where I lived until 1925. (Cornplanter 1936)

His description fits almost perfectly the classical Iroquois episode of the warrior who returns to find his village abandoned, his relatives dead, and the clearing overgrown with brush. In the depression of bereavement he wanders aimlessly in the forest, tries a number of settlements, and finally comes to rest in a community in which he is a stranger.

For the next decade he was in and out of Veterans' Hospitals. The details do not concern us, although he says he was cheered by receiving "smokes" from veterans' groups with which he was now affiliated, and which provided him with a continuing identity. Back home on the reservation his contemporaries tired of hearing about the war, and he grew impatient with them. A Clansman at Allegany told me in the thirties that Jesse was irritable, that he tried to play lacrosse again but soon got winded, that he drank too much and criticized the longhouse people for not running the ceremonies properly, and that he was impatient with the singers. It was just no fun to be around him. It was during this period that I first saw him while he was giving the Indian touch to a trading post run by an old friend, Ed Countryman, in the Allegany State Park, adjacent to the reservation. Jesse was the big feature at campfires for the summer campers, singing and telling stories.

IV

His unique ability to communicate with the White world coupled with his deep roots in the religion and culture of his ancestors made him an extraordinary interpreter and informant for an ethnologist fresh out of the university. Show business and the war had been Jesse's education. He had gone south on a tour in 1928 as far as Florida; enroute he paused at the Smithsonian to meet J. N. B. Hewitt, the distinguished Tuscarora ethnologist at the Bureau of American Ethnology, which reawakened his interest in preserving the culture of his people and resulted in a lively correspondence between the two men. Hewitt was working on the Condolence Council and other matters relating to the League at Six Nations Reserve. Jesse was moved to learn the "good message" of Handsome Lake, his father's specialty. Hewitt had criticized Parker for publishing Newhouse's version of the Constitution (Parker 1916), without acknowledging previous work or appearances; and Parker now the Director of the Rochester Museum had time for neither controversy nor ethnology. Jesse was ready for a new vehicle.

Having tried the hand to mouth existence of Indians living on Seneca Street in Buffalo during 1929, when the Depression set in, Jesse and Elsina Billy or Yowehˊsonh, who had called him back to Tonawanda, withdrew to her house near the longhouse where I found them in 1933. Perhaps he was willing to work with me because he felt himself an outsider there, and could see things objectively with a comparative viewpoint of Newtown and Coldspring where I had worked, and I trust because the work challenged him. I believe it did. When he saw that I could write Seneca phonetically (phonemics came later), and he realized I had some grasp of main ritual patterns at Coldspring Longhouse, he responded with enthusiasm. During my absences in New Haven, we commenced to correspond, and I conceived the notion that in Jesse Cornplanter I had at last found Boas's George Hunt. He sent me answers to questions concerning my very first paper on ceremonialism (Fenton 1936), and I sent him what few dollars I could spare from a meager Yale fellowship out of which one then paid tuition. After Benedict and Mead had invited me to attend their now famous seminar on Competition and Cooperation in Primitive Society (Mead 1937; 1961), for which Buell Quain was preparing the chapter on the Iroquois, in trying to satisfy their questions, I learned what it is to be an informant, sent some questions on to Cornplanter, and followed up on my return to the field that winter with a long running commentary that appears as footnotes to the Quain article. Jesse received an honorarium, and I learned something about the kinds of questions that would yield answers and those which are unresearchable two hundred years after the fact.

Another good thing came out of the experience. Because some of the questions were beyond his scope, Jesse impaneled a committee of old men who met more or less regularly with us and they became my Tonawanda doctoral committee, although I submitted the dissertation on the Eagle Dance to another committee of beloved men at Yale. Twenty Kettles, Dáhon and "Scroggy" (the latter a Sachem chief) were as pleased as any of my faculty when I finished.

I had returned to Tonawanda as Community Worker for the U.S. Indian Service, at the behest of John Collier, and I stayed there for two and one-half years. I saw Jesse and his neighbors "down below" daily. My regular work was to assist them to generate projects of self-help. I was supposed to do the dissertation on my own time. We started with the committee, worked through the chiefs and longhouse leaders, and we were soon into a number of projects.

The most obvious agency was the Salt Creek Singers, a mutual aid society, which was already in being and which I joined and kept the minutes. We cut wood for widows and ill persons, held practice sessions to learn social dance songs, traveled to other longhouses, and assisted at funerals. Jesse was a prominent member, and the singers frequently met at his house.

Indeed he was the proper Clerk, but since I had a typewriter, he delegated the writing of minutes to me. The business of the "Salt Creek Mutual Aid Society," as it was named on March 3, 1935, was carried on in Seneca, which I was learning, and motions were made and seconded in conformance with Roberts' rules. Obviously, Jesse had to go over the minutes with me carefully so that they represented what actually went on during the meetings. It was a mutually agreeable arrangement.

Ga'neho is what the Senecas call going out on an Indian Show, the special songs that belong to show business, and the war and social dances that may be used for show purposes. Occasionally, Feather Dance or a demonstration of the False Faces may be put on, but this is frowned upon as "selling our religion." Jesse and his friend Nick Bailey, a Tonawanda entrepreneur, excelled at these arts, and once or twice I went along for the experience. In turn, I invited Jesse to help me present a paper on Seneca ceremonialism before the Morgan Chapter of the New York State Archeological Association at the Rochester Museum, where Dr. Parker had invited us. Jesse illustrated my talk with the appropriate song styles. He remained enthusiastic about this experience for long afterward and mentioned it in letters.

Our Rochester appearance had an interesting consequence that would affect both our careers. Carl Carmer, the writer and folklorist, who had attended our lecture, came out to the reservation for the Midwinter Festival, saw the False Faces and heard the beautiful songs of the Little People in the Dark Dance. (In his book he says I introduced Cornplanter to him at an Akron, N.Y. camp meeting). In May, the three of us went to Newtown to hear the origin legend of the Dark Dance from James Crow, Sanoń'kai:s, "Long Horns," of the Deer Clan. Jesse interpreted and I later shared a duplicate copy of my transcribed notes with Carmer, which he reworked and published (Carmer 1936:25, 96–98). Although I had given away field notes that were afterward copyrighted, I was to discover on going to teach in a small college that everyone knew me from Carmer's book, and virtually no one knew my own publications. This experience with ethnologists and writers was to put Jesse in mind of doing his own book.

Just what Jesse had in mind when he borrowed my old Corona portable typewriter I was never certain. He said he had decided to do his own book of legends and accounts of the ceremonies. He said that if I could write from his telling, he could do it himself. I urged him to go ahead. Official duties were preventing my spending much time on ethnology, and this was one way to get it done. Jesse, who was then employed on the Rochester Museum's WPA Arts Project, was discovering that he no longer liked to draw, but he was turning out finely carved and polished False Faces in the distinct Spoonmouth style of Newtown. I think he regarded writing as a new experience in learning. Moreover, starting with Mrs. Converse, then Arthur Parker, myself and Carmer, he had been dealing with the learned world all his life through intermediaries, and he was tired of it. One thing he had learned from his varied dealings with such people was how to manipulate one to influence the other.

Among the competing agencies and enterprisers at work to assist the Tonawanda Senecas in these Depression years, besides the U.S. Indian Service under the "New Deal" which I represented; and the WPA Arts Project, which Dr. Parker directed; the N.Y. State Social Welfare Department programs which Helen A. Wayne supervised from Buffalo; and the Akron School Board, which ran the first integrated school; was Mrs. Walter A. Henricks, a lone woman from Penn Yan of formidable energy who styled herself "The White Sister." I was never certain whether she was the reincarnation of Mary Jemison, the White woman of the Genesee, or Jemima Wilkinson, the prophetess; but while I was writing and defending a dissertation, Saˀ´ni:we:, "It is walking," having now been adopted into the Beaver Clan, persuaded Jesse to cast his book in the form of letters to her. She also found a publisher, talked Carl Carmer into writing the Introduction, and had Professor Harold Thompson of Albany edit the manuscript. This was no mean achievement.

The book consists of 16 letters that emerge successively from the author's "story bag" which holds the repertoire of the Cornplanter family. They represent a long winter of thought, recollecting childhood memories "When the earth slept," commencing in October 1936, and appropriately closing in May 1937, in time to plant; for winter is the season of story telling. They cover the familiar Iroquoian cosmology, the origin of the Little Water Medicine, later described by Edmund Wilson (Wilson 1960), long in the literature and now thought to be "super secret"; the Dark Dance legend repeats what we had from James Crow with embellishments; the bears who adopted the lost boy who founded the Bear Society is a companion piece; there is a selection from the trickster cycle; two cannibal myths—Stone Coats and Naked Bear; and a delightful animal tale, "Rabbit and Pussy-willow." Several of these he had dictated to me, but only Jesse who thought in Seneca and wrote in "Reservation English" could achieve his terse and graphic style (Fenton 1938).

Both Cornplanter and Mrs. Henricks wrote me letters in appreciation of my review in New York Herald Tribune Books (1938).

As his writing advanced Cornplanter found my typewriter inadequate to his task. One late winter day he stopped me to tell me that he now had a new machine of his own, which he had arranged through his agent from an advance of royalties. "Here take your machine, Hanyonˀon (Pale Face), it is no good anymore." I knew when he called me that pejorative term, and not by my adopted clan name, I was being put in my place. Indeed I wondered who was being exploited.

Jesse now discovered that being a published author changed his life. Disillusioned and somewhat despairing that he would complete the one book, he now struggled not to be a "one book author." He was traveling hither and yon promoting the first book, writing to Mrs. Roosevelt to whom a copy was sent, and now signing his letters "Your Seneca author and Friend." He now had no time for his friends on the reserve: he quit the singers. He withdrew from all activities. There was to be no more free information to ethnologists. His hypertension increased. The Cornplanters installed the "Electric," and this would lead to other improvements in their menage, including an electric refrigerator. But when the first big royalty check came in he blew it on a binge of several days. Strangely enough and with characteristic tolerance Yowehˊsonh did not put his boots, his ax, his typewriter or his manuscripts out on the lawn. After that things returned to normal for a while.

Jesse discovered that "one can't live on fame alone." But despite his best efforts, he could not make progress on the second book. Instead he wrote letters, which often cover the same ground—his father, the war, his claim, his publisher, his health, etc.—enlivened by accounts of ceremonies, visits to other longhouses, and other news, and these constitute his art form. The number of his correspondents increased and some of them he used productively.

After my departure to teach and then to the Smithsonian, which pleased him because he was partly responsible for my appointment, we maintained a cordial correspondence mainly on subjects for research. He helped me to shoot down Hrdlička's hypothesis of ritual tooth ablation in America by compiling data on old lacrosse and hockey players who had lost their incisors from cross-checking. He wrote about a Condolence Council for installing chiefs which he had observed and which I was then studying at Six Nations Reserve. We discussed rates of pay now that he was famous.

Harold Conklin became his next protégé. Jesse reaffirmed his strong belief in the longhouse way by returning to Newtown whenever possible to attend ceremonies. Returning to the fire of his old people was an emotional experience, as I observed on occasions when we went there together; and the people responded by raising him to moiety leader among the Faithkeepers, a kind of "Super-Hodiont," as he explained to Conklin (2/1/43). In March he suffered his first stroke, which partially paralyzed his face, and by June he ascribed its cause to an old Eagle Dance curse, reiterating his early dream and vision (JC to WNF 6/18/43; Fenton 1953:127).

Within a year he took two ceremonial friends: a Sioux Indian and a Canadian Seneca, who was also a prominent singer. The Veterans Hospital in Batavia was adequate when you were in serious trouble, but it was safer to rely on the old ways, and a lot more reassuring.

Along with going back to Newtown for the "doings," the Cornplanters commenced to attend the ceremonies at Coldspring where they stayed with Yendi Abrams of his wife's clan. On one of these visits, when I was present in 1942, I introduced him to Charles Congdon, the noted attorney of Salamanca, and historian of the Allegany Oxbow. Congdon had us up for dinner. Since both men were gifted craftsmen, they were soon in correspondence, exchanging articles they made, which produced a contretemps over a drum tightener for which Jesse could never extract a substantial payment. But he did get some free legal services that he very much needed to obtain a divorce under Indian custom law from his legal wife, Effie Killbuck, and make the "Little Beaver" (Yoweh´sonh) the beneficiary of what he termed his "moth-eaten compensation." No one enjoyed twisting the tails of bureaucrats more than Congdon who enabled Jesse to subsist as a seventy-percent disabled veteran during his declining years.

Although it disturbed him that his surviving sister had become a Christian, Jesse himself, during the 1940s, frequently mentioned withdrawing his participation from Tonawanda Longhouse activities, including the singers; but as if to hedge his bets, he joined the Order of Moose and the D.A.V. (Disabled Veterans) in addition to the American Legion, and he took up with a California-based cult named *Psychiana*, which he wrote me was a kind of "Science" with a developed literature. In the closing years he was giving the "Rosecrucians" a whirl. These passing experiments with alternate faiths recall how he, having once taken peyote when visiting the Winnebago as a young man, could still sing the song that came to him during his vision. Indeed Cornplanter was the only Iroquois I have known who participated in a peyote meeting, but he never tried to introduce the cult to his own people.

Having suffered two strokes in his late fifties, he mentions that he awaits death, and as with the passing of other great Longhouse leaders, notably Elijah David and Lyman Johnson of Tonawanda, he instructed *Yoweh ˊsonh* to throw his manuscripts into his grave: his knowledge would go with him. He was much concerned that he have a full military funeral, confident that a Longhouse funeral service would be forthcoming anyway.

Jesse lived a final decade teetering on the brink of the grave before "Death, the Faceless," that follows men on the trail, overtook him. Meanwhile, in classical Iroquois terms, he sought the return from his friends of various objects of ethnological art that he had given or loaned to them or knew that they possessed. It was as if these objects were tokens of his soul's desires. It did not please him or lessen his wish that some of these objects were then in museums. He recalled that Jonas Snow, my Coldspring host, in 1933 had made for me a particularly fine turtle rattle of convenient size for keeping tempo in Great Feather Dance, Jesse's specialty; I had observed and photographed the stages of its manufacture, published, and deposited the rattle in the Yale Peabody Museum. He refused to accept the fact that I could not get it back once it was accessioned without an elaborate procedure involving the Yale Corporation. At this point he had little sympathy for me and my museum research, concluding: "To me, any 'ologist' is some animal with queer ideas."

And then there was the matter of wampum for Newtown Longhouse, the keeper having lost it in a fire. After long and involved correspondence with Heye, Speck, Deardorff and others, I located a quantity in the hands of a private collector who was systematically excavating historic Seneca graves. The man wanted a wooden corn mortar and pestle. Jesse remembered that his friend Ed Countryman from his Allegany State Park days had obtained from him the one that his mother had at Newtown. Somehow he got it back and traded it for enough wampum to fulfill the commission which the Newtown Faithkeepers had charged him to accomplish when they elevated him to "Super-hodiont." On his next visit there he carried the wampum which he had now strung to resemble the old, but in the longhouse he heard another man report on his own small success in obtaining one string. Jesse wrote that he kept quiet, and I am uncertain what disposition he ultimately made of his unfulfilled commission.

Both Jesse and Elsina were in fragile health, but there were periods of remission when he felt like singing, working at his crafts, visiting other reserves, and going on the Ganeho circuit. This is the period of his voluminous correspondence with hobbyists and collectors. Elsina who had taken to working in the Heinz pickle factory when he had his strokes, came down with pneumonia in 1945 and almost tasted the berries on the heavenly road. Jesse did the housework. His letters sometimes dated 5:30 a.m., mention angina attacks in the night: "In my age and condition," he wrote to Jiskoko (M.R. Harrington), "I sleep all by myself" (2/4/53). Of his housekeeping, he remarked: "It's a fright the way things are scattered in our house" (11/16/51). On a day when he was not annoyed with "ologists," he was holding me up as a model to Conklin. But he found the hobbyists less taxing, they could swap things with him freely, and they posed no threat to his "prestige." And Yoweh´sonh too was tired of what she termed "Museum stuff."

With the advent of tape recorders, which have revolutionized field work, I went up to see Jesse at Green Corn time in 1948, fully prepared to meet his fees, with what I thought was a bright idea. I wondered whether the tape recorder might not free him as the typewriter had not to produce the oral documents for that second book which he had been unable to write. After the usual avuncular lecture, which reduced me to under-graduate dimensions, and informed me of his unique position in his culture, Jesse announced that he was ready to cooperate with me as an old friend on the old basis.

Jesse was in fine voice that day and we recorded the chants and speeches of the "Uncles, the Bigheads" announcing the advent of the Midwinter Festival at Newtown, the Adónwenˀ of Handsome Lake, as his father performed it, and related material. We had plugged the recorder into the same circuit as the Cornplanters' new refrigerator, which was already a maze of wires. Within twenty-four hours the refrigerator quit, spoiling ten pounds of hamburger, which Jesse wrote was reduced to "cat food," and all on account of my "lousey machine." I sent him a check, although the appliance guarantee covered the failure, and Jesse later wrote that all was in good working order and he was well-compensated.

Soon afterward, at my suggestion, the Library of the American Philosophical Society offered to buy the manuscript of his Seneca song texts, and Jesse agreed to sell, with the understanding that he was to receive a xerox copy for his use. Such institutional acquisitions never move rapidly, and Jesse grew impatient for his check and then for the copies. He wrote that he could not understand why the A.P.S. wanted his songs anyway when no one there could sing them. I suggested that the A.P.S. make a tape recorder available to him and Tony Wallace, who was going up to Coldspring for the Midwinter Festival, was kind enough to deliver it, instruct Jesse in its use, and leave him to record at his leisure. He set aside a room in his house for the purpose, vowed that his neighbors should not know of his activities, and then commenced to worry. It didn't work without an audience, or someone to prompt him, and run the machine. The rate per song and per recording was too small, and he began to write abusive letters to me, to the Society, and to Dr. Wallace. He even wrote to Tony's father, Paul Wallace. It was too much. My experiment failed. Jesse wanted the machine out of the house. His Tonawanda neighbors were accusing him of selling his religion, but he vowed they should not have the songs, and once more he instructed Yoweh´sonh to tie up his manuscripts with a black ribbon and toss them into his grave.

During this fracas, my monograph on the Eagle Dance (1953) appeared. He acknowledged a presentation copy with a letter I treasure, praising my accomplishments as a fieldworker, and in a postscript recounting his vision as a sick child just as he had told it to me twenty years earlier. He complained that the order was declining, and signed "Your old informant and Friend." The next day he found "silly" my translation into English of Seneca clan names to protect my sources. He recognized all of the people and said I should have used their actual names.

V

Before going the long trail to the westward, Jesse was more than once within sight of the berries that grow by the path. His angina attacks increased in frequency and severity. Nitroglycerine helped somewhat, but he felt that the etiology might lie in his own culture. What had he neglected to fulfill? On five separate occasions his friend Dr. Charles Bartlett of Castile drove him to Grand River to consult a Cayuga medicine man. "On one occasion he took me along behind the cabin to see the tobacco burning and hear the Cayuga-Seneca ritual—all of which was unintelligible to me" (Bartlett to Fenton 5/2/58). Like many of his people Jess was almost certain that he was being witched, and wrote a long letter to Bartlett on his experiences. Bartlett persuaded him to consult a physician friend who took him off salt (which he hated) and gave him medication to reduce his body fluids. Jess immediately felt better. Thanks to Attorney Congdon, his compensation had reached the maximum allowable ($135.45), and as the recipient of "9 medals," he was assured of a military funeral. There was at least one false alarm. In January 1956, Cephas Hill, a neighbor and former foreman of the Arts Project, wrote me that "Jesse has gone to his maker." Having written condolences to Elsina, a few days later, I learned from Hill and Bartlett that it was a rumor, that "Firmly ensconced on a veritable sea of snow-white pillows at the Vets Hospital is friend Jess. In this land of combination hearse and ambulances, it was the sight of one of these at the home of Jesse that started the luscious rumor. . . ." (C. D. Hill 1/30/56)

When Jesse died a year later on March 18, 1957, I was unable to attend the funeral, which was well-covered by the press. He received both the rites of the Longhouse and the honors due him by an all-Indian American Legion honor guard. Solon Jones and Dean Gardner of Newtown represented the Keepers of the Faith where Jesse had grown up, played lacrosse, and was raised-up to office. George Buck, a famous singer, attended from Six Nations Reserve in Canada. Chief Corbett Sundown of the Hawk Clan at Tonawanda spoke the bare words of condolence to lift up the minds of the mourners.

Burial was not in the cemetery behind the Longhouse, as one might expect, but in his wife's plot in the triangle at the Four Corners, near the Council House and Baptist Church (Kidd Smith to WNF, 7/16/76). "Elsina wanted to be buried in that cemetery rather than the Longhouse one as it was too swampy" (E. Tooker, Field Notes; p.c. 6/25/76), and that is where they both repose. And Jesse's manuscripts did not go into the grave. Instead, Elsina gave them to Dean Gardner who went up to Tonawanda the same day Jesse died. He and Jesse used to sing ˀohki:we together and he naturally wanted the song texts. Elsina asked him to decide for her whether to transport Jesse to Newtown for burial at his birthplace, or at Tonawanda. "DG thought the widow should decide, but she insisted DG do it. Dean and Jesse were the same clan (Snipe), friends ("he called me 'cousin'"). Dean told Elsina it would cost $40 to remove the body to Newtown. So at least partly for this reason he was buried at Tonawanda." (Dean Gardner to W. C. Sturtevant, 9 June 1957; Sturtevant p.c. 6/17/76.)

Chief Sundown told me afterward that Jesse gave them a hard time even after he died: there was not only the question of where he should be buried, but there was some hitch at the graveside in lowering the coffin at the right moment. Perhaps this was symbolic of his whole career.

Jesse Cornplanter had a foot in two worlds. He was what the sociologists call "a marginal man." He had great talent as an interpreter, he was learned and he was critical of himself and others. His life and career epitomize the culture of the Longhouse people in the twentieth century. In many ways I owe him my career, and I am grateful. Nyawenh!

NOTES

1. M. H. Deardorff's papers are in the Pennsylvania Historical Commission Archive Harrisburg.

2. Possibly Mrs. Walter A. Henricks of Penn Yan, New York, owns his book plates.

3. W. C. Sturtevant's informants at Newtown—Solon Jones, Dean Gardner, Mrs. Charlie Funn, and Roy Button—believe that Edward Cornplanter was indeed descended from the old chief of that name and not from the "Joe" line (WCS to WNF 6/17/76).

LITERATURE CITED

Carmer, Carl

1936 Listen for a Lonesome Drum. New York: Farrar & Rinehart.

Congdon, C. E.

1967 The Allegany Ox-Box. Little Valley, New York (published by the author).

Cornplanter, Jesse J.

1903 Iroquois Indian Games and Dances. Drawn by Jesse Cornplanter, Seneca Indian Boy (Frederick Starr: published privately.) 1–15.

1936 "Autobiography," Rochester Democrat and Chronicle.

1938 Legends of the Longhouse. Philadelphia; New York: J. B. Lippincott.

1941 "Jesse Cornplanter, Chief of the Senecas," Marius Risley, ed. St. Bonaventure Alumni Magazine 42(8): unpaged.

Fenton, W. N.

1936 An Outline of Seneca Ceremonies at Coldspring Longhouse. Yale University Publications in Anthropology, No. 9.

1938 "A Story-Bag of the Senecas" (Review: Jesse J. Cornplanter, Legends of the Longhouse), New York Herald Tribune Books: Sunday, March 20.

1953 The Iroquois Eagle Dance: an Offshoot of the Calumet Dance. Bureau of American Ethnology Bulletin 156. Washington: The Smithsonian Institution.

1968 Parker on the Iroquois. Syracuse, New York: Syracuse University Press.

Jaffe, Irma B.

1975 John Trumbull: Patriot-Artist of the American Revolution. Boston: New York Graphic Society.

Mead. Margaret, Ed.
1937 Cooperation and Competition Among Primitive Peoples. First Edition. New York: McGraw-Hill.

1961 Cooperation and Competition Among Primitive Peoples. Second Edition. Beacon Paperback 123. Boston.

Parker, A. C. and H. M. Converse
1908 Myths and Legends of the New York State Iroquois. Ed. and annotated by A. C. Parker. New York State Museum Bulletin 125, Albany.

Parker, A. C.
1909 "Secret Medicine Societies of the Iroquois," American Anthropologist XI:161–185.

1910 Iroquois Uses of Maize and Other Food Plants, New York State Museum Bulletin 144, Albany.

1913 The Code of Handsome Lake: The Seneca Prophet. New York State Museum Bulletin 163, Albany.

1916 The Constitution of the Five Nations. New York State Museum Bulletin, 184, Albany.

1923 Seneca Myths and Folk Tales. Buffalo Historical Society Publications XXVII.

1968 Parker on the Iroquois. W. N. Fenton, ed. Syracuse, New York: Syracuse University Press.

Wilson, Edmund
1960 Apologies to the Iroquois. New York: Farrar, Straus and Giroux.

CHAPTER FOURTEEN

SYLVESTER LONG, BUFFALO CHILD LONG LANCE

Catawba-Cherokee and adopted Blackfoot, 1891–1932

HUGH A. DEMPSEY

Sylvester Long, or Buffalo Child Long Lance, was an author, newspaper reporter, movie actor, and athlete of the 1920s and '30s. During his day, he was acclaimed throughout the continent; was a member of the Explorers' Club in New York, and was friends with people like Douglas Fairbanks, Irving S. Cobb, Jack Dempsey, Lowell Thomas, and Viljalmur Stefansson.

Yet his main impact—particularly among historians and ethnologists—was derived from his book *Long Lance: The Autobiography of a Blackfoot Indian Chief*, published in 1928 by Cosmopolitan Book Corp. of New York. Let me quote from the first page of this book:

> The first thing in my life that I can remember was the exciting aftermath of an Indian fight in northern Montana. My mother was crying and running about with me in my moss bag-carrier on her back. I remember the scene as though it were yesterday, yet I was barely a year old. Women and horses were everywhere, but I remember only two women: my mother and my aunt.
>
> My mother's hand was bleeding. She was crying. She handed me to my aunt and jumped on a pony and rode away. My infant mind told me that something tragic was happening, and though Indian babies seldom cry, I cried for my mother when she ran away and left me. It seemed that I should never see her again. (Long Lance 1928:1)

And later on, Long Lance made these comments about a trip to a trading post:

> As we rode into the post we passed some stables with some cows in them. We had never been around cows before, and the smell of them made us sick. We all had to hold our hands over our noses as we rode by this stable. We youngsters had always thought that the cow would smell strong like the buffalo, but they smelt sweet, like milk; and that made us want to vomit.
>
> When we arrived at the post the traders came out to meet us. The white men came up to our fathers and started talking. . . . We boys had never been close to white people before; so while they were talking with our fathers, we and some of our braves walked up behind them and smelled of them to see what they smelt like. They smelt different from the Indians; they smelt just like those cattle, and it made us sick. (Long Lance 1928:172)

With this kind of first hand observation it is little wonder that Long Lance's book was an instant success, going into three printings within a short span of time. And over the years Long Lance has been widely quoted by historians and ethnologists, both for his impressions of early life allegedly as a Blackfoot Indian, and also for his observations about neighboring tribes.

In 1933, another volume, entitled *Redman Echoes*, was published by admiring friends in Los Angeles. This limited edition contained some of Long Lance's best writings from *Cosmopolitan*, *Good Housekeeping*, *McClure's*, *Century Magazine*, and *Mentor*.

The title *Long Lance: The Autobiography of a Blackfoot Indian Chief*, should be looked at, one segment at a time. Long Lance, the main title, was not the author's true name. He was born Sylvester Long, and at various times during his career he was known as Sylvester Long Lance, Sylvester Chahuska Long Lance, Sylvester Clarke Long Lance, and Buffalo Child Long Lance.

The next part, *The Autobiography*, is equally erroneous, for the book is not an autobiography. The final part of the sub-title is . . . of a *Blackfoot Indian Chief*. Long Lance was not a Blackfoot Indian. And his claim to being a chief is based upon an honorary chieftainship which was conferred upon him by the Blood Indians in 1922. Obviously, then, the title of Long Lance's book poses a number of significant questions. Although the main purpose of this paper is to examine Long Lance's literary contributions, this cannot be done without looking at the total man. The understanding of Long Lance is essential to the assessment of his works.

Long Lance was born Sylvester Long in Winston, North Carolina, in 1891, the son of Joe and Sally Long. Recently, Professor Donald Smith of the University of Calgary made a trip to Winston-Salem and verified some valuable facts about the family's background (Smith 1976 a and b). The father, Joe Long, was part Catawba Indian and part Black, having been taken into the family of the Reverend Miles Long as a slave. It was from his master that he received his surname of "Long."

Long Lance's mother, Sally Carson Long, was of mixed descent, her mother Adeline Carson, being classified as a Croatan, or Lumbee Indian. Long Lance's grandmother, was said to have been the offspring of Robert Carson, nephew of the famous "Kit" Carson, and an Indian woman from South Carolina.

Long Lance, then, had mixed racial background including Catawban, Croatan, Black, and White blood. And in North Carolina in the 1890s, that meant he was Black.

Culturally, too, the family appeared to be Black. When they moved from their hill country farm in Iredell County to Winston a year before Long Lance was born, Joe Long became a "colored" caretaker in a White school. In later years, Long Lance's brothers both married Black girls, one of the brothers becoming the manager of the "colored" section of a local movie theatre, and the other operating a detective agency in the Black community.

Under normal circumstances, Long Lance would have faced the same limited opportunities available to other Blacks of that period and place. But there was one difference: Long Lance looked like an Indian.

After attending a Black school until the age of 12, Long Lance joined a Wild West show where he mixed with Cherokee Indians and learned some of their language. At the age of 18, he applied for admission to Carlisle Indian School in Pennsylvania, enrolling as a Cherokee. According to one of the White teachers:

> The legitimate Cherokees were indignant at his posing as an Eastern Cherokee and a delegation of their number went to the Superintendent and protested his enrollment. I remember well that one of their number indignantly exclaimed, "Cherokee nigger!" (Smith 1976a)

Partly to offset the accusations of being Black, the boy was encouraged to change his name to the more Indian-sounding Sylvester Long Lance. As he gradually adjusted to the new life, he devoted his attention to athletics, also proving to be an exceptional student in English and history. He graduated at the head of his class in 1912, spent a year at nearby Dickinson College and then won a scholarship to St. John's Military Academy, near Syracuse, New York.

In 1915, Long Lance was a candidate to West Point, something that could never have happened if he had been identified as Black. At this time, he had completely cut himself off from his family, preferring to live the life of a "Cherokee Indian."

Instead of entering West Point, Long Lance went north to join the Canadian Army, as that country was already at war with Germany. Shipped overseas with the Canadian Expeditionary Force, he rose to the rank of staff sergeant and was wounded twice in action. When asked where he wanted to be demobilized, he chose the city of Calgary, in the heart of the Canadian prairies.

Shortly afterwards, under the name of S. C. Long Lance (presumably the S. C. stood for Sylvester Clarke, or Sylvester Chahuska) he became a reporter for the *Calgary Daily Herald.* Travelling across western Canada, he wrote numerous articles on the native peoples, looking both at their history and their current mode of life. During this time, he became a friend of Archdeacon S. H. Middleton, the Anglican missionary on the Blood Reserve, who accepted him completely as a Cherokee Indian and introduced him to many Indian elders. In 1922, Middleton arranged for Long Lance to be inducted as an honorary chief of the tribe. In an article of February 14, 1922, entitled "Cherokee Given High Honor by Blood Indians," the *Calgary Herald* stated:

> In sacred and solemn terms his own tribal name, In-Nus-Tuan Long Lance, was changed to En-Ui-Pok-Kau, Buffalo Child, by which name he will henceforth be known by the Bloods.

However, lest anyone think he was changing a Cherokee name for a Blackfoot one, it should be explained that *In-Nus-Tuan* is simply the Blackfoot word for "Long Knife" or "Long Lance."

From that time on, for the public at least, Long Lance became a Blackfoot chief. He was a man with an engaging personality, a tremendous charisma, particularly with women, and he had the ability to draw about him a wide circle of devoted friends and admirers. Leaving the Calgary *Herald* for freelance work, he soon had articles appearing in newspapers and magazines all across Canada and the United States. In some cases, magazines even surpassed the author himself in trying to establish his image as a noble Indian. For example, 1926, Long Lance wrote to a friend:

> Did you see my article in "Cosmopolitan" for the current month? My friends tell me that it was good, but I wasn't entirely pleased with the way they changed my lead and put in one or two paragraphs along towards the end, giving them first person and making me appear proud and boastful of myself; also taking for granted that my A.B.C.'s were learned on "the Blackfoot Indian Reserve in Southern Alberta." (Letter to W. M. Graham, May 22, 1926, Long Lance Papers, Glenbow Alberta Institute.)

In 1928, after publishing his "autobiography," Long Lance became the social lion of New York. Dubbed the "Beau Brummell of Broadway," his portrait was painted by the Kaiser's daughter-in-law and his name was romantically linked with women in the social set. In letters to friends back in western Canada, he was a shameless name-dropper:

> Jack Dempsey and his wife live just two blocks from me, and I frequently go up to his apartment for dinner. (Letter to W. M. Graham, August 17, 1928, Long Lance Papers.)

> I am going tonight with Viljalmur Stefansson to hear Madame Juliette Gaultier de la Vendrye give a recital of her Eskimo and Indian songs. (Letter to W. M. Graham, December 16, 1929, Long Lance Papers.)

> I had a very nice time the short while I was in California. Fannie Hurst sent a letter about me to Douglas Fairbanks, and after my work was through he took me in town and gave me a wonderful time. . . . I liked Charlie Chaplin, too; he was with us a lot. And Doug and I golfed one afternoon with Harold Lloyd. . . . (Letter to Alice Tye, April 24, 1930, Long Lance Papers.)

> I work out with Bob Fitzsimmons . . . and I frequently go down and visit with him and Edna, their little daughter Jean, and their youngest daughter . . . I gave her the Blackfoot name, *Napi*. Do you like it? (Letter to Alice Tye, July 17, 1930, Long Lance Papers.)

Interestingly, *Napi* is a man's name, actually the trickster-creator of the Blackfoot, and hardly suitable for a little girl.

Partly as a result of his publicity, Long Lance was invited to star in a film, *The Silent Enemy*, which was being sponsored by the American Museum of Natural History, and released by Paramount Pictures. Filmed in Ontario, it was a silent fiction thriller about a brave hunter who saved his people from starvation—the "silent enemy." Released in 1930, it was acclaimed a dramatic success, but reached the markets just as the new talking pictures were pushing silent films right out of the movie theatres.

But the film industry liked Long Lance and he was invited to star in a talking film dealing with the exploits of an Indian flying ace during the great war. Long Lance quickly mastered the art of flying and enjoyed a romantic interlude in Europe with one of the leading female fliers of the day. Returning to California in 1932, he was preparing for his Hollywood debut when he suddenly died of gunshot wounds in the home of Anita Baldwin, daughter of a wealthy mining magnate. A revolver was found beside the body and the coroner ruled that Long Lance had committed suicide.

The coroner's inquest files cite a witness who said that Long Lance had spoken of suicide, and some people are convinced that he did indeed take his own life. According to Professor Smith, Long Lance's past began to catch up with him in 1930, when his Black detective brother approached him in New York to tell him that his father had been ill and that the family had been caught up in the Depression (Smith 1976b).

Yet the story still persists in Western Canada that Long Lance was murdered. In a way, the added confusion about his death is simply in keeping with his entire life. Was he a charlatan and a fraud, or was he simply a man who desperately wanted to break out of the chains that society had cast upon him?

Long Lance cannot be considered a native recorder in the usual sense of the term. Rather, he was a gifted journalist and writer who happened to be part-Indian, but who culturally brought nothing to his work. In my estimation, he was no different from a non-Indian writer who chose to write about the North American Indian. The only difference may have been that his acceptance by the missionaries, and later by the Indians themselves, could have opened doors which would have been closed to other journalists.

Yet even this view is open to question for although he was made an honorary chief of the Bloods, all tribes in the Blackfoot nation did not approve of him. As a one-time Indian Agent noted:

> The Blackfoot band would never accept him as an Indian. . . . They treated him kindly but must have had their doubts. When he requested that I arrange for him to attend the Sun Dance the leaders were noncommittal and insisted that he live, while attending the ceremonies, *outside* the circle of the Sun Dance camp. Even his "blood brother" relationship with the Blood band was overdrawn,

> while many of his stories were of dubious authenticity. (Gooderham 1958:8)

In some ways, it is unfortunate that Long Lance's reputation must stand or fall on his so-called "autobiography." Yet such is the case, for it is the only hardcover work completely authored by him, and it has been widely distributed throughout the world as a work of non-fiction written by a Blackfoot Indian.

In the publication of the book, Long Lance may have been a victim, albeit a willing victim, of his publishers. As he said in a letter to a friend:

> My publishers asked me last year for a "Boys' Book" on the Indian, explaining pretty well what they wanted—lots of adventure and a goodly amount of Indian customs. I connected up my own experiences and those of many other Indians I know and made a running story out of it, such as they asked for. But when they received the copy they thought it was "too good for a boys' book," and forthwith decided to run it as a straight book. (Letter to W. M. Graham, August 17, 1930, Long Lance Papers.)

In other words, what started as a semi-fictional juvenile book became a supposedly authoritative autobiography. While Long Lance may not have set out deliberately to mislead the reading public, he made no attempt to have the book classified as fiction, nor did his public statements after it was published lead anyone to believe that they were reading anything but his own life story.

Yet Long Lance's other works, his newspaper and magazine articles, reveal that he was carrying out valuable field work at a time when few ethnologists, and even fewer journalists, were concerned about the history of the Indian. For example, in 1923 he interviewed a number of Ojibwa Indians who related stories of battles with Sioux in the mid-nineteenth century, and described in some detail the Midewiwin ritual as practiced in Manitoba (Boys' Own Tribune, Winnipeg Tribune, March 10, 1923). Similarly, an interview with the Cree chief Masqua brought out an interesting tale which traced the migration of the tribe from eastern Canada after its contact with White traders. This data was considered significant enough to be reprinted in the Archaeological Report of the Province of Ontario for 1923 (Long Lance 1933:143).

Unfortunately for the historian, Long Lance realized that his own identity as an "Indian journalist" helped to sell his stories. As a result, he often injected a personal element into his articles which, while perhaps not totally inaccurate, certainly left the wrong impression with his readers. For example, when telling a correct account of the flight of an Indian fugitive, Almighty Voice, in 1895, Long Lance said that the man's mother, Spotted Calf, "is also my adopted mother, and that is why I am able to record the inside story of this famous man-hunt." (Long Lance 1933-172.) At best, Long Lance's "adoption" was little more than an honor bestowed upon him as a visiting journalist when he went to interview the elderly couple.

In some ways, Long Lance's writings can be compared with the fictional works of James Willard Schultz, a White man who was married to a Piegan girl. He wrote some 37 books about the Blackfoot and although four or five of these were entirely non-fictional, the rest were written as juvenile fiction. Even though many details in the latter books were based upon Schultz's own experiences, no historian can seriously cite them as factual sources.

Long Lance, rather than writing pure fiction, often used journalistic license which makes much of his work suspect. While there is a sharp line between Schultz's fiction and non-fiction, such is not the case with Long Lance. A few of the latter's articles, particularly his newspaper accounts, appear to be quite accurate, while those in magazines often suffered from a combination of the author's ego and the editor's heavy hand. And, at the extreme end of the spectrum is Long Lance's only book, his so-called "autobiography," of which about 80 percent is probably accurate information from native informants. But which 80 percent?

A few of Long Lance's handwritten field notes exist in the Glenbow-Alberta Institute in Calgary. They reveal the firm and confident hand of a good newspaperman. If more such notes existed, they might be sufficient for a new Long Lance book which could establish his reputation as a competent observer and recorder of Indian lore. But even then, the fact that Long Lance was an Indian—or claimed to be—would be only incidental.

LITERATURE CITED

Gooderham, George H.
1958 Chief Buffalo Child Long Lance. In Glenbow-Alberta Institute, ed., Northern Plains Tribes. Calgary: Glenbow-Alberta Institute.

Long Lance, Buffalo Child
1928 Long Lance, The Autobiography of a Blackfoot Indian Chief. New York: Cosmopolitan Book Corporation; London: Faber and Faber.

1933 Redman Echoes; Comprising the Writings of Chief Buffalo Child Long Lance and Biographical Sketches by His Friends. Los Angeles: Frank Wiggins Trade School.

Smith, Donald B.

1976a The Legend of Chief Buffalo Child Long Lance. Toronto: The Canadian, February 7, 1976.

1976b Long Lance's Last Stand. Toronto: The Canadian, February 14, 1976.

Newspapers and Periodicals

Boys' Own Tribune. (Weekend supplement to Winnipeg Tribune, March 10, 1923.)

Calgary Daily Herald, February 14, 1922
Boys' Own Tribune.

Documents

Long Lance Papers. Calgary: Glenbow-Alberta Institute.

CHAPTER FIFTEEN

JOHN JOSEPH MATHEWS

Osage, 1894–1979

GARRICK BAILEY

One afternoon, while still an undergraduate at the University of Oklahoma, I had a chance meeting on the street with a fellow student who was an Osage Indian. I quickly judged that he was returning and possibly still recovering from a night of revelry. His hair was uncombed, his clothes were wrinkled, and his eyes were bloodshot. Before I could make some sarcastic remark about his unkempt appearance, he excitedly started telling me about a book he had just finished reading a few minutes prior to our encounter. The book was John Mathews' *The Osages* (1961) which had been published a few weeks before by the University of Oklahoma Press. By chance he had bought a copy the day before, and he had become so engrossed in reading it that he had stayed up all night and even cut his morning classes so that he could finish it. For the reader unfamiliar with the book I might add that it is 788 pages long. Never before, nor since have I seen him as excited as he was that afternoon telling me about *The Osages*. The comment he made that I always remembered was, "Now I know who I am." He of course didn't mean this in a literal sense, but in the sense that now he knew for the first time what it truly meant to be Osage. While Mathews' work, *The Osages*, is an important contribution to anthropology, Mathews himself did not regard it as an anthropological study. In fact Mathews was not writing the book for the academic community. It was a book written for the Osages by an Osage.

John Joseph Mathews is, and has been, an impossible person to categorize. He is or has been an aviator, a scholar, a naturalist, a rancher, a geologist, and a tribal council member. He has always been an adventurer, individualist, and an individual self-confident of his own worth and abilities. Some individuals have described him as an English country gentleman (Logsdon 1972:70) but what these individuals may have failed to recognize is that his aristocratic bearing is possibly more typical of the Osage than of the English.

John Joseph Mathews was born in 1894 in Pawhuska, the governmental and commercial center of what was at that time the Osage Nation. His father was William Shirley Mathews, one quarter degree Osage, while his mother was of French descent. The mixed-blood Osage family from which John Mathews is descended, traces its origin back to the marriage of William Shirley Williams, an early day missionary to the Osages, and A-Ci'n-Ga, a Buffalo Clan woman from the Big Hill band of Osages. William Williams and A-Ci'n-Ga had two daughters before A-Ci'n-Ga died. The daughters, Mary and Sarah, still children at the time of their mother's death, were sent to a girls' boarding school in Kentucky. Williams then joined a party of fur traders headed for New Mexico. In the Rocky Mountains, William Shirley Williams became famous not as a missionary to the Indians, but as "Old Bill" Williams the mountain man (Mathews 1961:ix).

While at school in Kentucky the eldest daughter became acquainted with John Mathews, a native of Kentucky, who operated several trading posts among the Osages and Cherokees. Mathews married Mary Williams, but she died not long after they were married. Shortly after her death he married her sister, Sarah (Mathews 1961:ix–x). At the outbreak of the Civil War John, Sarah, and their two sons, were living on the Osage reservation in southern Kansas where John Mathews had a trading post. Mathews, a southerner and a slaveowner, was an ardent supporter of the Confederacy. Realizing the troubles which were going to engulf Kansas, he sent his two sons, under the care of a trusted slave, to live with relatives in east Texas. He then organized the Southern sympathizers in southern Kansas into an "army." Their attempt to seize part of Kansas for the Confederacy failed, as Mathews and his "army" were defeated. Mathews himself was hunted down and eventually killed while fleeing from his burning home. After the war the two sons rejoined their mother on the reservation in Kansas, and were removed to Indian territory with the rest of the tribe in 1872.

One of the two sons, William Shirley Mathews, the father of John Joseph, followed in his father's footsteps. He established a trading post (which later evolved into the Osage Merchantile Company) on the Osage reservation. Later he established the Citizens' Bank in Pawhuska. In the 1890s the William Mathews family was one of the more prosperous families in the Osage Nation.

John Joseph was born in 1894 in his family's large two-story stone house on Agency Hill in Pawhuska. The world into which he was born included a strange mixture of traditional Indians, mixed-bloods, cowboys, squatters, traders, agency personnel, missionaries, whiskey peddlers, and horse thieves. Like most frontier communities in the American West, Pawhuska contained both the best and the worst of mankind. From his home near the top of Agency Hill John Joseph could see the rustic western town of Pawhuska along Bird Creek, as well as the mat lodge village of the Thorny Thicket band of Osage on Soldier Creek.

Five years before Mathews was born, in 1889, the so called "Unassigned Lands" in the central part of Oklahoma were opened. This was only the first in a series of land rushes. Pressure soon developed for the allotment of Indian reservations in severalty, and the opening of "surplus" lands for White settlers. Indian reservations in central and western Oklahoma were dissolved and in rapid succession opened to White settlement. Even though the Osage Nation was not included in these, numerous Whites migrated into the Osage Nation to await the day when the Osage lands too would be allotted, and the surplus opened to White farmers. But the Osage, together with the Five Civilized Tribes, adamantly refused allotment until it was forced on them in 1906 (see Bailey 1973:84–85 and 89–90).

The Osage Nation in the 1890s consisted of two distinct worlds: the White world and the Osage world. Most of the mixed-blood Osage "aped" White society and were openly contemptuous of the traditional Osages. Mathews (1961:772) states that to the mixed-bloods, "the full-bloods appeared as stupid, stubborn, 'blanket Indians.' They were 'uncivilized' and had 'no get up and go.' This attitude of contempt did not escape the full-blood leaders. . . ." The attitude of the mixed-bloods toward the Indians approximated the attitude held by many of the White squatters living in the Nation. However, those mixed-bloods attempting to shed their Indian heritage tended to be more adamant and overt in expressing their anti-Indian sentiments. There were notable exceptions among the Whites; many of the former agency employees, missionaries, and older traders, had a great deal of respect for the traditional Osages, and these feelings were reciprocated. However, in the 1890s these individuals constituted a small minority of the resident White population.

Unlike other tribes during this period the Osages were wealthy. Although most individuals today know of them as an oil rich tribe, few realize that they were wealthy even before oil was discovered on their reservation in 1897. The tribe had 1,400,000 acres of the best grasslands in the Plains, and over $8,000,000 in the U.S. Treasury. The $8,000,000 came from the sale of Osage reservation lands in Kansas starting in 1872. The interest from the money in the U.S. Treasury and the income from the leasing of grassland to ranchers was divided every three months among tribal members. During the 1890s every Osage man, woman, and child received about $200 a year from these sources (Bailey 1973:80–81). Their landholding and income led Special Agent White in the 1880s to declare them the "richest people in the world" (White 1965:203) While the traditionalists may have been living in mat lodges and wearing their traditional clothes, they were wealthy and they knew it. They had something the White man wanted, money, and thus the full-bloods were openly as contemptuous of the Whites and the mixed-bloods as the latter two groups were of them. The full-bloods possibly had more contempt for the mixed-bloods than the Whites, since the Osage word for mixed-blood translates "little White man," and the diminutive here is one of contempt.

The Mathews family was atypical as a mixed-blood family in a number of ways. Most importantly, they were respected by most groups. The full-bloods respected them as they do even today. Culturally the Mathews family was White; they did not participate in traditional Osage ceremonial or social life. The Osage clan system was patrilineal, and the Osage ancestry of the Mathews family had passed through a matrilineal line; thus they were not part of the clan system. While culturally White the Mathews family still psychologically identified, at least in part, with the Indian community. Through their store and by choice, they maintained strong personal ties with the traditional Osages. William Shirley Mathews could speak Osage fluently, and even John Joseph could speak Osage, although he could not speak it fluently. While the Mathews family did not participate in Osage traditional life, they were close observers of it, and the entire family maintained an active interest in Osage culture and history.

John Joseph grew up knowing both the White and the Indian worlds intimately. He was born and grew up in an upper class White house surrounded by material things from the White world. He went to public school, not an Indian school, and was educated as a White among Whites. However, at the same time the Indian world was never far away. From his father's house, "at night one could hear the giant pulse-beats of the kettle-drum when they dance the I'n-lon'schka" (Mathews 1961:x). John Joseph loved to hunt and to ride. At every opportunity he would take his horse, his dog, and his gun and ride over the reservation. At these times he visited the traditionalists in their camps to eat with them, and sometimes attended their dances. He also met them in town and in his father's store. He grew up in constant association with the full-bloods and counted them among his closest friends.

He was in an unusual position in that he could objectively judge both the White and Indian worlds, and in his judgment the White world placed a poor second. In *The Osages* he gives the following contrast between the White man and Indian:

> It was odd that the Amer-European should have, in his illusions about himself, created standards of Christian ethics which he couldn't possibly live up to and yet be natural and sincere. He created criteria, for ethical actions and relationships among men made of him a hypocrite . . . their (White) transgressions, were transgressions only through their own illusions about themselves as Christians, following Christian principals. The Osages had no standards against which to judge them, and therefore the Heavy Eyebrows (White men) judged themselves against their own standards, and if finding themselves transgressing their own moral laws, they could hide their transgressions from their Christian God with words implying their humanitarianism, in which they could make themselves believe. They used words in the preambles of all their treaties with the Osage to make their God believe that they were honorable men, and only interested in protecting the Osage. The Little Old Men had used words too, not to hide their transgressions from Wah-Kon-Tah but for mysticism, and the word became sacred and not a screen; but the Heavy Eyebrows believed in his screen as much as the Osage believed in the mystic sacredness of his words. (Mathews 1961:776–77)

The Osage world was changing, and their traditional way of life was coming to an end. Osage resistance to allotment was futile as the government policy was set and the Osages could not resist it. In 1906, when John Joseph was twelve, the Osage Nation was allotted and his name was placed on the final allotment roll. As an allottee he received 560 acres of land and a headright. Oil had been discovered on Osage land in 1897, and thus at allotment the tribe had retained its mineral rights. The headright Mathews received entitled him to l/2229th of the mineral royalty income of the tribe. This oil income has meant that Mathews has been financially independent for his entire life.

After graduating from public school in Pawhuska he enrolled at the University of Oklahoma in 1914 to study geology. However, his education was interrupted by the entrance of the United States into World War I. At first Mathews, naturally enough, enlisted in the Cavalry, but he soon changed to the aviation branch of the Signal Corps and served as an aviator in France. After the war he returned to the University of Oklahoma to finish his education. The returning soldiers seem to have placed an added burden on the university and the university attempted to process the veterans through as quickly as possible, much to Mathews' dislike. Course credit was given to veterans on the basis of training in the military; Mathews himself was given credit for aerodynamics on the basis of service in the Air Corps. In 1920 he was graduated from the University of Oklahoma with a degree in geology. According to Mathews he did not feel as if he were qualified. Deciding that he was in need of additional study, he went to England to study natural science at Oxford. He graduated with a B.A. in 1923. Before Mathews graduated, he and one of his friends were contacted by Harry Sinclair of the Sinclair Petroleum Company who intended to do a survey in Angola. However, before this came to pass the Teapot Dome scandal broke, and Sinclair decided to cancel the Angolan project.

The cancellation of the Angolan project was a disappointment, but it really did not affect him financially. In 1923, Osage oil production was at its height, and from his own headright Mathews had a tax free income of slightly more than $12,000. Thus he was able to go to Switzerland and enroll in the School of International Relations of the University of Geneva. At this time the League of Nations had its headquarters in Geneva. Mathews took a part time job as a League of Nations correspondent for the *Philadelphia Ledger*, as he says, filling in when their regular correspondent was absent, thus not covering the more important sessions.

After a year Mathews was awarded an International Relations Certificate from the University of Geneva. Still he didn't know what he wanted to do with his life, income from his headright making him financially independent. In a conversation with Guy Logsdon concerning this period he said,

> I was aimless. I didn't know what I wanted. I wanted to go on reconnaissance for some oil company—the wilder, the better. I roamed around, toured France on a motor bike—all that sort of thing. I wasn't too proud of myself. I was active physically and mentally, but aimless. (Logsdon 1972:71)

His travels took him over Western Europe, the British Isles, and North Africa. The love of hunting which he had developed as a young boy in "The Osage" stayed with him, and many of this trips including those to Scotland and North Africa were hunting expeditions.

In North Africa he developed an interest in archaeology. The ruins of ancient Roman colonies in North Africa fascinated him. While exploring the ruins of the Roman officers' club in Timgad, he found the broken marble lintel from over the main entrance. Putting the pieces together he was able to read the Latin inscription, "To Hunt, To Bathe, To Play, To Laugh, That is to Live." Mathews adopted this inscription as his personal motto, and the lintel is now the mantel over the fireplace in his home.

On one of these trips in North Africa an incident took place which ended his aimless wandering and gave direction to his life.

> I remember very distinctly one evening, when we were preparing our meal, suddenly it came to my guide and my cook that it was time to worship. So they fell on their knees, faces toward Mecca, as usual. In this situation you feel so clumsy, so out of things—you feel that you are an absolutely sinful person. About this time some Kabyles, a wild tribe of Arabs, came up who were not Mohammedan and had not known religion at all—wild! they came across the sand. I think there were about six or eight of them firing their Winchesters, the model 1894 lever. I thought, here, we're in trouble. My guide and my cook were prostrate. They surrounded us shooting all the way—on their Arab horses—all mares, incidentally. Then they got off and ate with us. They were very friendly.
>
> That night I got to thinking about it, and I thought that's exactly what happened to me one day when I was a little boy, riding on the Osage prairies. Osage warriors with only their breechclouts and their guns had come up and surrounded us—firing. Of course, I knew some of them, about them; they knew me, who I was. That's what we called joy shooting, you see, just joy. So, I got homesick, and I thought, what am I doing over here? Why don't I go back and take some interest in my people? Why not go back to the Osages? They've got culture. So, I came back. . . . (Logsdon 1972:71)

From North Africa he went back to his home in Geneva, put his affairs in order, and in 1929 returned to Pawhuska.

The fifteen years he had been gone had brought many changes in him and in the Osages. The period that Mathews, in *The Osages*, calls "The Great Frenzy" was coming to a close. From 1916 until it peaked in 1925, oil production on the Osage reservation had increased rapidly. The increase in production had produced unbelievable wealth for the tribe. Whites flocked into Osage county by the thousands wanting to share in this oil bonanza. Some came in disguise as merchants, others as lawyers or doctors. It was a time of unparalleled excess on both the part of the Osages and the Whites. It was a time of drunkenness, debauchery, fear, and, not infrequently, murder. Many of the Osages succumbed to wild abandonment. The more stable turned to their new religion, peyotism, as a sanctuary. In either case Osage traditions and the old way of life were rapidly disintegrating (Mathews 1961:771–784).

The old men of the tribe whom Mathews had known as a boy had changed. Their confidence in themselves and their way of life had been shaken. Now they were fearful, not as individuals fearful for their own persons, but fearful of the survival of their people. The younger Osages didn't care about their culture, their history, or their traditions, and the old men sat by themselves seeing the cultural disintegration of their people. The old men who had not talked to Mathews as a boy were ready and willing to talk to him as a man. As Mathews said:

> They were afraid that their moccasin prints would be washed by the sheetwaters of oblivion. Then they started talking; they wanted to live in word symbols. That's the only chance that they had; they thought that they would be gone. They weren't afraid about getting to Spirit Land—their faces could be painted and Wah'Kon-Tah would see them. They could go to Spirit Land, but the point was that they might lose their culture. They might be absorbed by (the) I'n-Shta-Heh, the white man. So, they started talking. (Logsdon 1972:72)

Out of this change in the Osage and this fear expressed by the old men Mathews found the direction to his life for which he had been searching. After his return in 1929 Mathews focused his efforts on what he called "Osage culture rescue."

Although he was obsessed with the idea of preserving Osage culture, he initially did not know exactly how he was going to go about it. However, his interest in the Osages had not gone unnoticed by Laban Miles, an old friend of the family. Miles, a Quaker and uncle of President Herbert Hoover, had been an agent to the Osages during the late nineteenth century and upon retirement had made his home in Pawhuska. During his time as agent Miles had kept a diary. Shortly before his death in 1931 Miles gave his diary to Mathews. Mathews mentioned the existence of the diary to Joseph Brant, a close friend, who was the editor of the newly established University of Oklahoma Press. Brant encouraged Mathews to rewrite the diary in a publishable form. To rewrite the diary was a major undertaking since the diary consisted of "plain old Quaker facts," and Mathews had had little experience as a writer. For almost five months he did nothing but fish and write. The result was *Wah'Kon-Tah: The Osage and the White Man's Road. Wah'Kon-Tah* was published by the University of Oklahoma Press in 1932 and became the first university press book ever chosen to be a selection of the Book-of-the-Month Club, selling over 50,000 copies (Logsdon 1972:73).

The success of *Wah'Kon-Tah* brought Mathews to the attention of the publishing industry. The Book-of-the-Month Club took him to New York as part of its promotional campaign. In the series of parties which he attended as part of this campaign he was besieged by representatives of a number of publishing houses. As he says, he really didn't want to write another book at that time. However, he met the representatives of Longmans, Green, and Company and he personally liked them, so on this basis he agreed to write another book.

His second book was a novel, *Sundown* (1935), the story of a young Osage struggling between two cultures. As he says, "I just wrote the book and I've never read it." Although it was to him the least favorite of his books, others considered it one of the best novels written about the American Indian (Logsdon 1972:74).

By the time he had finished writing *Sundown*, Mathews' attention had been diverted to a new project, an Osage museum. With this as one of his objectives he ran for and was elected to the Osage Tribal Council in 1934. As a councilman he pushed hard for the creation of a tribal museum. He lobbied at home and in Washington where he received encouragement from John Collier, then Commissioner of Indian Affairs, and from the staff of the Smithsonian Institution. He found support from almost every quarter except from the Council. Most of the Council and most of the Osages didn't care. Finally he was able to secure a building on the agency grounds at Pawhuska, but because of lack of enthusiasm in the local community, he was forced to fill the museum with items loaned by the Smithsonian. The museum was opened in 1938. In its early years the museum languished because of lack of tribal support. At one time Mathews had to get money from the Pawhuska city council to keep the museum open. It was not until the 1950s that local Osage support for the museum developed. Local Osage families started donating items to the museum, and finally the Osage were able to return the items loaned by the Smithsonian. In 1957 the building was remodeled and the museum truly became the center of Osage culture rescue.

Ten years passed between the publication of *Sundown* and the publication of Mathews' third book. Most of this time had been spent either with the museum, tribal matters, or in the construction of his home, The Blackjacks, which he built himself on his allotment eight miles from Pawhuska. His third book, *Talking to the Moon* (1945), is primarily about himself, the land, and the Osage. It is concerned with his view of man, nature, and man's relationship to the earth.

In 1951 he published *Life and Death of an Oilman: The Career of E. W. Marland*. Governor Marland, an oilman from Ponca City, Oklahoma, had been a close friend of Mathews and a good friend of the Osage tribe. Marland's oil company had been involved in developing the oil fields in Osage county. So even though this is a biography of a White man, the book is at least in part concerned with Osage history.

Mathews' most important contribution to anthropology has been his study *The Osages* published in 1961. In his first four books Mathews had only lightly touched upon the margins of Osage culture and history. In *The Osages* he deals with the traditional Osages directly.

The book *The Osages* involved Mathews in a project that took more than 30 years from start to finish. As noted earlier, when Mathews returned in 1929 he found that many of the older Osage were more willing if not anxious to talk to him than they had been when he was a boy. They wanted their knowledge recorded so that it would not be lost. The idea of writing such a book first germinated during this period. However, Mathews didn't know the precise form such a book would take. With this general objective in mind, Mathews started interviewing the old men and taking notes on what they told him. He also initiated research on the written records. His research proceeded slowly during the 1930s and 1940s. Much of his time was devoted to other matters: the writing of his other books, the museum, tribal problems, and the building of The Blackjacks. To make matters worse, tribal oil production, and thus his income, dropped following World War II. The decline in his income seriously limited his ability to undertake the expenses of research.

In 1949 Chief Fred Lookout died. His death left a vacuum in the tribe, and a feeling of uncertainty as to the future of the Osage. He had been chief of the tribe for 25 years and his death marked the end of an era. Lookout's death seems to have stimulated Mathews' research and writing on the Osage. Mathews had been a close friend of the chief and his family, and Chief Lookout had been a major source of information. The collecting of oral histories from the few remaining old men had to be done immediately, or much of it would be forever lost. Using a tape recorder Mathews collected data for his study. In addition he had to travel to various libraries throughout the country to gather published and manuscript materials. The collecting of data and writing on the Osage occupied him for most of the decade of the 1950s. Although oil production, and thus his personal income, increased during this period, research expenses depleted his personal resources. Fortunately financial assistance came from some of his old friends: Frank Phillips (of Phillips 66), Allen Oliphant (Oliphant Oil), and W. G. Skelly (of Skelly Petroleum). This assistance allowed him to finish the study about two years earlier than anticipated (i.e., if he had been forced to rely solely on his own resources). Finally in 1961 *The Osages* was published, and a significant part of Osage culture had been "rescued" from oblivion.

Since *The Osages* is his major contribution to anthropological literature it is important to examine the materials he utilized and his method of analysis. Since it was to be on Osage history, he wanted to use only Osage oral histories. However, this proved to be impossible since they were incomplete. Thus, he was forced to rely upon what he calls "Amer-European" materials to fill in gaps in the oral data. In using this non-Indian data he makes a statement concerning the problems inherent in the use of such materials with which most ethnohistorians would agree:

> One had to keep constantly in mind the basic interest of the writers of military reports, trappers' letters and stories, Spanish, French and American official reports, and mission journals and letters home. One had to make allowances for the smugness of the traveler whose interest was chiefly academic. No matter how sincere, honest, and objective the Europeans and Amer-Europeans were, their unconscious economic, political, military, social, and religious interest often nullified all three. One had to know something of the background of the writers of private letters, official reports, verbal witnesses, and travelers, . . . ambition to advance one's personal interest, either politically or economically; military ambitions and Christian intolerance and the settlers' struggle for existance could not live with untainted academic interest . . . (1961:xiii)

Having little formal training in history and virtually none in anthropology, Mathews' overall analytical framework was not that of a social scientist but that of a natural scientist. He states (1961:xiv):

> I thought of myself as a paleontologist searching for a lost femur, a lost tarsus, several vertebrae, or ribs. In assembling the fact-bones for my reproduction, I had to supply the missing ones with the plaster of 'instinctive knowledge.' I had much more than merely a jaw bone and a femur: I had bones from every part of the skeleton.

> More than that, when covering the finally reproduced skeleton with flesh and hide, I could use the material of my personal experiences and the experiences of my father and grandfathers, and I, myself, had seen my dinosaur walking.

The end product of his study is a book which starts with Osage creation myths and ends with the death of Chief Lookout in 1949. The book covers a wide range of topics: mythology, history, and culture. These diverse topics are integrated around a central theme, the relationship of the Osage to an ever changing world. What Mathews attempts to demonstrate is how the Osage viewed themselves in relationship to God, nature, and other men. He makes no attempt at being neutral with regard to the Osage and their relationship to other societies, particularly White society. To have done so would have defeated the primary purpose of the book. This is an Osage history, written from an Osage point of view, with events interpreted from an Osage cultural perspective. Because of this factor some people have said that *The Osages* is not a history, but rather a saga. In defense of Mathews and his approach to Osage history, I am reminded of that oft-quoted dictum, "History is only mythology taken seriously, while mythology is merely some one else's history." Regardless of whether *The Osages* is a history, a saga, or a myth, it is one of the greatest examples of Native American literature and scholarship.

Much of the material presented here is from personal interviews with John Joseph Mathews. The Osage Tribal Museum, which he founded, remained one of his main interests until his death in 1979. Even when he was no longer active in research himself, he was a major source of encouragement and support for those individuals active in recording and preserving Osage culture. In the last few years of his life, he moved from the Blackjacks into Pawhuska, living on Agency Hill, a few blocks from the museum he founded and from the house in which he was born. And on June nights, he could still "hear the giant pulse-beats of the kettle-drum dance of I'n-lon'schka."

LITERATURE CITED

Bailey, Garrick A.

1973 Changes in Osage Social Organization: 1673–1906. University of Oregon Anthropological Papers, No. 5.

Logsdon, Guy

1972 "John Joseph Mathews—A Conversation." Nimrod 16:70–75.

Mathews, John Joseph

1932 Wah'Kon-Tah: The Osage and the White Man's Road. Norman: University of Oklahoma Press.

1935 Sundown. New York: Longmans, Green and Co.

1945 Talking to the Moon. Chicago: University of Chicago Press.

1951 Life and Death of an Oilman: The Career of E. W. Marland. Norman: University of Oklahoma Press.

1961 The Osages: Children of the Middle Waters. Norman: University of Oklahoma Press.

White, Eugene E.

1965 Experiences of a Special Agent. Norman: University of Oklahoma Press.

CHAPTER SIXTEEN

FLORA ZUNI—A PORTRAIT[1]

Zuni, 1897–1983

TRILOKI NATH PANDEY

The recent appearance of many biographical and autobiographical studies of the American Indians has misled us into believing that the life history is a natural and universal narrative form among these people. It might not be too much of a parody to say that the prevailing public as well as the anthropological view is as follows: place a tape recorder in front of Mr. or Miss American Indian and he or she will tell the "real truth" about his or her life. As far as the Pueblo Indians are concerned, nothing could be further from the truth. Although there are biographical and autobiographical studies of the Pueblo Indians, such as Leo Simmons' *Sun Chief* (1942), Polingaysi Qoyaway-ma's *No Turning Back* (1964), Helen Sekaquaptewa's *Me and Mine* (1969), Alice Marriott's *María: The Potter of San Ildefonso* (1948), and John Adair's "A Pueblo G. I." (1960), interest in autobiography is relatively rare among the Pueblos. The Pueblo traditions do not provide any model of such confessional introspection, as people hardly remember individuals after their death. After all, traditionally an individual is not that important in Pueblo culture.

Given this situation, one could wonder how I managed to get material for a biographical sketch of Flora Zuni. Let me briefly describe what led me to this undertaking.

I met Flora Zuni in September of 1964, when, at the end of my first fieldwork season, I went to see her daughter whom I had met earlier in the summer while I was with the Ramah Navajo. I lived with Flora Zuni's neighboring family whose members often asked me about the anthropologists whom they had known. Although I knew little of their anthropologist friends, I had learned from my hosts that Flora Zuni had worked for such anthropologists as A. L. Kroeber, Ruth Benedict, and Ruth Bunzel. So I began to visit with her occasionally, discovering that Flora Zuni and her family members were more cooperative toward and sympathetic to my research than members of my host family. As a result, on my return to Zuni next summer, I moved in with them. I have spent more than two years with Flora Zuni's family, and she and her daughter have come to visit me in Santa Cruz. Flora Zuni assumed a maternal role with me, and helped me to learn the ways of her people. Without her support, it would have been difficult for me to do my research in Zuni.

I believe Flora Zuni's earlier association with anthropologists was useful to my work. She would tell me "stories" about Bunzel, Benedict, Kroeber, Elsie Clews Parsons, and other anthropologists she had helped, asking me what I knew about them. This led me to investigate systematically how anthropologists who had worked in Zuni were viewed by the people of the pueblo (see Pandey 1972). During the course of this investigation, I would ask Flora Zuni questions about her own life, which she always answered graciously. However, it was not until December 1971, when she was 74, that I decided to collect material for her biography. It was suggested to me by one of Flora Zuni's favorite granddaughters that it would be good for her "people" to know about her grandmother's "life" and "times." When I explained what the project entailed, Flora Zuni burst into laughter and said, "What is this book you want to write about me? I did not know that I was such an important person!"

Flora Zuni was quite conscious of her position in her society, but avoided becoming conspicuous in the eyes of her fellow Zuni. I suspect that she did not want to be accused of being a *newista*, a White-lover, and of selling her "secrets" to outsiders.[2] However, I believe that she rather enjoyed talking about her life and times and did not mind my asking questions about certain individuals and events from her past.

In this paper, I have tried to present a portrait of Flora Zuni based on my informal conversations with her and with other members of her family. I have also relied upon the information that was collected by other fieldworkers and visitors to the pueblo.

Flora Zuni is one of the most respected members of Zuni Pueblo. She was born on July 1, 1897, and was the third child of her parents. She had three younger siblings—two of them, a brother and a sister, are still living. She is from the Badger clan that "owns" many powerful religious offices, including the high priesthood in the religious hierarchy of the pueblo. Her father was from the Bear clan, and child of Badger, and an accomplished artist. Her mother was, according to Bunzel, "an excellent potter and a real artist."[3] Flora Zuni was married in 1915 to a man from the Sun clan who died in 1939, leaving her 700 sheep. Two years later she married a man from the Deer clan who was a prominent member of the pueblo. For many years he was a councilman and, until a year before his death in 1966, was a tribal judge.

Flora Zuni had six children, four of whom are living. Her eldest son was born in August 1913, when she was 16, and he takes care of the sheep. Her second son was born on May 10, 1915, and he works for the New Mexico Highway Department. Her only daughter, Vera, was born on August 1, 1925, and she has just retired from the BIA after 20 years of service. Her youngest son, born on August 6, 1928, is a college graduate and is now director of the tribal social service programs in Zuni. Flora Zuni had 27 grandchildren and 35 great-grandchildren. She was very proud of this record.

III

Flora Zuni enjoyed talking about her early life—her childhood and the early years of married life. She said:

> Just a few of us went to school those days. I went to the Boarding School at Black Rock.[4] I didn't get much education; just up to 6th grade. There were about 60 students in the school. I think there were about 20 girls. I am not sure now. It's hard to remember these things. But I started to speak English at the school. There were only a few Zuni who could speak English then. Nick Tumaka was one of them. Later in 1918, when I started to work at the Day School, I had to speak English with the teachers there.[5]
>
> Those days I stayed in my mother's house in the village. I had lots of sisters and brothers and nephews and nieces. I took care of them all. I bought clothes and other things for them. Those days we had very little money. I worked very hard and that's what I tell my children to do.

One thing which impressed me about Flora Zuni when I first met her, was her ability to do hard work. Every day she got up at six o'clock in the morning and worked until eleven at night. In March of 1976, when I saw her last, I noticed that even at 79 she still maintained the same routine.

Obviously, this is the way she was all her life. In August 1924, Bunzel mentioned in a letter to Franz Boas that Flora's "chief regret is that each day has only 24 hours that she can work in."[6] Her hard work indeed served her well. She had one of the best homes in Zuni, and her family was certainly one of the five most prosperous families in the pueblo.

Early in her life Flora Zuni came to realize that she would have to cooperate with "outsiders" in order to improve her economic situation. Since she was fluent in English, she became an interpreter for different groups of outsiders—anthropologists, BIA employees, PHS employees, missionaries, and teachers. She was Kroeber's informant when he did fieldwork in Zuni in the summers of 1915 and 1916 for his book, *Zuni Kin and Clan* (Kroeber 1917). Once when I told her that Zuni had changed a lot since Kroeber's time, her immediate response was, "So have anthropologists. You are not asking me what Mr. Kroeber used to ask." Kroeber did not live in her house; Mrs. Margaret A. Lewis, the Cherokee school teacher who named her, was his hostess. But he did work with Flora Zuni who received shell, feathers, and other household material from him for her father.[7]

As I mentioned earlier, Benedict and Bunzel stayed with Flora Zuni when they were in the pueblo during the 1920s. They collected folk tales, prayers, and linguistic material from Flora Zuni and found her both a great story-teller and a good interpreter.[8] Flora Zuni also became very fond of them, in particular of Bunzel, "who was just like a sister" to her. She recalled that:

> Mrs. Benedict and Bunzel lived together for a while in the old house and then moved to this new house. During the summer they slept on the roof of that house.
>
> Mrs. Benedict was . . . deaf. She always put her right hand on her ear while she talked with somebody and often asked them to speak louder. . . . Bunzel was very hardworking like me. She used to grind cornmeal for our doings, go to the field with men to work there, and helped my nieces with their homework. . . . But Mrs. Benedict was a nice lady. She was more polite and generous than Bunzel. She spoke gently and gave more money. Some weeks I earned two hundred dollars. Mrs. Benedict came to me in the evenings when I returned home from work and asked me to translate stories and tales into English. We would work for three to four hours and Mrs. Benedict would give me 10 dollars for that. Bunzel was giving me only 50 cents per paragraph.

This indicates that Flora Zuni was quite concerned about money. She often asked me how much money I would make when the "story" of her life would be published. At any rate, the amount she reported that she received for her work seems to be exaggerated. Nonetheless, she made the most of the opportunity offered by Benedict and Bunzel and, with the money she earned from them, she was able to buy some land on the edge of the pueblo and build a small house where anthropologists could stay more comfortably. This also gave her some freedom from the constraints of a close community.

When there were no anthropologists in the pueblo, Flora Zuni rented the place to anyone who was willing to pay. Thus, during the late 1920s Miss Elizabeth Duggan, the field nurse, stayed with her for several years (Duggan 1928). She named Flora's only daughter. Mrs. Clara Gonzales, who came to teach at Zuni Day School in 1923 and retired in 1965, also stayed with Flora Zuni for a few years. They became good friends and supported each other. Flora Zuni considered Mrs. Gonzales "the best friend I have among the Anglos." This feeling was mutual, since, in talking of Flora Zuni, Mrs. Gonzales once said:

> She was different from other Zunis of her age group. She always cooperated with Anglos in Zuni and this helped her. She got a job at the school and her children were able to get some education. They are well off today. When people asked me, "How come everything goes to Flora and we get nothing?" I had to tell them that, because she has been good to the outsiders and has worked hard for them. You also work and you will get the rewards.

This was confirmed by an examination of the BIA and church records which show that Flora Zuni's was one of the very few families that would take outsiders as "boarders." Since there were quite a few government and church employees who needed such facilities, Flora Zuni's house was full most of the time.

During the last World War, when more than 200 Zuni men went overseas to fight, women took up making jewelry in order to support their families (Adair 1944). Flora Zuni also did so for two years, but she did not enjoy it. As she said, "I didn't like sitting at the machine all the time. It was because of my diabetic condition that in 1939 I had to retire from the Day School. I didn't feel good making jewelry." Luckily, one of the traders asked her to sell turquoise for him on a 20 percent commission, and that is what she has been doing since 1940. This has made her quite wealthy, and, as a result, conspicuous in the eyes of her fellow Zuni. Even her own brother, who is the High Priest of the South, became "jealous" of her and started to sell turquoise on credit. He was not as successful as Flora Zuni, so he spread the rumor that since she did not want any competition, she asked people not to buy any turquoise from him. He was so furious with her that, according to Flora Zuni, "he wanted to have a court" for her and discontinue her license. Flora Zuni and her husband went to the Tribal Council members and explained that he was selling Lone Mountain turquoise and people did not want to buy it, preferring to buy Morenci from Flora Zuni. She was so upset by this incident that she went to all her relatives and explained what her brother had done to her. She said, "Willie did mean things to our brothers and sisters, but this is the first time that he has done this to me." Flora Zuni and her brother did not talk to each other for several years, and there was not much interaction and reciprocity between them.

I suspect that Flora Zuni was always worried that she might be accused of witchcraft. In a closed society like Zuni, if anyone is either rich or poor—conspicuous, different from others—he or she is suspected of witchcraft. She must have done it at the cost of her fellow members of the society, goes the reasoning. It is understandable why, whenever I went to see someone with whom Flora Zuni or any member of her family was not on good terms, I was invariably asked on my return what was said about them. Once, when I jokingly told her that they were saying that Flora was rich, her face fell and she said, "You must be lying. No one says that. We have no money. We are poor people." On the other hand she herself reported to me on another occasion that her granddaughter's husband's niece told her great-granddaughter that she would not talk to her because she came from a "rich family."

This made me aware of how well integrated Flora Zuni was in her culture. She always wore her traditional Zuni costume and regularly fed her *kachinas* either before or after eating. If we were eating at home, she would put some food in the fireplace. "I gave food to the dead ones," she said. If we went to a restaurant, she would leave some food on the plate. "This is for my gods," she observed. "My mother told me that if we don't give food to the dead ones, something bad will happen. I also tell this to my children," she added.

This shows that Flora Zuni was very particular about the performance of rituals and her participation in religious "doings." She built a *Shalako* house in 1946 and sponsored several initiations into the *kachina* cult and her medicine society. She often went to the summer and winter dances and regularly gave food, clothing, and money to the *Koyemshi*. When her brother, the high priest, went into retreat twice a year for "rain," she, along with other members of the family, kept *teshkwi* by abstaining from eating certain kinds of food and refraining from buying and selling (see Kroeber 1917:165–174; Bunzel 1932:501–502; and Benedict 1934:65–74).

IV

Flora Zuni was a very kind and generous person and it gave her genuine pleasure to feed people and share what she had with them. She often gave gifts of turquoise bracelets, necklaces, and rings to her relatives and friends. Several of my students who took care of her when she visited Santa Cruz were pleasantly surprised by such generous gifts. Her cultural model for this was her mother who was, as she put it, "very nice to everyone." In talking of her daughter, Flora Zuni remarked that "Vera is just like me. She is good to everyone. I raised my sister's children, my brother's children, and many of my grandchildren. Now Vera is raising (her son's) children." The way in which Flora Zuni spoke of her parents and her children was particularly compelling and revealing of her conception of the formation of character structure. She believed that her children were "good" because she was good and because she took good care of them. She said, "I don't drink, nor do my children." When I reminded her that it was only her daughter who does not drink, all other members of her family do (Pandey 1975: 209), she thought for a moment and then said, "Yes, you are right. I meant only Vera and (her daughter) Geraldine."

Flora Zuni took a great deal of pride in her children. She always mentioned the good things they did for her and she often gave them presents (cf. Bunzel 1938:354). In return, she was greatly loved and admired by them. Her sons visited her regularly, bringing her groceries and other provisions, and her daughter drove her around, taking her in her car to see her "customers," friends, and relatives.

Flora Zuni enjoyed going to town and visiting her friends in other pueblos. Her daughter said, "She starts complaining if we don't take her to town for a few days." She attended most of the important ceremonies and feasts and fairs in the Southwest, trading with Indians and non-Indians. She was often visited by her friends from the Hopi, Isleta, Jemez, and Santo Domingo Pueblos. Her relatives often called on her, bringing such things as Zuni bread, watermelon, corn, peaches, green chilli pepper, piñon, and candies.

Flora Zuni was a very shrewd person. I have noticed that with everyone she met, she was the same—tactful, smiling, and friendly.[9] She was a gracious hostess; she was very courteous to all my friends and students who visited Zuni. She always asked me about them and mentioned what she thought of them. She was very observant and loved mimicking the people whom she found interesting. I will never forget her mimicking some of the characters of Star Trek, her favorite television program, and Ruth Bunzel carrying a basketful of bread over her head. Her face glowed when she spoke of the people she had known.

I might mention that Flora Zuni did not express any animosity toward any of the White people she had known. There was some misunderstanding between her and one of the school teachers, but it was resolved amicably.[10] Her attitude toward White people was basically friendly. Once, when she learned that I was going to see the local Catholic priest, she observed, "Give him my regards and tell him that I used to go to the church when I was young, but now I don't. I am old now and I have my own religion." When I told this to Ruth Bunzel, who had known Flora as a young woman, she said, "It's incredible! Flora was a Catholic, but she sent her children to the Protestant school because 'they gave them better clothes there'!"

I believe that in this respect Flora Zuni changed little. Beginning in 1964 I recorded several events which illustrated her statement: "I am two-faced like a pancake."

V

There are certain themes which clearly emerge from the foregoing portrayal of Flora Zuni's life. Let me briefly mention a few of them.

It is obvious that Flora Zuni had a remarkable aptitude for entrepreneurial enterprise. When she was born, her family was not economically well off, but the pueblo was opening up to Whites and "by the end of the last century, some 30 Anglo Americans had come to stay in Zuni" (Pandey 1977:201). She took advantage of the opportunities offered by them, becoming first a schoolteacher, then an interpreter, and later a saleswoman. Thus, she was able to move up economically and make her family one of the most prosperous in Zuni.

However, she remained a well-integrated person with a strong sense of social responsibility and a commitment to her family and to her "people." She lived her life in an orderly, restrained, and well disciplined way, representing the classic "Apollonian" type of personality popularized by Ruth Benedict (Benedict 1934:79). In Flora Zuni's "story" of her life there is hardly any boasting of her achievements, while the idea of family welfare and of carrying traditions from one generation to another is strongly expressed.

She was concerned with maintaining proper inter-personal relationships. In this connection, it should be recalled that Flora Zuni became very upset when she discovered that rivalry had appeared between her brother and herself. I suspect she had no idea that it was due to the economic competition that was generated by the new opportunities which became available to more Zuni in recent years. Cooperative attitudes, essential for an agrarian economy, have been modified in a market-oriented society.

Finally, let me conclude this paper with a personal observation. I hope that I have made it clear that it was my special friendship with Flora Zuni which made it possible for me to collect material for her biographical sketch. I am well aware that this might have influenced my understanding and interpretation of her life history. But it should be mentioned that Pueblo women have a special position in their society. They are less concerned with religion and politics and possibly have a more detached, "objective" view of what takes place in the pueblo. Flora Zuni knew a great deal about her society and I am grateful to her for making me her pupil.

NOTES

1. This paper is a preliminary exploration of the life history of Flora Zuni. I wish to gratefully acknowledge the support of a small grant from the Phillips Fund of the American Philosophical Society that aided in its preparation. I am indebted also to Professor Fred Eggan and Mrs. Gail Ghose for their comments on an earlier version of this paper.

2. It had happened to her in the past. For more information, see an unpublished letter from Ruth Bunzel to Franz Boas, Zuni, July 5, 1926. The Boas Papers, American Philosophical Society, Philadelphia, Pennsylvania.

3. Unpublished letter from Ruth Bunzel to Franz Boas, Zuni, August 6, 1924. The Boas Papers, American Philosophical Society, Philadelphia, Pennsylvania.

4. It used to be the headquarters of the Agency of the Bureau of Indian Affairs until the Tribal Council took over the BIA in July 1970. The Public Health Service (PHS) and the airport are still in Black Rock.

5. Ruth Bunzel confirms this in her letter to Franz Boas. *Supra* Note 3.

6. Ibid., p. 1.

7. Unpublished letter from A. L. Kroeber to Flora Zuni, August 29, 1916. The Kroeber Papers, Bancroft Library of the University of California, Berkeley.

8. Unpublished letter from Ruth Bunzel to Franz Boas, Zuni, August 6, 1924. The Boas Papers, American Philosophical Society, Philadelphia.

9. Bunzel makes a similar observation in her letter to Boas cited above. *Supra* Note 8.

10. I have excluded all information which could be embarrassing to Flora Zuni or her family.

LITERATURE CITED

Adair, John J.

1944 The Navajo and Pueblo Silversmith. Norman: University of Oklahoma Press.

1960 A Pueblo G. I. In In the Company of Man. Joseph B. Casagrande, ed. New York: Harper and Row.

Benedict, Ruth

1934 Patterns of Culture. Boston: Houghton Mifflin Company.

Bunzel, Ruth L.

1932 Introduction to Zuni Ceremonialism. 47th Annual Report of the Bureau of American Ethnology 47:467–544.

1938 The Economic Organization of Primitive Peoples. In General Anthropology. Franz Boas, ed. New York: D. C. Heath and Company.

Duggan, Elizabeth V.

1928 Health Work Among the Zuni Indians. Public Health Nurse 20:20–22.

Kroeber, A. L.

1917 Zuni Kin and Clan. Anthropological Papers of the American Museum of Natural History 18:39–204.

Marriott, Alice

1948 María: The Potter of San Ildefonso. Norman: University of Oklahoma Press.

Pandey, Triloki Nath

1972 Anthropologists at Zuni. Proceedings of the American Philosophical Society 116:321–327.

1975 "India Man" among American Indians. In Encounter and Experience: Personal Accounts of Fieldwork. A. Béteille and T. N. Madan, eds. Honolulu: University of Hawaii Press.

1977 Images of Power in a Southwestern Pueblo. In Anthropology of Power. Raymond D. Fogelson and Richard N. Adams, eds. New York: Academic Press.

Qoyawayma, Polingaysi
1964 No Turning Back. Albuquerque: University of New Mexico Press.

Sekaquaptewa, Helen
1969 Me and Mine: The Life Story of Helen Sekaquaptewa as Told to Louise Udall. Tucson: University of Arizona Press.

Simmons, Leo
1942 Sun Chief: The Autobiography of a Hopi Indian. New Haven: Yale University Press.

CHAPTER SEVENTEEN

ORAL HISTORIAN OR ETHNOLOGIST? THE CAREER OF BILL SHAKESPEARE

Northern Arapahoe, 1901–1975

LORETTA FOWLER

In July of 1975, while I was on the Wind River Reservation in Wyoming, Bill Shakespeare, a Northern Arapahoe,[1] was buried. The afternoon before the funeral, while he lay in his coffin in an old frame house no longer inhabited, but on his nephew's allotment, the priest from the Indian mission arrived to pray over his body. The day was bright and warm, the sky clear blue. With the first words of the priest, the sky darkened and opened. Flashes of lightning, terrible thunder, and a wrath of huge hailstones descended on that frail little house, and the din made the words of the priest inaudible. We few friends and relatives sat there, I for one feeling increasingly apprehensive and uneasy, as the stones beat against the house like a thousand fists, and the day darkened. By the end of the prayers, an interval of about thirty minutes, the storm vanished as abruptly as it had come.

When I subsequently mentioned the incident to elderly Arapahoes, they quietly explained that Shakespeare had kept his grandfather's medicine bundle, and that although he never used the medicine, the storm had been a sign of the power still residing in the bundle. Another unusual aspect of the funeral ritual surrounding the death of Shakespeare was the fact that very few people were in attendance during the ceremonies for the 74-year-old man. This was so despite the fact that the tribe invariably turns out en masse for funerals of elderly persons, and that deaths of individuals of any prominence in tribal affairs ordinarily draw hundreds of Arapahoes. In my mind, the ambivalence of Arapahoes toward Shakespeare and the ambiguity surrounding his role as a member of the tribe and an authority on Arapahoe culture are aptly symbolized by the events of the mortuary ritual which accompanied his death.

Bill Shakespeare was born in May 1901 on the Wind River Reservation. In his youth, he was a Hollywood actor and a world traveler, and in later years he was an informant for anthropologists studying Arapahoe language and culture. Towards the end of his life he spoke on Indian culture and history in many schools around the country, and he tried to establish his credentials with his own people as a "Tribal Historian." The life of this man is interesting not only because it is an illustration of how the aid an informant gives to anthropologists may have repercussions for that individual personally, but also because it points to the ways that some Indian communities—that of the Wind River Arapahoe, in this case—both are and are not receptive to scholarly study of their way of life and to the concept of tribal historian.

GROWING UP ARAPAHOE

Shakespeare was born in an era of flux and transition. His father, War Bonnet, went to Carlisle Indian Industrial School in 1881 at the age of 16, and during his three year attendance learned to read and write English (Records of the Carlisle Indian Industrial School, 1879–1918: File 156). His readjustment to reservation life initially was problematic, as this letter of April 19, 1917, to the Carlisle Superintendent seems to reveal:

> Now I just wanted to express myself at the Carlisle Arrow that I am still alive out here in Wyoming where I am located and doing very well on my farm only now I am kind of over-or-run down by hard-works. It's a long time since I left there. The year was (1872) and the Supt. was General R. H. Pratt and the more I thank him for what he has taught me. I only were at second reader and that help me well. I can talk with a business man alright. The reason I left the school so soon is I were in very ill health.
>
> Now I will tell you about my pass present years since I left the school and how I mistake from my own people. When I started my living I was well off, have lot stock such as horses pigs cattle chickens and my Indians when so foolish on account that what they call Ghost dance I been giving big feast and I thought I was a big chief then and when I broke no body give me a feast then.[2]

> When I first came back that is returning home I start to teach my people the way of white people education farming and I was the first one in my people to wear a hat but my people were still had a feathers on their head and few years after I show them how school means. I have been wishing to visited the Carlisle once more but I am getting old now.[3] (Records of the Carlisle Indian Industrial School, 1879–1918: File 156)

He married, and accepted employment as a policeman, government herder, and interpreter throughout most of his adult life. He served on the council of Arapahoe leaders, and frequently spoke for his tribe in dealings with federal agents, on one occasion writing to the Secretary of the Interior to request an investigation of financial irregularities on the part of the Indian agent.[4] Too young to have been a warrior in pre-reservation days, War Bonnet, whose name was William Shakespeare at Carlisle, was an important go-between, serving as a communication link between tribe and agent in the days when few Arapahoes spoke English.[5] In the letter of April 29, he characterizes these years of service in a more positive light than his initial readjustment period:

> I have seven children. Five are married and two are attending school yet. Their are growing very well. I support them by my own hand and raise them in doing agriculture from my own land too. I have living at my allotment few years after I returned home and still I am located here as my father found this place for me to own. (Records of the Carlisle Indian Industrial School, 1879–1918: File 156)

War Bonnet was a strong influence on his son Bill, and Bill emerged bilingual under the tutelage of his father. In fact, until Bill's death, he was acknowledged as one of the few Arapahoes who spoke "old time" Arapahoe, a man who could communicate fluently and eloquently in the Arapahoe language. At the same time, he was very articulate in English, speaking with style and wit, and he acted as interpreter for the Arapahoe tribal council on many occasions. His father, who is credited with introducing (from Oklahoma) the peyote ritual to the Northern Arapahoe, also taught peyote songs to Bill, whose skill as singer was later to prove useful to ethnomusicologists.

Also instrumental in the direction Bill's life was to take was his grandfather Beaver Dodge. As a boy, Bill spent much of his time with his grandfather, an important medicine man and tribal elder. One day, when Shakespeare was talking with me about his youth, he mentioned an incident which he felt had assumed immense proportions in the course of his career:

> My grandfather, Beaver Dodge, he was the one that knew how to proceed with all these various Lodges (men's age-graded societies). Now, Beaver Dodge was not my grandfather through ceremonial or any other Lodge, but by blood relationship. And we were there camping with him. Now, some of these men would come out of their tipi and you were drafted. You could not refuse when they came and got you. They'd ask you in a nice way to come and join them, and if you did not want to, you were forced. They'd knock you out or carry you, pick you up bodily, and take you over there and you became a member. And you could not run away from there. If you did, they'd come and tear your tent up, destroy your property, beat you up, and carry you back into the tipi. So you had to be a member without trying to get away, because there was no use trying to get away; they'd get you anyway. . . .
>
> Now, one of the Lodges had intended or had planned to draft me into this Lodge, and we saw them coming as I was sitting in my grandfather's shade. And he said, "Don't move. Don't run." He says, "They will not come in and take you." He says, "They can't come into my tipi and draft you." He says, "It's against the laws of the tribe since I am one of the men that knows the proceedings of these ceremonies. Since I am the head of all these Arapahoe ceremonies." So I sat there. They came so far and turned around and walked back. They found out that they couldn't take me by force or any other way. So the dances went on in there; and I didn't know what happened in there. I didn't go around in there to peek in, but I saw them when they would come out, come out after sinew or something that they had to use to work with in the Lodge.[6]

Thus, Bill did not join with several of his peers in induction into the young men's society, and in the years to come did not become involved with other ceremonial groups. In short, his knowledge of the ceremonial sphere of tribal life was minimal. Even in later years his commitment to Arapahoe traditions was not expressed through participation in the religious rituals of the tribe, despite the early influence of Beaver Dodge. His interests were more parallel to his father's achievements in secular and particularly inter-cultural affairs.

THE SEARCH FOR A PLACE

Bill's middle years were characterized by a restlessness, possibly instigated in part by family difficulties in his early years. Bill's father had three co-wives, Bill's mother, Nevada, being the youngest and most recent. She died when Bill was four years old, and Will's second wife, Cassie, became dominant in the household. There was apparently ill will between the issue of Cassie and Nevada, and for several years Cassie, senior wife to Nevada, insisted on Bill's use of the name Whiting (Nevada's maiden name) (Estate of William Shakespeare, Probate Hearing, 1934).

Bill's early school days were spent at St. Stephen's Indian Mission operated by Jesuits on Wind River Reservation. Registered as Alphonse Shakespeare, he attended during 1908–1913, 1915, and for the 1916–1917 term (St. Stephen's Indian Mission, Student Records 1908–1917). These were trying years in many respects, given the Mission policy of suppressing Indian cultural expression. Parents attempted to ease the transition to school life in several ways, including the performance of liminal rituals such as hair cutting at tribal gatherings (Hilger 1952:43). Bill was fond of telling this story about such rituals:

> Now, one of my friends, who during the "give-away dance" was just one ahead of me, his father handed him fifty cents to give to some Ute Indian so that this Ute Indian would come and spank him because he was going to school that fall, and his father said that when he was attending school, the teachers would spank him if he didn't study or didn't do right in school. So he didn't want the teachers to be the first one to spank him; so he told his boy to give that half a dollar to the Indian, who was a Ute from Utah, to spank this boy. So after he got his spanking, he was told to give the money to the Ute, and he says, "Oh, no." He says, "I'm going to buy me something to eat with this fifty cents." And he took off and all you could see going down the road was dust. You couldn't see the Indian. He still had his fifty cents; he got away with that. So my turn came along. My father said that I was going to go to school and the teachers would cut my hair. So he got a Cree Indian to come and go through the motions of cutting my hair. So he did, and we gave him the horse. And whatever was on the pack, that was for him to take home.[7]

In October 1917, he enrolled under the name of Nestor Whiting at Haskell Institute Boarding School in Lawrence, Kansas, but about two months later, Bill (Nestor) and Ralph Antelope, also a Northern Arapahoe, fled—this following on the heels of the "desertion" of two other Northern Arapahoe boys (Quarterly School Reports, December 31, 1917, Haskell Institute). Bill next enrolled as Alfonzo Shakespeare at Genoa Boarding School, Genoa, Nebraska, in September 1918, which he attended until April 19, 1919, when the school records indicate that he left to enlist in the army (Quarterly School Reports, September 30, 1918, March 31, 1919, and June 15, 1919, Genoa Boarding School).

He returned to the reservation and throughout the next three decades made sporadic attempts to construct a role for himself in the reservation community, although he also made periodic forays into non-Indian society as an actor. On the reservation, he occasionally was able to use his bilingual skills as interpreter and secretary for tribal meetings, but for the most part he was alienated from the norms of Arapahoe society. His middle years are characterized by other Arapahoe as marred by heavy drinking and disruptive behavior, with long interludes of off-reservation residence. His tribesmen even point to his earlier failure to care for children as evidence of his irresponsibility in family matters. Most significantly, he made several marriages and temporary alliances with non-Arapahoe women (several of whom were non-Indian), thereby alienating himself from his tribesmen who saw his behavior as indicative of rejection of Arapahoe life style. He cut himself off from alliances with affinal kin who could be relied upon for support in attempts to improve status or assume new political and ceremonial roles. A few of Shakespeare's peers, also students at off-reservation boarding schools, did become important leaders in the Arapahoe community, but renounced their contacts and interests in non-reservation society.

Despite Bill's wide experience with non-Indian educational institutions and his familiarity with the off-reservation world, his efforts to contribute his skills to reservation society were not appreciated by his fellow Arapahoe. He recalled his accomplishments in this phase of his life as stemming from his film roles, his European travels, and his association with well-known non-Indians such as Tim McCoy, with whom he went on tour in Europe, and with whom he appeared on "This Is Your Life" in 1957.

ANTHROPOLOGICAL CONTACTS

Bill is listed as one of Inez Hilger's informants for her studies in 1936, 1940, and 1942, but it was his later activities that were of particular significance for him personally. In the 1950s, Bill became involved with several anthropologists, and this experience was a major turning point in his life, stimulating him to begin years of research into Arapahoe cultural tradition. His first experience as an informant was in early summer of 1952, when the linguist Zdenek Salzmann came to the Wind River reservation to work with John Goggles, who had been an informant for Salzmann and other linguists studying the Arapahoe language.[8] Goggles had died, and Salzmann was referred to Bill Shakespeare, who consented to come to Indiana University in Bloomington for the duration of the summer. Bill served as Salzmann's informant for his dissertation on the Arapahoe language (Salzmann 1963), and later in 1957 and again in 1961 he worked with Salzmann as a linguistic informant for several studies of Arapahoe phonology and grammar.[9] At the University he also was employed at the Linguistic Institute, serving as an informant for students in the linguistic field methods course taught by C. F. Voegelin, Henry Lee Smith, and C. F. Hockett.[10] In addition to his work with linguists, during this time Shakespeare was Bruno Nettl's major informant for studies of Plains Indian music (Nettl 1954; 1955). In the 1950s, he also served as informant for La Mont West's and Carl Voegelin's research on Plains sign language (Voegelin 1958; see also Kroeber 1958).[11]

Bill no doubt made a contribution to the careers of several anthropologists—not only the research of the 1950s but also my own 1967–75 studies of Arapahoe politics (Fowler 1970) and the research of ethnomusicologist Ron Lah. But, of equal importance was the transformation of his own life. Nettl observed that at Indiana University Bill became "quite interested in reading about Arapahoe culture," and that Bill showed "an increasing interest in an academic approach to his culture . . . ; as he resided at Indiana University, he became more acquainted with and perhaps intrigued by the kinds of things that professors and students do, something which he probably had not experienced earlier."[12] Salzmann taught Bill to read phonemic transcriptions,[13] and later when I was visiting Shakespeare in the late 1960s and early 1970s, I observed him writing the Arapahoe language and comparing it with transcriptions of other Algonkian languages which he made himself on visits to other reservations or which he found in the professional literature.

As a result of stimulation from work with anthropologists, he began collecting published sources on the Arapahoe, and he read extensively about Arapahoe and Plains culture history. He rarely attended an Indian gathering without a tape recorder, and attempted to record as many songs and ceremonies as Indian singers and officials would permit. In short, he virtually apprenticed himself to anthropologists and learned several of the skills and points of view which he employed in his subsequent studies of and lectures about Arapahoe culture and society. On a more personal level, his work with anthropologists was also a great stabilizing influence—his periodic problems with alcohol and family relations subsided and did not recur.

In the 1960s, he again sought to reintegrate himself into the Arapahoe community. He gained recognition from Arapahoes as a master of ceremonies and organizer of inter-tribal dances in the pan-Indian sphere, both locally and in his involvement with the Miss Indian America contest in Sheridan, Wyoming. The Arapahoe community elected him several times to the Arapahoe Entertainment Committee, which sponsored dances or other tribal gatherings, and which assumed an important role in "public relations" vis-à-vis the neighboring non-Indian community during Bill's years of service. Under the sponsorship of the Entertainment Committee led by Bill Shakespeare, Arapahoe singers and dancers traveled and performed throughout Wyoming. Shakespeare's talent in these pan-Indian, public relations activities brought him a fair measure of recognition by members of his tribe and contributed to the diffusion of pan-Plains musical and dance styles.

Coterminous with Shakespeare's interest in pan-Plains institutions was his deep commitment to his study of Arapahoe culture and history. The 1960s and early 1970s marked the culmination of his attempt to gain acceptance as a tribal historian. Coinciding with local "Indian Studies" projects, his self-proclaimed expertise brought him speaking invitations from local, non-Indian controlled schools with sizeable Indian enrollments. Of particular importance, however, was a manuscript entitled "Northern Arapahoe" which Bill distributed and "authorized" for workshops and classroom use (Hand 1962; see below). During the 1960s this paper was the primary resource for teachers of Arapahoe culture in the reservation area, and it has been used as a text at the University of Wyoming. As Shakespeare's recommendation accounts for the extensive use made of this manuscript, the authorship and history of "Northern Arapahoe" is of considerable interest in light of Shakespeare's struggle to gain acceptance as a tribal historian.

One prominent educator in the reservation area knew Bill and was familiar with the manuscript, which was 64 pages single spaced on mimeograph and which had a drawing of Bill Shakespeare on the cover sheet. He recollects Bill's part in the dissemination of "Northern Arapahoe" thusly: "I came across someone who said, 'Have you seen the material William Shakespeare prepared on the Arapahoe tribe?' I said that I had not seen it so this person loaned me a copy. As I recall, this person said to William Shakespeare, 'Why don't you have your name on this? You should have this printed as a book.' As I recall it, William Shakespeare made the material available but said that the material came from many sources and he was reluctant to claim authorship. He seemed to feel that it belonged to many people."

"Northern Arapahoe" summarizes the linguistic, archeological, ethnohistorical, and ethnological research completed on the Arapahoe tribe through 1959. The most important sources—Kroeber, Dorsey, Hilger, etc.—are quoted and cited. The view of Arapahoe culture and history which Shakespeare advocated was clearly one based on anthropological theory and method. None of Shakespeare's recollections were included.

The manuscript—originally titled "The Northern Arapahoe"—was actually written in a graduate anthropology seminar in 1962 at the University of Illinois by James Hand.[14] Each student in the class wrote on a different Indian group, and the intent was to compare results at the end of the term. Hand—although he omitted his name from the manuscript—refers to the companion studies of his co-participants Michael Hoffman and Judith Hellewell (Hand 1962:50), who mentions Hand's paper on the Arapahoe in her own work (1962:1). Hand informed me that after leaving the University of Illinois, he returned to his native Wyoming, and there attended the Arapahoe Sun Dance of 1962. He distributed three copies of his paper to young Arapahoes, and had earlier mailed three copies to the Arapahoe Business Council.[15] He received no acknowledgement from the Council, and no response from any of the tribal members. I assume that Bill Shakespeare received his two copies of the paper[16]—unsigned by Hand—from the youth at the Sun Dance because, although he made inquiries as to the authorship of the paper, he apparently was not informed of Hand's correspondence with the Business Council. Shakespeare had the paper typed on mimeograph and provided copies to local workshops and schools, leaving the manuscript unsigned or "authorless," and entitling it "Northern Arapahoe."

Shakespeare appears to have found the laudatory viewpoint taken in the manuscript compatible with his own. Several of the conclusions in "The Northern Arapahoe" appealed to Shakespeare: the Arapahoe language is particularly difficult and also significantly different from other Algonkian languages, "'a stock in the making'" (pp. 3–4); the Arapahoe were first and longest on the Plains (pp. 13, 15–16); scalping was not an original practice with the Arapahoe (p. 21); the Arapahoes, who were skilled traders, "hired" the Cheyennes as "body-guards" to "preserve and protect the valuable Arapahoe horse herds and supply line to the southwest while leaving the Arapaho free to engage in peaceful trade with the surrounding tribes" (p. 21); most of the attacks on White settlers in the latter

19th century were attributable to White "renegades" and not to the Arapahoe who were blamed for the attacks (pp. 53–56). The only alteration Shakespeare made was to add a final page—a synopsis of the story of the tribal medicine bundle, the Sacred Pipe. The addition was probably made because Arapahoe mythology was not treated in "The Northern Arapaho," despite the collection of oral tradition compiled by Dorsey and Kroeber (1903). And he substituted a drawing of himself in costume for one of his film roles, for the original cover of "The Northern Arapaho"—a somewhat abstract drawing of the Keeper of the Sacred Pipe flanked by tribal members.

Bill Shakespeare's respect for the approach taken in the paper "The Northern Arapaho" was to have important, and ironic, repercussions. Sometime between the summer of 1962 and 1964, Bill's half-brother Tom (the son of William Shakespeare and Cassie) copied the manuscript, which he had borrowed from Bill, in long hand on tablets—but since his few years of schooling were in the mission school on the reservation and he had no knowledge of bibliographic citation or other academic conventions, he omitted the citations and, in most cases, the quotation marks." Years later, in 1969, Tom's son was successful in having this manuscript (which came to 110 pages double-spaced) typed and published as *The Sky People* (Shakespeare 1971).[18] Tom's manuscript began with three and one-half pages of his own recollections about Arapahoe origins, technology, and oral tradition, then incorporated the "Northern Arapaho" text almost in its entirety, followed by 19 pages of Tom's own observations of Arapahoe family life.

A comparison of a passage from each of the four manuscripts illustrates the relationship of each to the other:

> In 1880, Chief Little Raven told Capt. W. P. Clark (1885, 40): "Before we crossed the Missouri River we used to plant and raise corn. The Arikarees stole the corn and the art of raising it from us. Before we went hunting so much we lived on what we raised from the ground." Clark regarded this as "very reliable tradition" although it was given to him in sign language. (In "The Northern Arapaho" by James Hand, p. 12)

> In 1880, Chief Little Raven told Capt. W. P. Clark (1885, 40): "Before we crossed the Missouri River we used to plant and raise corn. The Arikarees stole the corn and art of raising it from us. Before we went hunting so much we lived on what we raised from the ground." Clark regarded this as "very reliable tradition" although it was given to him in sign language. (In "Northern Arapaho," pg. 12)

> Another story I heard told by Chief Little Raven, an Oklahoma old timer, "Before we crossed the Missouri River we used to plant and raise corn. The Arikarees stole the corn and art of raising it from us before we went hunting. We lived on what we raised from the ground." This is regarded as very reliable tradition.[19] (In Tom Shakespeare's manuscript for *The Sky People*, p. 15)

> Another story I heard was told by Chief Little Raven, an Oklahoma old timer. "Before we crossed the Missouri River we used to plant and raise corn. The Arikarees stole the corn and the art of raising it from us before we went hunting. We lived on what we raised from the ground." This is regarded as very reliable tradition. (In *The Sky People*, p. 20)

What is significant about the relationship between "Northern Arapaho" and its successor *The Sky People* is that the latter, which is now the most frequently used publication in teaching Arapahoe studies locally and the book most accessible to the general public, was indirectly a product of Bill Shakespeare's association with anthropologists and his internalization of their point of view. What is also important is that Bill's credentials as a tribal historian (from the perspective of non-Indians) were based on his familiarity with anthropological sources. In the view of other Arapahoes, he was not a Tribal Historian. None of Hand's original copies is to be found at Wind River (Shakespeare's two copies were lent and not returned), nor are the copies Shakespeare mimeographed currently in the possession of Arapahoes. Shakespeare, acknowledging his fellow Arapahoes' feelings about his lack of qualifications for Tribal Historian status, did not purport to publicly recount tribal oral tradition or speak of his own personal recollections of important events in Arapahoe history (although he gave such information to anthropologists). Rather, he acted to disseminate the research of the anthropological community. When informed of the course his student paper had travelled, James Hand wrote:

> It is my hope that the overall effect of the paper adequately conveys the pride of all humanity in the fact that a portion of it is Arapaho. If there can be a touching on the human spirit level, the tribes of man may somehow fuse so that all may share the pride of each. William Shakespeare took this common goal of men as his personal objective and led us all toward its attainment. (Letter to Loretta Fowler, October 25, 1976)

ARAPAHOE VIEWS ON THE TRIBAL HISTORIAN: SHAKESPEARE'S DILEMMA

Shakespeare's concept of self, and his sense of personal accomplishment, were shaped in large part by his association with anthropologists and the interest in Arapahoe traditions that that association encouraged. Among his own people, he was not accorded the status of Tribal Historian. Shakespeare's case points to an interesting question, and that is, how do Arapahoes define the role of Tribal Historian, and how does this role differ from the Arapahoe view of the anthropologist as a tribal historian? Those who achieve the status of Tribal Historian have been reared in a milieu of kin relationships wherein they are in close, constant, and enduring contact with elderly individuals specially endowed with spiritual power. To be recognized as Tribal Historian one must demonstrate an uninterrupted lifetime of ceremonial participation and close genealogical links to individuals who have been important in tribal religious rituals. An individual must also demonstrate a life-long association with the Arapahoe community so that his loyalty to that community and his reliability as a participant in the network of communal sharing and reciprocal ceremonial obligations are not questioned. And he must have a recognized skill as an orator in the native language. Not anyone can learn oral history, and no one individual is considered qualified to learn all aspects of tribal history. Each Historian has the socially recognized right to include some stories in his repertoire for his exclusive use, but he cannot legitimately relate all tribal oral traditions. And, especially important, the subject matter of the Historian's field of expertise is the *spiritual* realm of Arapahoe cultural process. For example, the repertoires of Tribal Historians do not include stories about post-reservation political events or economic changes, nor do they include stories traditionally told by women.[20]

The anthropological approach to tribal history and culture lacks legitimacy in the view of Arapahoes. While resentment of outsiders has a bearing on the rejection of the anthropological contribution, most certainly so does the lack of credentials in the ceremonial, social, and oratorical realms, and so does the fact that historical documentation and analyses of structural relationships or ecological variables are not relevant to Arapahoe history as Arapahoes see it. Rather, Arapahoes see their history as a mythological process, which operates as a conceptual framework for interpreting and shaping social action and is not necessarily related to events as recorded by observers.

Shakespeare's disassociation with the Arapahoe community in the days of his youth and his marriages to non-Arapahoe women isolated him socially. And his informal training in anthropological perspective and method was alien to the understanding the Arapahoe community has of historical interpretation. To Arapahoes, those entitled to be called Tribal Historians have come up through the ceremonial ranks, have a long-term and deep commitment to kinship ties, and view historical process through oral tradition. Arapahoe society now precludes development of native ethnohistorians and ethnographers, although Bill Shakespeare came the closest to achieving such a position at Wind River.

When the Arapahoes established an Indian-controlled high school in 1973, because of his advanced age and his experience in local educational workshops, Shakespeare was included in invitations to tribal elders to contribute to the program. He recorded recollections about his role as interpreter and secretary during the second decade of this century, but because of his lack of participation in sacred Arapahoe ceremonies his role in the school's oral history project was viewed as minor; he was not perceived as knowledgeable in the more important areas of Arapahoe culture. Other elders were called upon for this task. Often, when outsiders, such as local non-Indian school teachers or clubs, would ask questions of Arapahoes about their culture and history, the non-Indians would be directed to see Bill Shakespeare. This was both a way of putting off unwanted questions and, at the same time, categorizing Shakespeare as an "outsider." There are strong sanctions against "real" Tribal Historians speaking about Arapahoe tradition to non-Arapahoes.

In the last days of his life, Shakespeare found his greatest source of personal satisfaction in his consultation work away from the reservation. For example, he taught sign language at Haskell in 1975 (*The Indian Leader* 1975:4). At home in Wyoming, he was somewhat embittered, particularly because he failed in his efforts to persuade the Indian-controlled high school to complete literal translations of tape recordings of other elderly Arapahoes' accounts of oral tradition. Most of these tapes currently cannot be used effectively since many of the students cannot understand the narratives, and teachers disagree concerning the accuracy of those English summaries of the narratives which presently exist.

Shakespeare's life, its course and direction, its twists and turns, is reflected and expressed in the names by which he identified himself. Born "Strikes Again," he was named Alphonse Shakespeare when he entered school—the name Shakespeare was that of his father, who was given the name William Shakespeare at Carlisle Indian school in 1881. Upon returning to the reservation as a young man, Alphonse was unable to attain acceptance and make a place for himself among his peers. During these years, he used the name Nestor Whiting (Whiting was the English name given his mother, Nevada Whiting), in part rejecting the Arapahoe heritage—signified in the career of his father in early reservation history—and the personal failure it represented. When he began to work with anthropologists he consistently used the name William Shakespeare, which symbolized both Arapahoe heritage and stature in the non-Indian world.

The events surrounding Bill Shakespeare's funeral point dramatically to the personal conflicts in his life, as well as to the ambivalence felt toward him by other Arapahoes. His ties to the Arapahoe past—to the old ways, as symbolized by the power of his grandfather's medicine bundle—were never severed. His commitment to recording as objectively as possible, oftentimes with the tools of anthropologists, his tribe's culture and history was strong even in the face of opposition, opposition reflected in part by the small attendance at his funeral.

Shakespeare—living much of his life in association with non-Arapahoes and lacking commitment to the ceremonial sphere—was caught in a dilemma, a dilemma shared in large measure by the anthropologist. The anthropological perspective he acquired was personally enlightening to Shakespeare himself, but not recognized as valid by his Arapahoe peers whose recognition he vainly tried to acquire throughout much of his life.

NOTES

1. The spelling "Arapahoe" is used by the Northern Arapahoe tribe today, although in much of the literature the form "Arapaho" appears.

2. In 1917 William Shakespeare made application for a patent in fee (Central Files of the Bureau of Indian Affairs 190939: File No. 312, Shoshoni 37567, 1917). He may have been presenting his involvement with the Ghost Dance in an unfavorable light in order to influence the judgment of BIA officials in the matter of this application.

3. I have not altered Shakespeare's original spellings, but have added punctuation where necessary for clarity. Shakespeare gives 1872 as the date he entered Carlisle, but this is incorrect.

4. Letter to the Secretary of the Interior, January 23, 1912. Central Files of the Bureau of Indian Affairs 1909–1939. File No. 20395, Shoshoni, 1912.

5. In fact, Friday (the agency interpreter) died in 1881, and the agent at Wind River wrote that with Friday's death the agency lost its only interpreter (Annual Report to the Secretary of the Interior, October 24, 1881).

The importance of school attendance must have been quite apparent to all concerned.

6. Narrative of William Shakespeare. Recorded August 20, 1972, by Loretta Fowler at Arapahoe, Wyoming.

7. Narrative of William Shakespeare. Recorded August 20, 1972, by Loretta Fowler.

8. Letter from Zdenek Salzmann to Loretta Fowler, August 26, 1976.

9. Salzmann's publications on his Arapahoe research completed in consultation with Shakespeare include Salzmann 1954; 1956; 1957; 1959; 1960; 1961; 1965a; 1965b; 1967a; 1967b; 1967c.

10. Letter from Zdenek Salzmann to Loretta Fowler, August 26, 1976.

11. La Mont West's recordings of his sessions with Bill Shakespeare are on deposit at Archives of the Languages of the World, Indiana University (107.21.2.1–12; and 112.11.1.1).

12. Letter from Bruno Nettl to Loretta Fowler, August 23, 1976.

13. Letter from Zdenek Salzmann to Loretta Fowler, August 26, 1976.

14. I would like to thank Edward Bruner and his former students in Anthropology 451, Spring 1962—Michael Hoffman, Stephen Thompson, Norris Lang, and H. Russell Bernard—for their efforts in aiding me to identify Hand as the author of "The Northern Arapaho."

15. Letter from James Hand to Loretta Fowler, October 25, 1976.

16. Carol Hensley, Bill Shakespeare's granddaughter, recalls that Bill had two copies of the paper, that he had the paper typed and duplicated on mimeograph, and that he lent one of the original copies to his half-brother Tom Shakespeare, Sr. (personal communication, December 15, 1976).

17. The Tom Shakespeare, Sr. (1890–1964) manuscript contains occasional, minor stylistic changes, and sporadically there are brief personal observations which appear as comments on the accuracy of "The Northern Arapaho" or as anecdotal embellishments. There are no indications in the work that material from "The Northern Arapaho" was used, although on Page 64 he writes "once I happened to see a written history of the Arapahoes and also saw the diagram of relationship." The "diagram" he refers to is in "The Northern Arapaho," Page 37e and 37f. (The page numbering is due to the fact that Hand's paper was typed by two individuals who each numbered pages separately.)

18. Parts of the manuscript for *The Sky People* were eliminated from the published version; specifically the first six paragraphs. These passages identify the author of the manuscript as Tom Shakespeare, Sr., attribute the stories to Tom's grandfather Scarface, and describe Tom's unpleasant experiences at the mission school. In lieu of these six paragraphs is a three para-

graph description of the "crossing of the ice," when the tribe separated into two divisions. I do not know who wrote this section, but assume it was done after Tom died.

19. The punctuation change here was possibly made by the typist as Tom Shakespeare rarely separated sentences with punctuation in his manuscript.

20. Women as storytellers are important in Arapahoe life, and, in fact, form a "society" in themselves, but do not tell the stories of male Tribal Historians.

LITERATURE CITED

Central Files of the Bureau of Indian Affairs
1909–1939 Record Group 75. Records of the Bureau of Indian Affairs. The National Archives.

Dorsey, George, and A. L. Kroeber
1903 Traditions of the Arapaho. Field Museum Anthropological Series 5. Chicago.

Estate of William Shakespeare
1934 Probate Hearing No. 59636. Billings Area Office, Billings, Montana.

Fowler, Loretta
1970 Political Process and Socio-cultural Change Among the Arapahoe Indians. Ph.D. Dissertation, University of Illinois, Urbana.

Hand, James
1962 "The Northern Arapaho." Unpublished manuscript.

Hellewell (Nagata), Judith A.
1962 "A Comparison of the Differential Rates of Change of the Religious and Family Structures of the Northern and Southern Arapaho." Unpublished manuscript.

Hilger, Inez
1952 Arapaho Child Life and Its Cultural Background. Bulletin of the Bureau of American Ethnology 148.

Kroeber, Alfred
1958 "Sign Language Inquiry." International Journal of American Linguistics 24:1–19.

Nettl, Bruno
1954 "Text-Music Relationships in Arapaho Songs." Southwestern Journal of Anthropology 10(2): 192–199.
1955 "Musical Culture of the Arapaho." Musical Quarterly 41:325–331.

"Northern Arapaho"
n.d. Unsigned manuscript. William Shakespeare Papers. Native American Archival Center. Department of Anthropology. Indiana University.

Quarterly School Reports
1910–1939 Record Group 75. Records of the Bureau of Indian Affairs. The National Archives.

Records of the Carlisle Indian Industrial School
1879–1918 Record Group 75. Records of the Bureau of Indian Affairs. The National Archives.

St. Stephens Indian Mission
1908–1917 Student Records. St. Stephens, Wyoming.

Salzmann, Zdenek
1954 The Problem of Lexical Acculturation. International Journal of American Linguistics 20(2):137–139.
1956 Arapaho I: Phonology. IJAL 22(1):49–56.
1957 Arapaho Tales III. Midwest Folklore 7:27–37.
1959 Arapaho Kinship Terms and Two Related Ethnolinguistic Observations. Anthropological Linguistics 1(9):6–10.
1960 Two Brief Contributions Toward Arapaho Linguistic History. Anthropological Linguistics 2(7):39–48.
1961 Arapaho IV: Interphonemic Specification. IJAL 27(2)P:151–155.
1963 A Sketch of Arapaho Grammar. Ph.D. Dissertation. Indiana University, Bloomington.
1965a Arapaho V: Noun. IJAL 31(1):39–49.
1965b Arapaho VI: Noun. IJAL 31(2):136–151.
1967a Arapaho VII: Verb. IJAL 33(3):209–223.
1967b On The Inflection of Transitive Animate Verbs in Arapaho. Contributions to Anthropology: Linguistics I: 135–139. Canada, National Museum, Bulletin 214.

1967c Some Aspects of Arapaho Morphology. Contributions to Anthropology: Linguistics I:128–134.

Shakespeare, Tom
1969 Untitled manuscript for The Sky People.

Shakespeare, Tom
1971 The Sky People. New York: Vantage Press, Inc.

The Indian Leader
1975 Haskell Indian Junior College. Lawrence, Kansas. Vol. 78(13).

Voegelin, C. F.
1958 Sign Language, Analysis on One Level or Two? IJAL 24(1):71–77.